SEVEN SEAS ENTERTAIN

CAPTAIN HA
SPACE PIRA
DIMENSIONAL VOYAGE VOLUME 1

story by LEIJI MATSUMOTO   art by KOUITI SHIMABOSHI

TRANSLATION
Zack Davisson

LETTERING
Meaghan Tucker

COVER DESIGN
Nicky Lim

PROOFREADER
Shanti Whitesides

ASSISTANT EDITOR
Jenn Grunigen

PRODUCTION ASSISTANT
CK Russell

PRODUCTION MANAGER
Lissa Pattillo

EDITOR-IN-CHIEF
Adam Arnold

PUBLISHER
Jason DeAngelis

CAPTAIN HARLOCK: DIMENSIONAL VOYAGE VOL. 1
© LEIJI MATSUMOTO 2015, KOUITI SHIMABOSHI 2015
Originally published in Japan in 2015 by Akita Publishing Co., Ltd..
English translation rights arranged with Akita Publishing Co., Ltd. through
TOHAN CORPORATION, Tokyo.

Seven Seas books may be purchased in bulk for educational, business, or pro-
motional use. For information on bulk purchases, please contact Macmillan Cor-
porate & Premium Sales Department at 1-800-221-7945 (ext 5442)
or write specialmarkets@macmillan.com.

Seven Seas and the Seven Seas logo are trademarks of
Seven Seas Entertainment, LLC. All rights reserved.

ISBN: 978-1-626925-69-4

Printed in Canada

First Printing: September 2017

10 9 8 7 6 5 4 3 2 1

FOLLOW US ONLINE: www.gomanga.com

READING DIRECTIONS

This book reads from *right to left*, Japanese style.
If this is your first time reading manga, you start
reading from the top right panel on each page and
take it from there. If you get lost, just follow the
numbered diagram here. It may seem backwards at
first, but you'll get the hang of it! Have fun!!

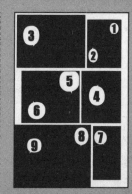

PROFILE

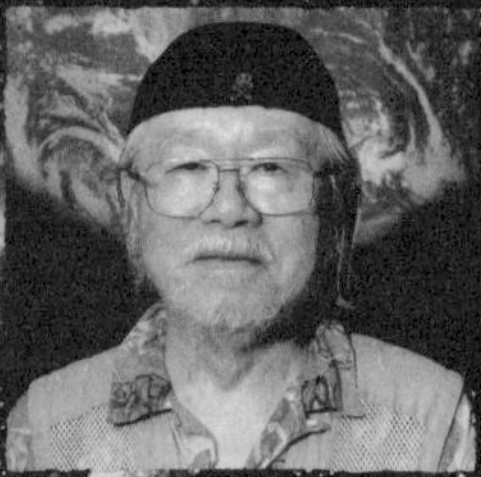

Original Story and Design

LEIJI MATSUMOTO

Born in 1938 in Kurume, Fukuoka. In 1954, he made his professional debut with *Adventure of a Bee* (*Hachimitsu no Boken*). Some of his many works include *Space Battleship Yamato* (*Uchū Senkan Yamato*), *Otoko Oidon*, *Space Pirate Captain Harlock*, *Galaxy Express 999*, *Battlefield Manga Series* (*Senba Manga Shiriizu*), *Queen Emeraldas*, and *Queen Millennia* (*Shin Taketori Monogatari: Sennen Joō*). One of the main figures in the worldwide anime and manga boom, Matsumoto now plays a leadership role for the next generation of artists and enthusiasts.

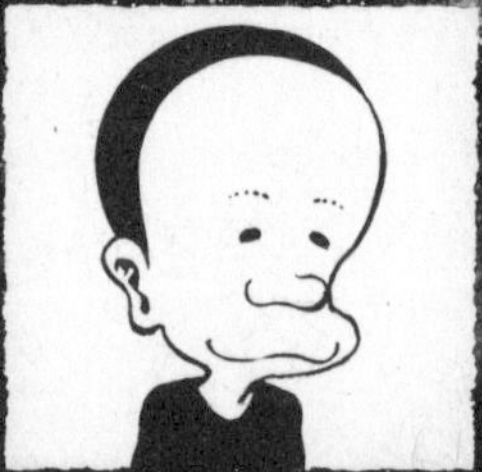

Artist

KOUITI SHIMABOSHI

A talent discovered by Leiji Matsumoto, Kouiti Shimaboshi makes his debut in *Captain Harlock Dimensional Voyage*. Under Matsutmoto's guidance, Shimahoshi has become immersed in this classic work beloved worldwide.

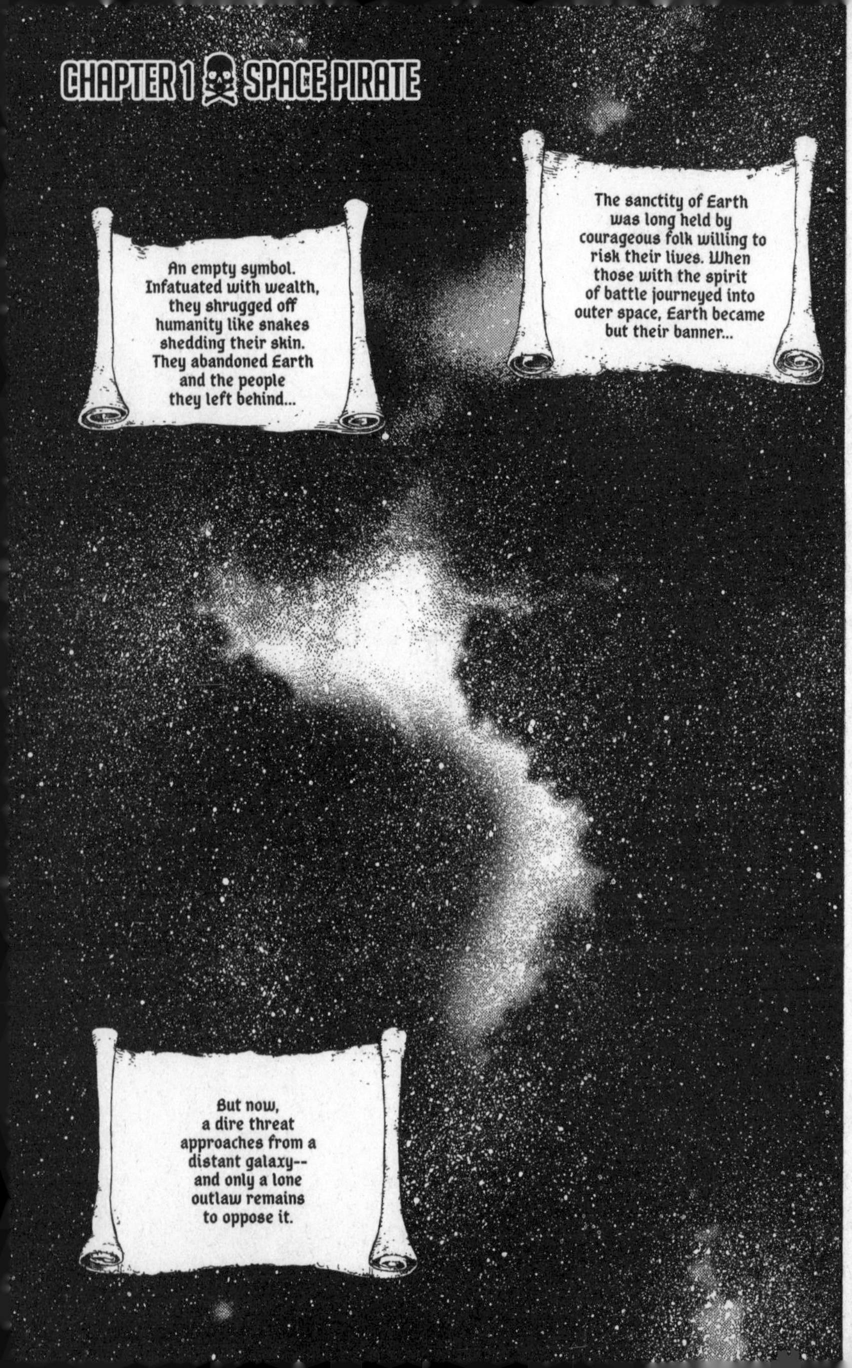
CHAPTER 1 SPACE PIRATE
The sanctity of Earth was long held by courageous folk willing to risk their lives. When those with the spirit of battle journeyed into outer space, Earth became but their banner...
An empty symbol. Infatuated with wealth, they shrugged off humanity like snakes shedding their skin. They abandoned Earth and the people they left behind...
But now, a dire threat approaches from a distant galaxy-- and only a lone outlaw remains to oppose it.

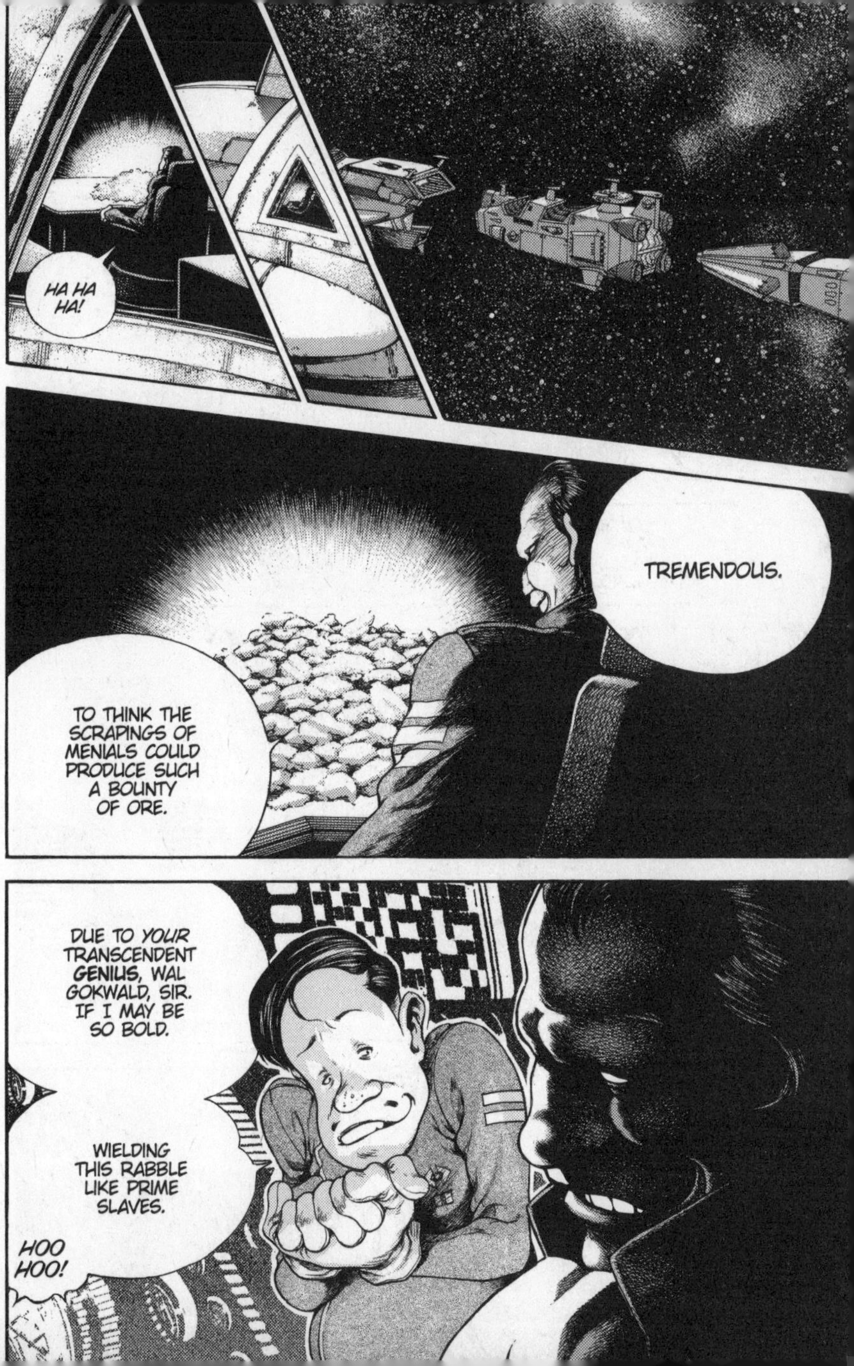
HA HA HA!
TREMENDOUS.
TO THINK THE SCRAPINGS OF MENIALS COULD PRODUCE SUCH A BOUNTY OF ORE.
DUE TO *YOUR* TRANSCENDENT **GENIUS**, WAL GOKWALD, SIR. IF I MAY BE SO BOLD.
WIELDING THIS RABBLE LIKE PRIME SLAVES.
HOO HOO!

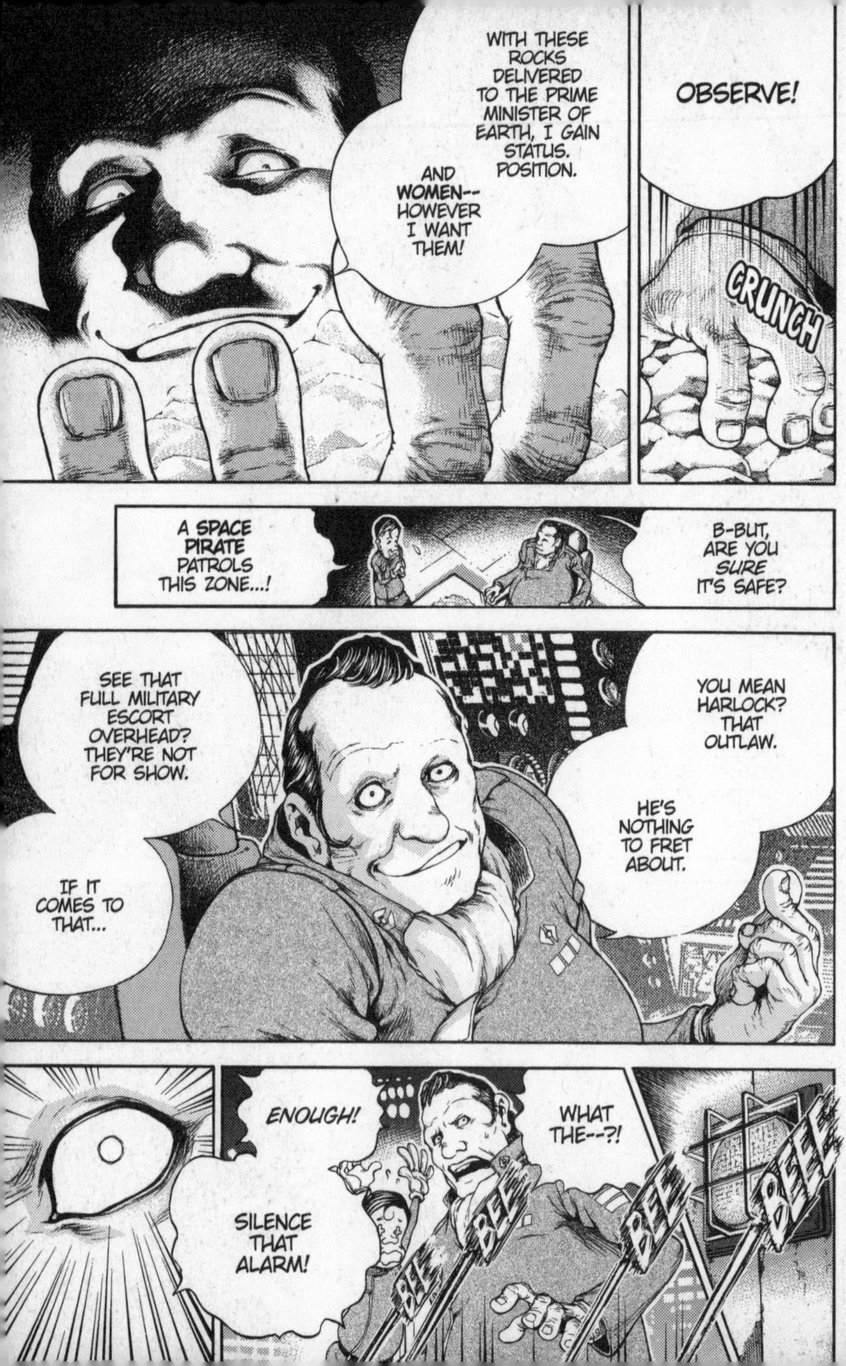

OBSERVE!
CRUNCH
WITH THESE ROCKS DELIVERED TO THE PRIME MINISTER OF EARTH, I GAIN STATUS. POSITION.
AND WOMEN-- HOWEVER I WANT THEM!
B-BUT, ARE YOU *SURE* IT'S SAFE?
A SPACE **PIRATE** PATROLS THIS ZONE...!
YOU MEAN HARLOCK? THAT OUTLAW.
HE'S NOTHING TO FRET ABOUT.
SEE THAT FULL MILITARY ESCORT OVERHEAD? THEY'RE NOT FOR SHOW.
IF IT COMES TO THAT...
BEEEE
BEE
WHAT THE--?!
BEE
BEE
ENOUGH!
SILENCE THAT ALARM!

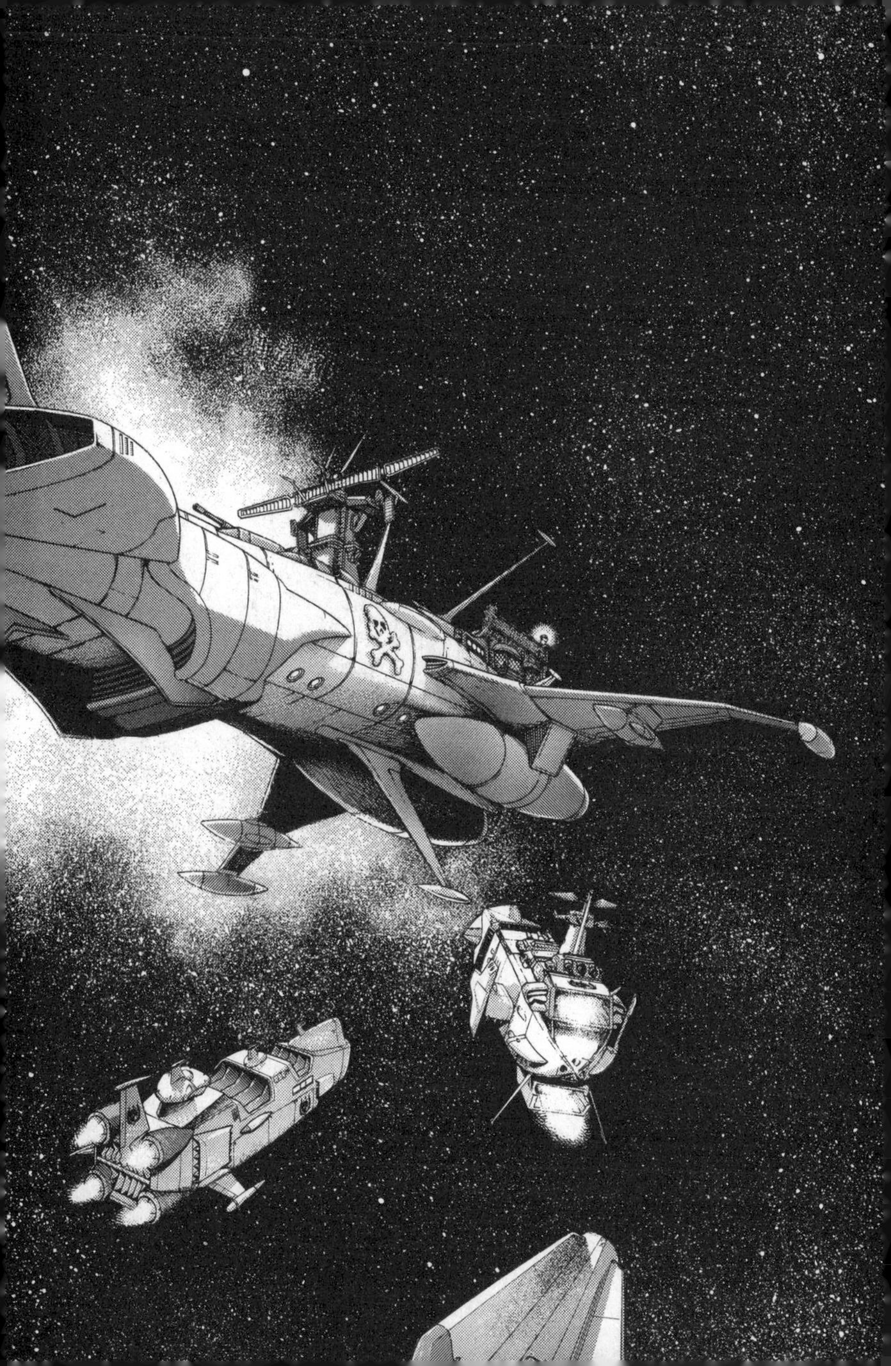

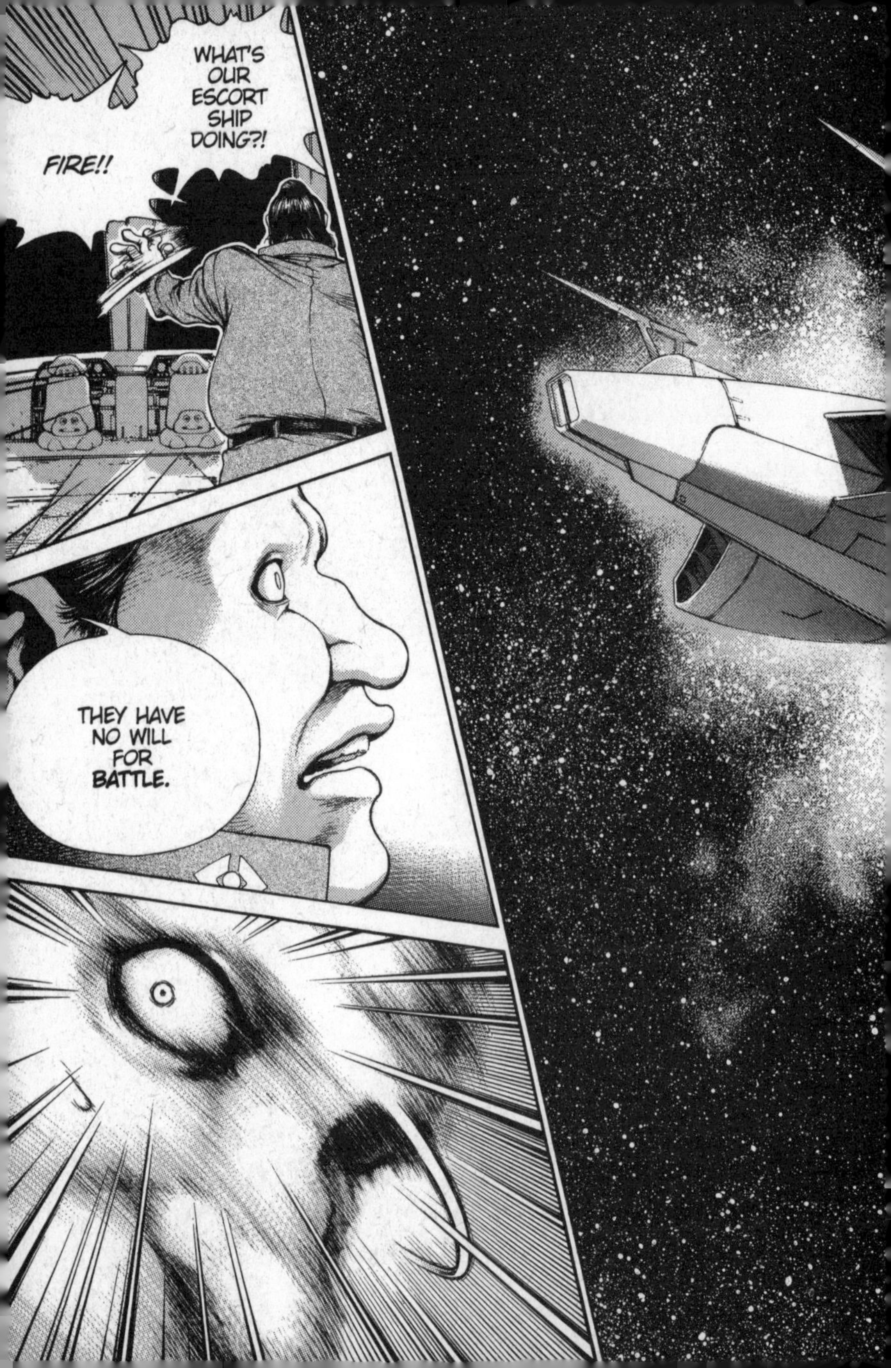
WHAT'S OUR ESCORT SHIP DOING?!
FIRE!!
THEY HAVE NO WILL FOR BATTLE.

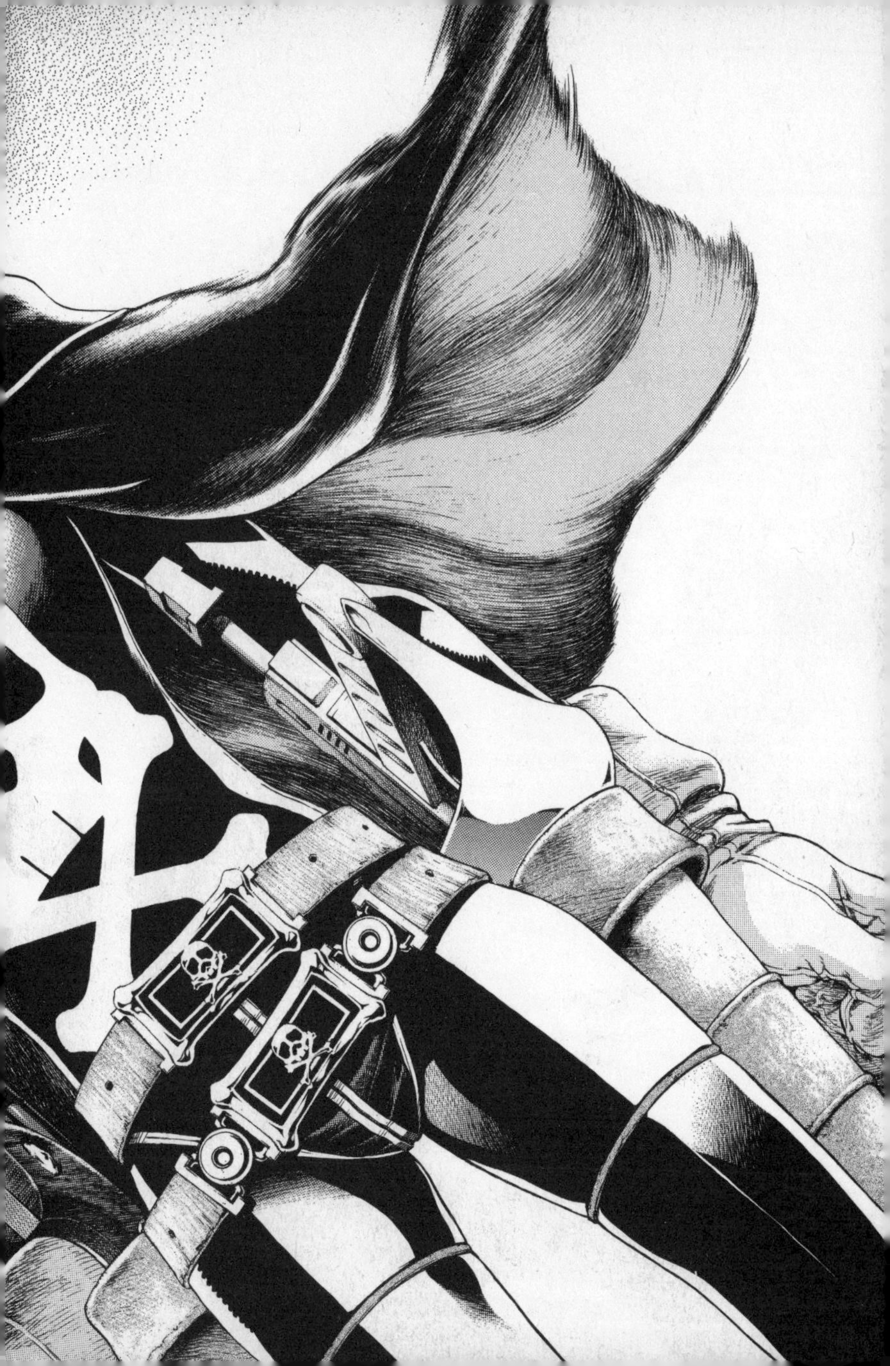

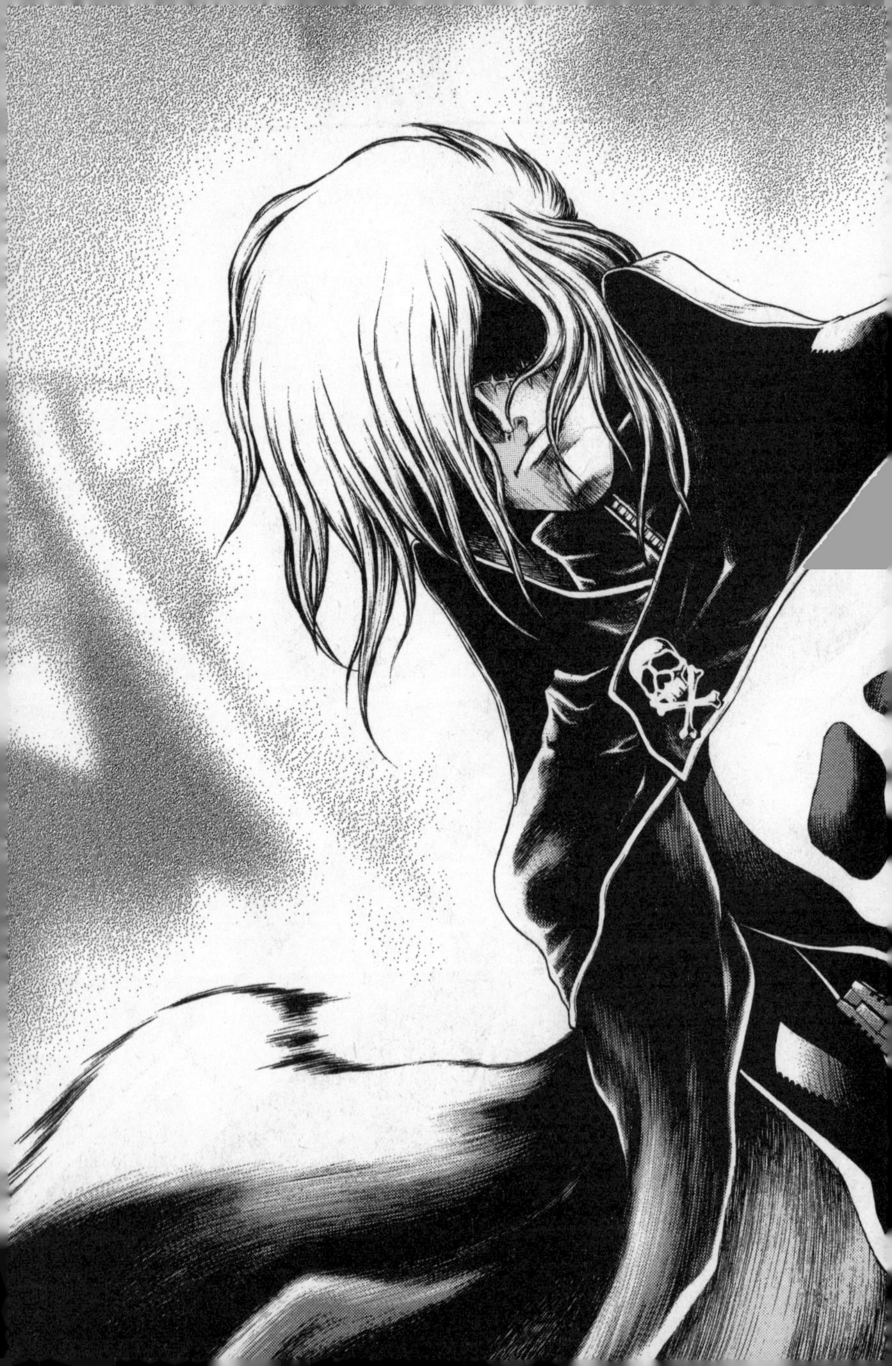

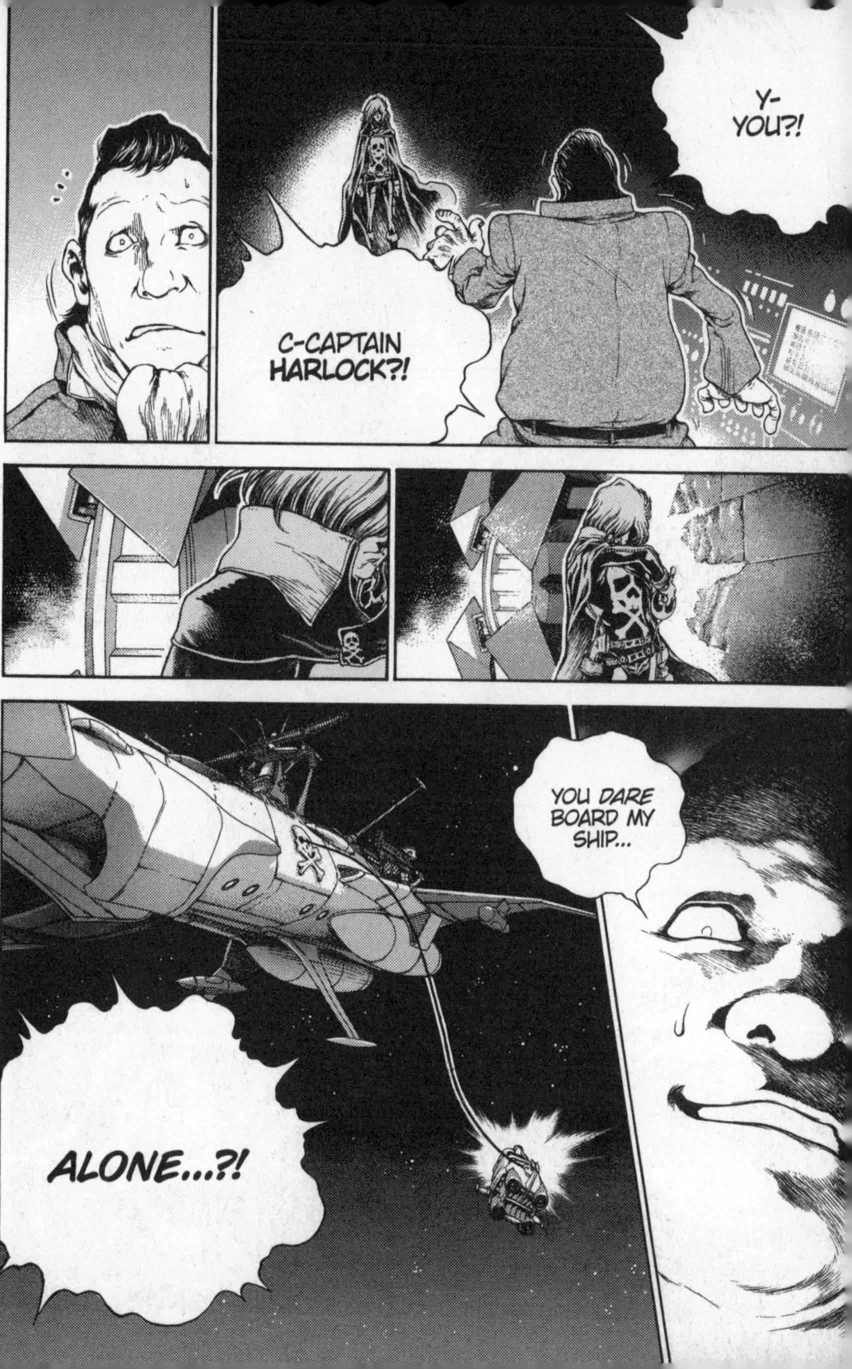
Y- YOU?!
C-CAPTAIN HARLOCK?!
YOU DARE BOARD MY SHIP...
ALONE...?!

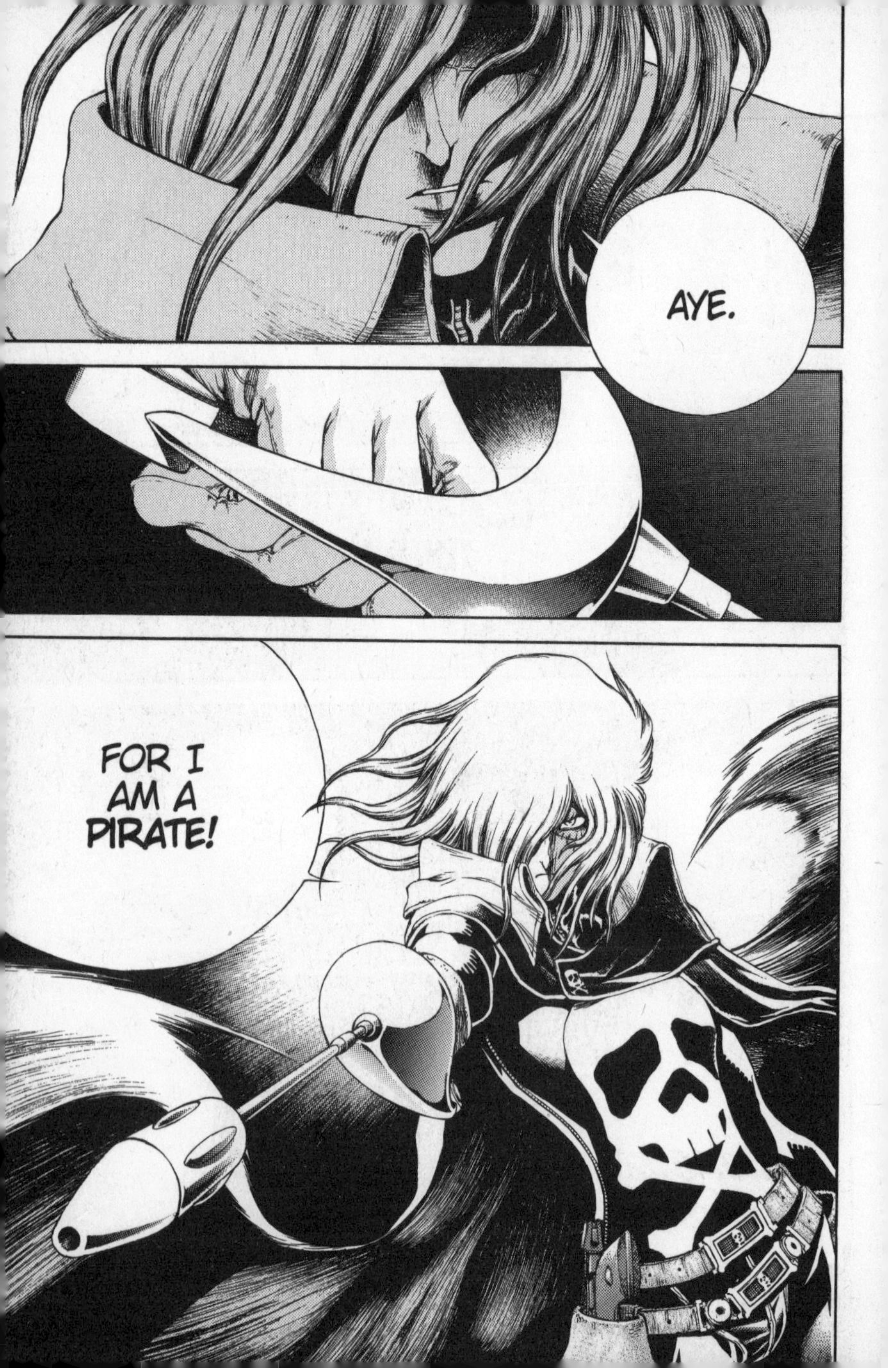
AYE.
FOR I AM A PIRATE!

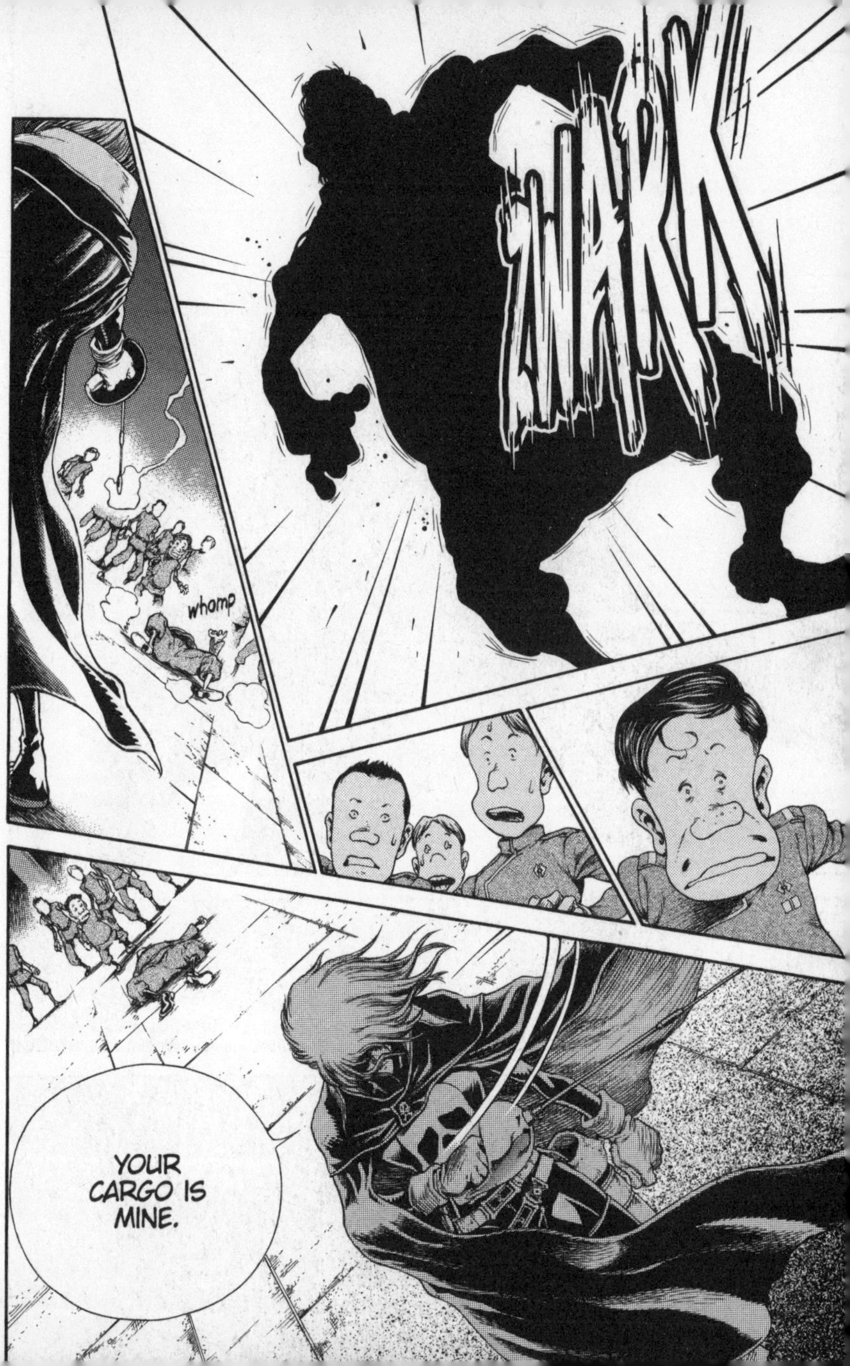
whomp
YOUR CARGO IS MINE.

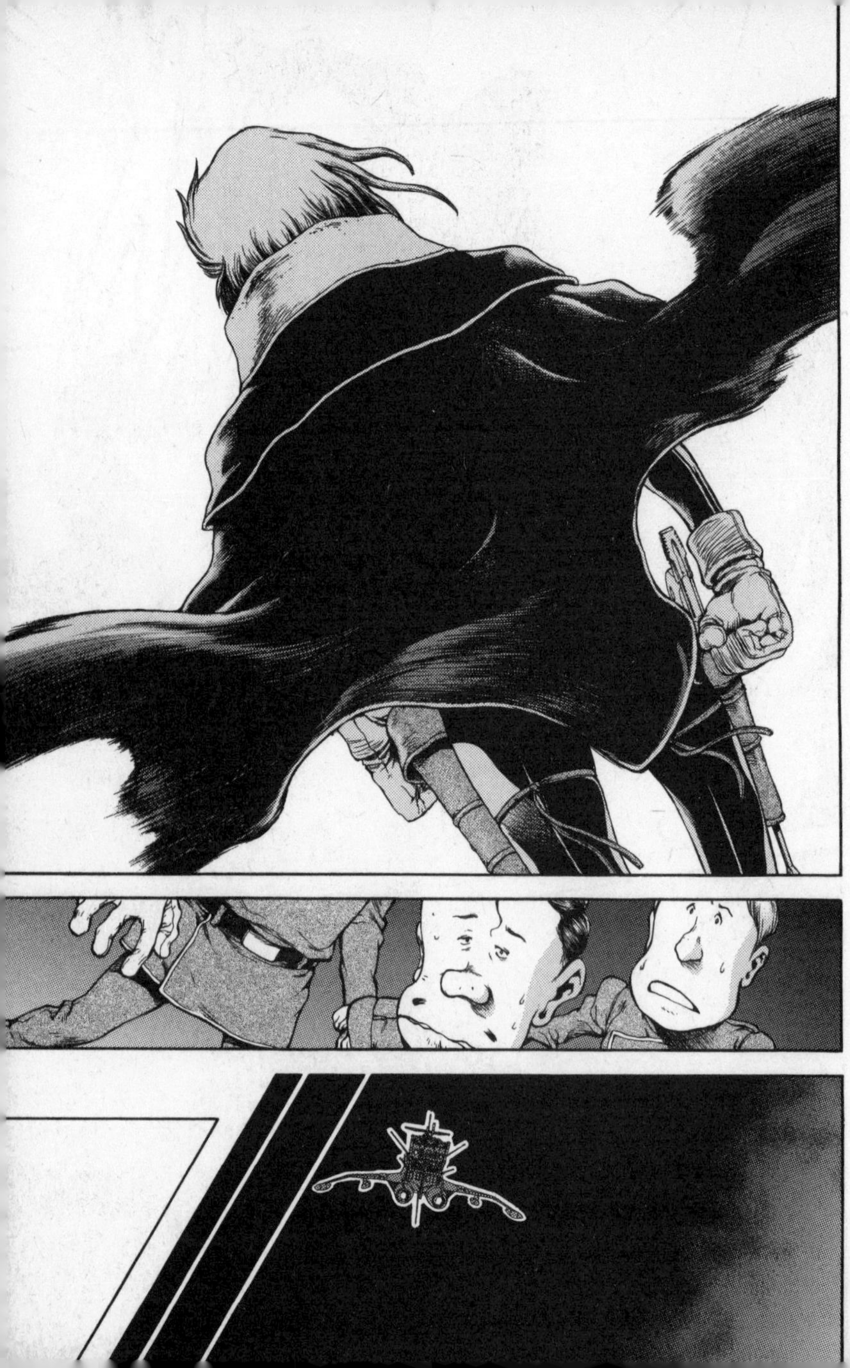

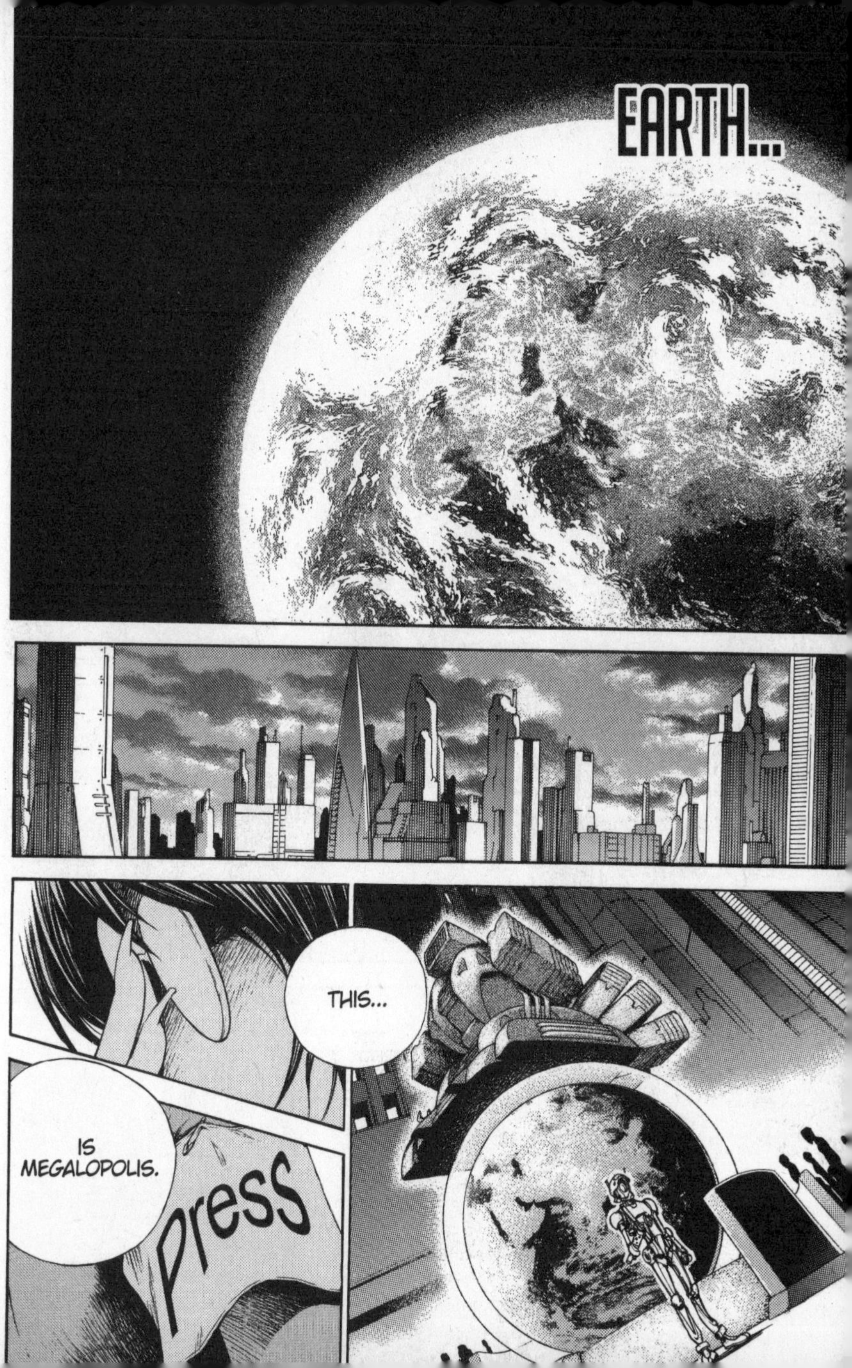
EARTH...
THIS...
IS MEGALOPOLIS.
Press

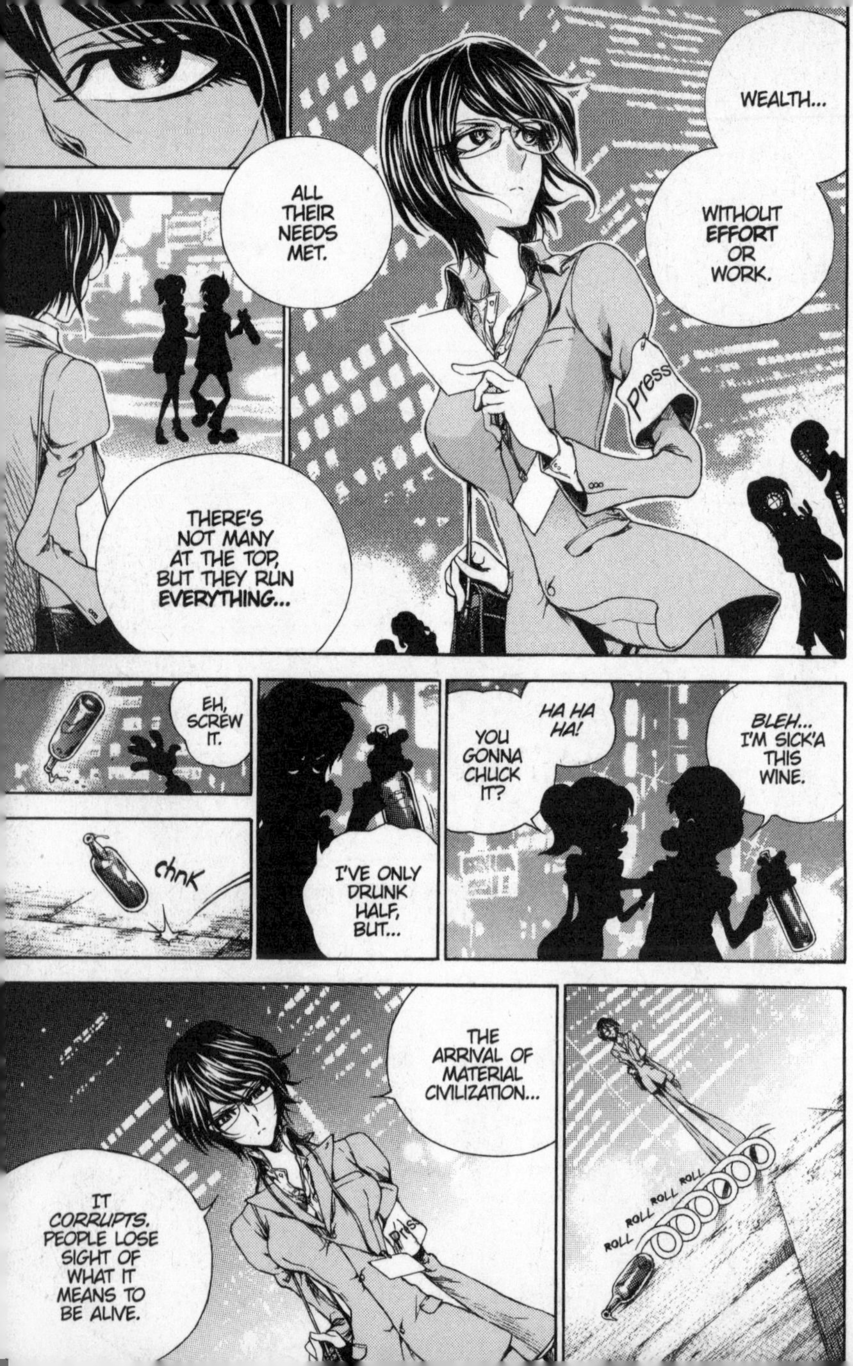
WEALTH...
WITHOUT EFFORT OR WORK.
ALL THEIR NEEDS MET.
THERE'S NOT MANY AT THE TOP, BUT THEY RUN EVERYTHING...
BLEH... I'M SICK'A THIS WINE.
HA HA HA!
YOU GONNA CHUCK IT?
I'VE ONLY DRUNK HALF, BUT...
EH, SCREW IT.
chnk
ROLL ROLL ROLL ROLL
THE ARRIVAL OF MATERIAL CIVILIZATION...
IT CORRUPTS. PEOPLE LOSE SIGHT OF WHAT IT MEANS TO BE ALIVE.

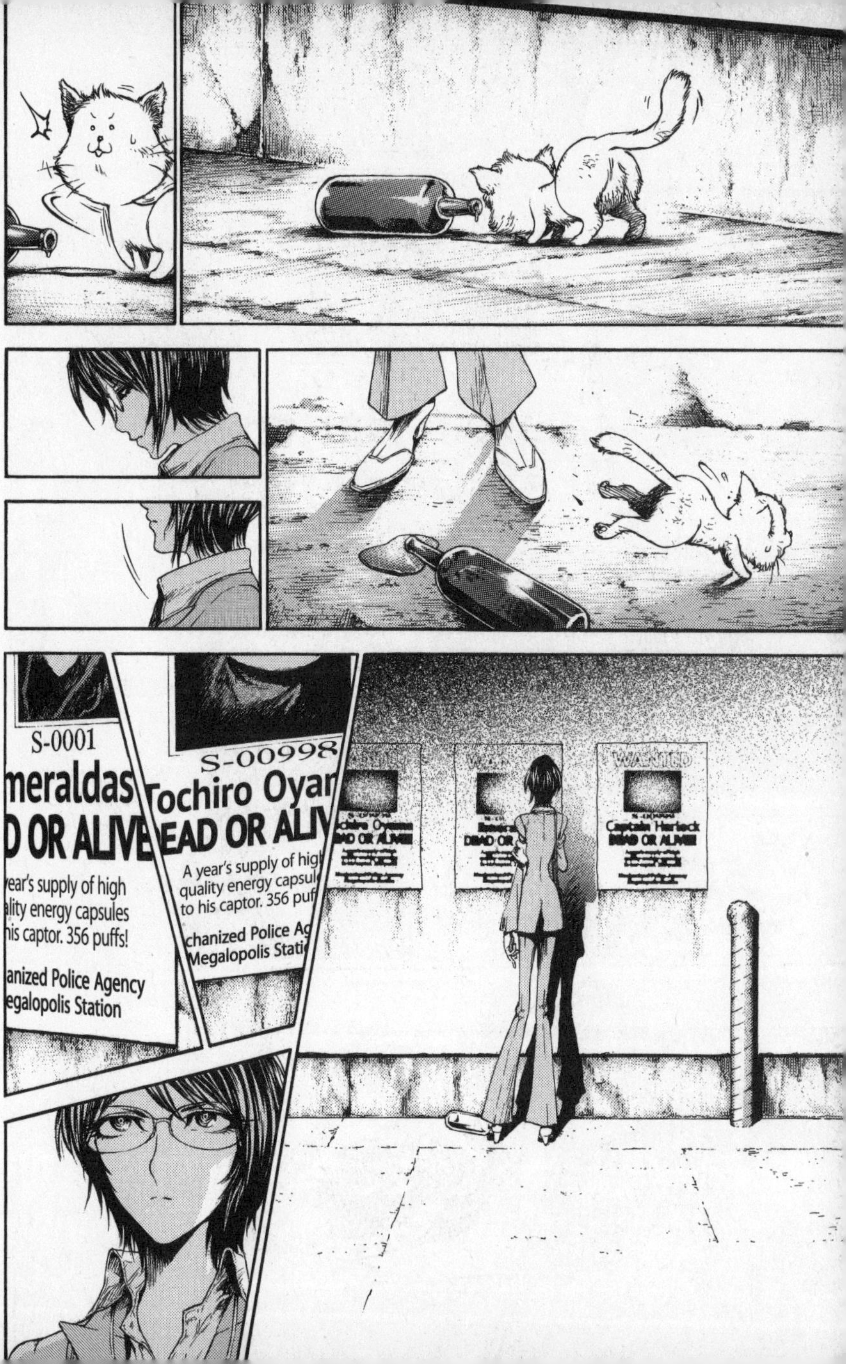
WANTED
Captain Harlock
DEAD OR ALIVE!!
S-00998
Tochiro Oyam
EAD OR ALIV
A year's supply of high
quality energy capsul
to his captor. 356 puf
chanized Police Ag
Megalopolis Statio
S-0001
meraldas
D OR ALIVE
ear's supply of high
ality energy capsules
his captor. 356 puffs!
anized Police Agency
egalopolis Station

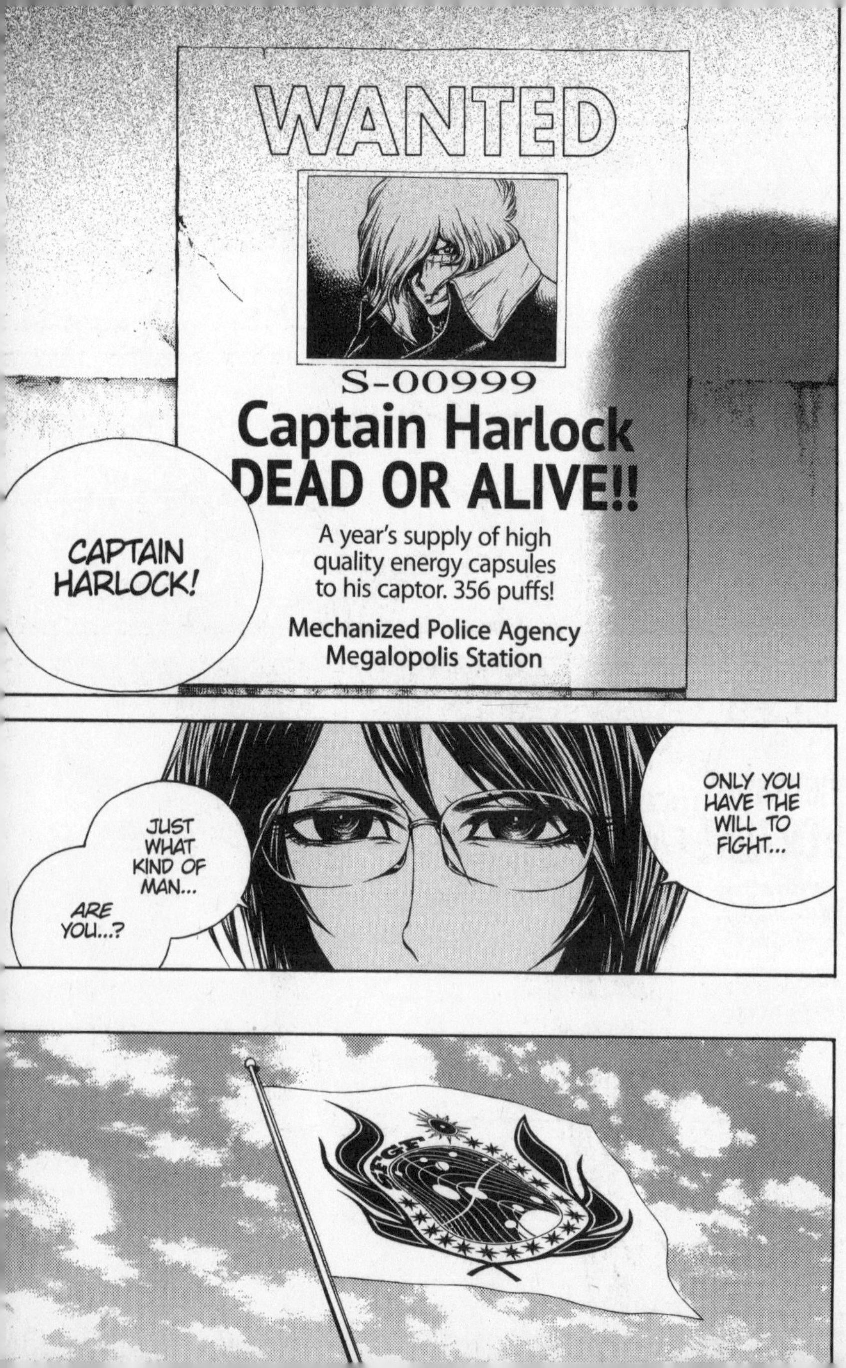
WANTED
S-00999
Captain Harlock
DEAD OR ALIVE!!
A year's supply of high quality energy capsules to his captor. 356 puffs!
Mechanized Police Agency
Megalopolis Station
CAPTAIN HARLOCK!
ONLY YOU HAVE THE WILL TO FIGHT...
JUST WHAT KIND OF MAN...
ARE YOU...?

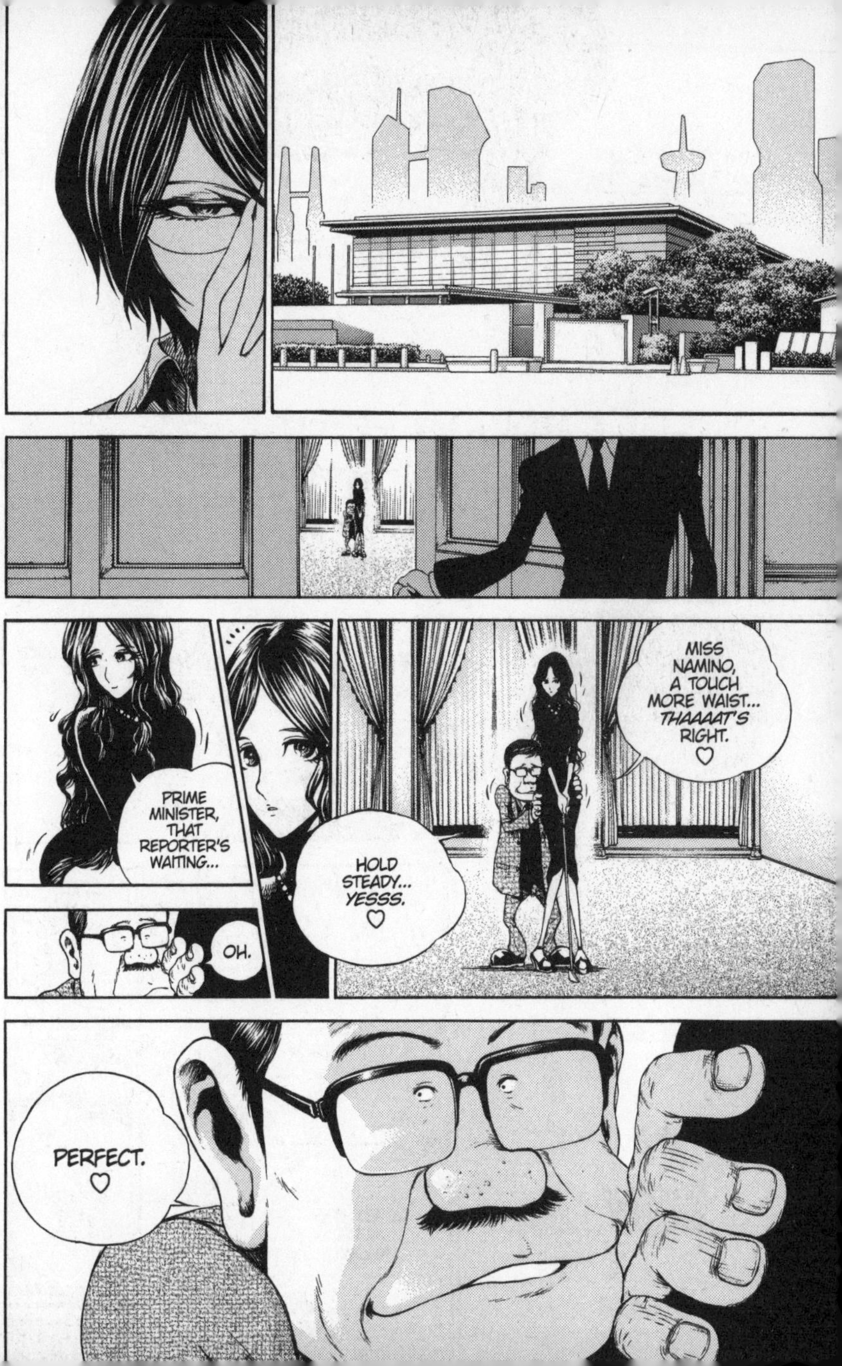
MISS NAMINO, A TOUCH MORE WAIST... *THAAAAT'S* RIGHT. ♡
HOLD STEADY... *YESSS.* ♡
PRIME MINISTER, THAT REPORTER'S WAITING...
OH.
PERFECT. ♡

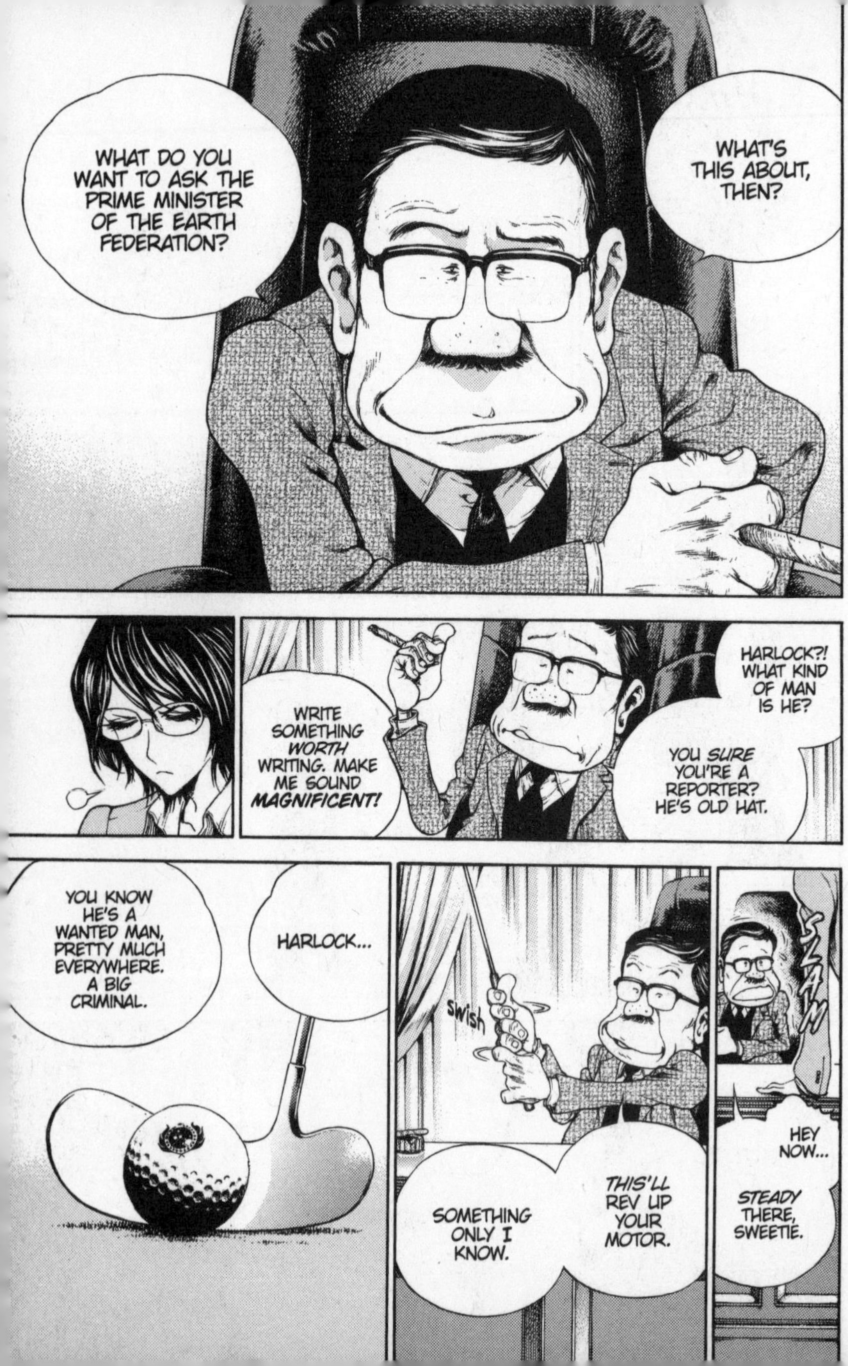
WHAT'S THIS ABOUT, THEN?
WHAT DO YOU WANT TO ASK THE PRIME MINISTER OF THE EARTH FEDERATION?
HARLOCK?! WHAT KIND OF MAN IS HE?
YOU *SURE* YOU'RE A REPORTER? HE'S OLD HAT.
WRITE SOMETHING *WORTH* WRITING. MAKE ME SOUND ***MAGNIFICENT!***
SLAM
HEY NOW...
STEADY THERE, SWEETIE.
swish
THIS'LL REV UP YOUR MOTOR.
SOMETHING ONLY I KNOW.
HARLOCK...
YOU KNOW HE'S A WANTED MAN, PRETTY MUCH EVERYWHERE. A BIG CRIMINAL.

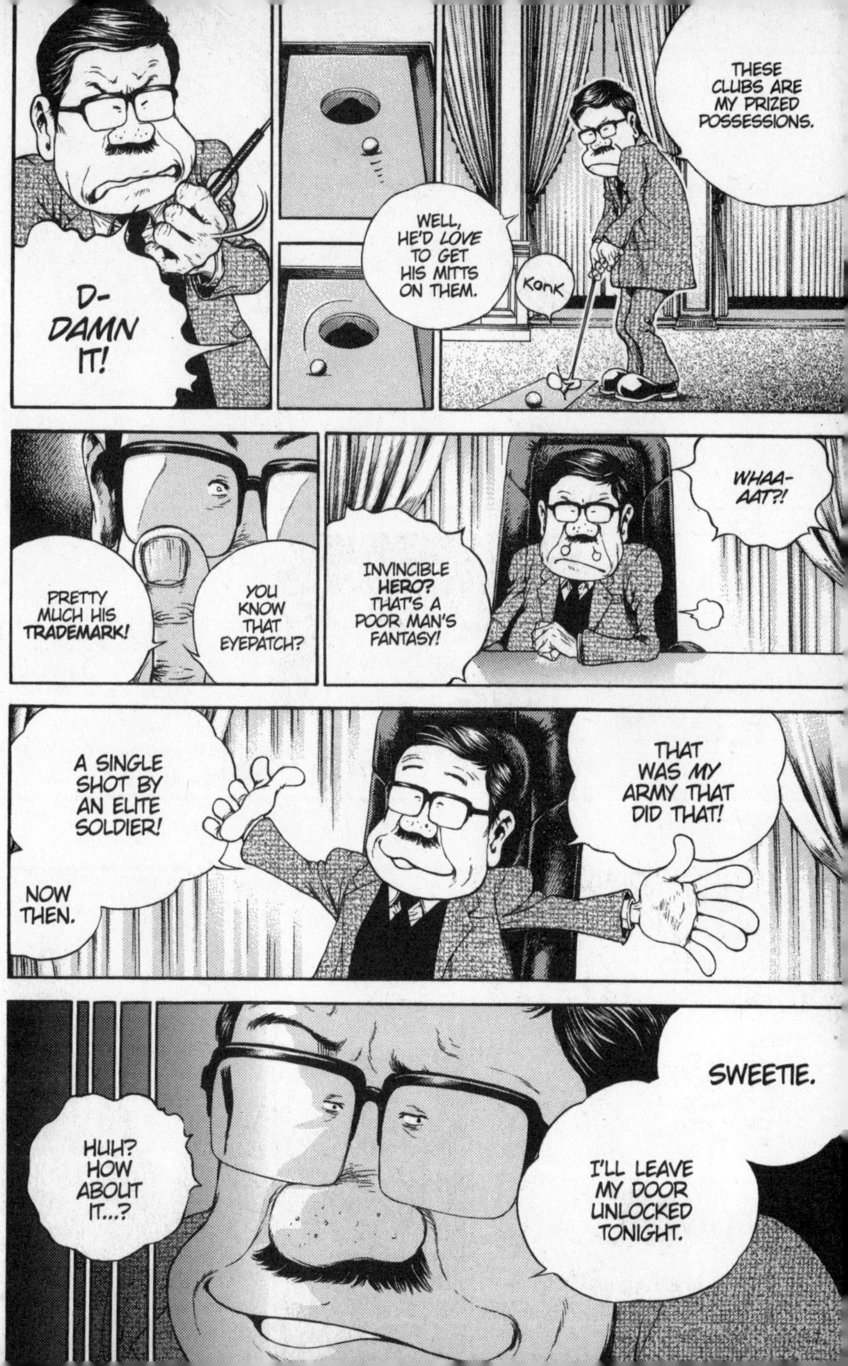
THESE CLUBS ARE MY PRIZED POSSESSIONS.
Konk
WELL, HE'D LOVE TO GET HIS MITTS ON THEM.
D-DAMN IT!
WHAAA-AAT?!
INVINCIBLE HERO? THAT'S A POOR MAN'S FANTASY!
YOU KNOW THAT EYEPATCH?
PRETTY MUCH HIS TRADEMARK!
THAT WAS MY ARMY THAT DID THAT!
A SINGLE SHOT BY AN ELITE SOLDIER!
NOW THEN.
SWEETIE.
I'LL LEAVE MY DOOR UNLOCKED TONIGHT.
HUH? HOW ABOUT IT...?

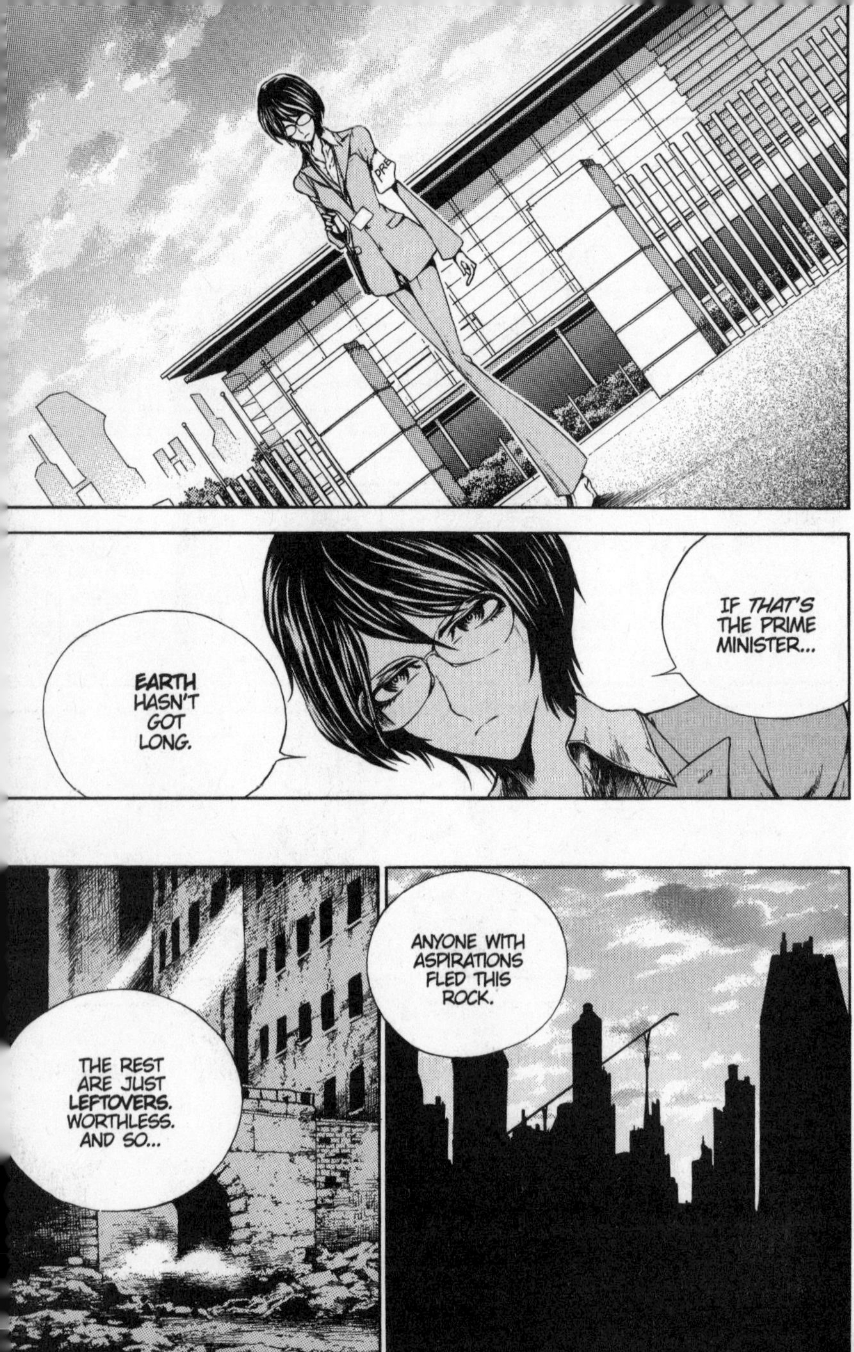
PRE
IF *THAT'S* THE PRIME MINISTER...
EARTH HASN'T GOT LONG.
ANYONE WITH ASPIRATIONS FLED THIS ROCK.
THE REST ARE JUST LEFTOVERS. WORTHLESS. AND SO...

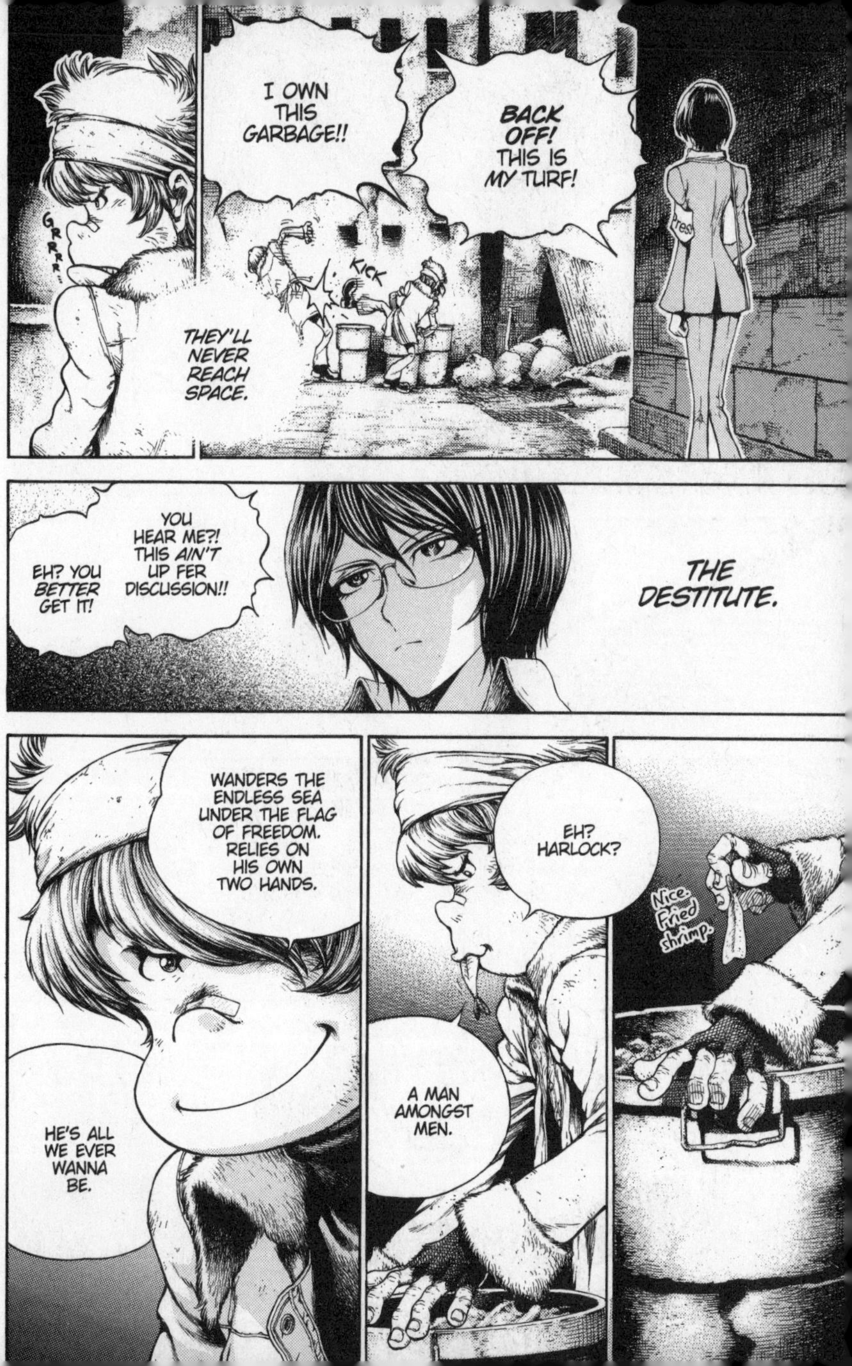
BACK OFF! THIS IS MY TURF!
I OWN THIS GARBAGE!!
KICK
THEY'LL NEVER REACH SPACE.
GRRRR...
THE DESTITUTE.
YOU HEAR ME?! THIS AIN'T UP FER DISCUSSION!!
EH? YOU BETTER GET IT!
Nice. Fried shrimp.
EH? HARLOCK?
A MAN AMONGST MEN.
WANDERS THE ENDLESS SEA UNDER THE FLAG OF FREEDOM. RELIES ON HIS OWN TWO HANDS.
HE'S ALL WE EVER WANNA BE.

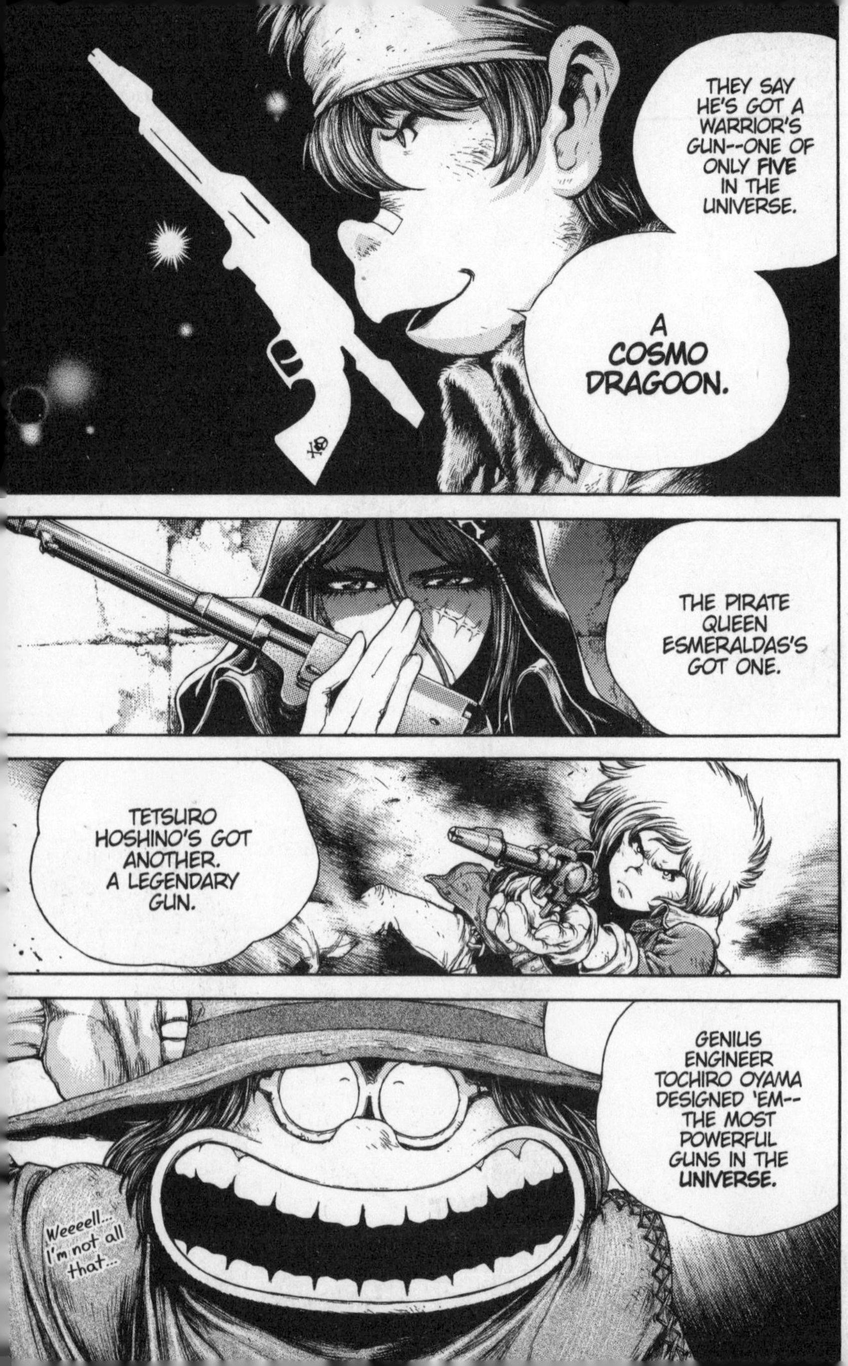
THEY SAY HE'S GOT A WARRIOR'S GUN--ONE OF ONLY FIVE IN THE UNIVERSE.
A COSMO DRAGOON.
THE PIRATE QUEEN ESMERALDAS'S GOT ONE.
TETSURO HOSHINO'S GOT ANOTHER. A LEGENDARY GUN.
GENIUS ENGINEER TOCHIRO OYAMA DESIGNED 'EM--THE MOST POWERFUL GUNS IN THE UNIVERSE.
Weeeell... I'm not all that...

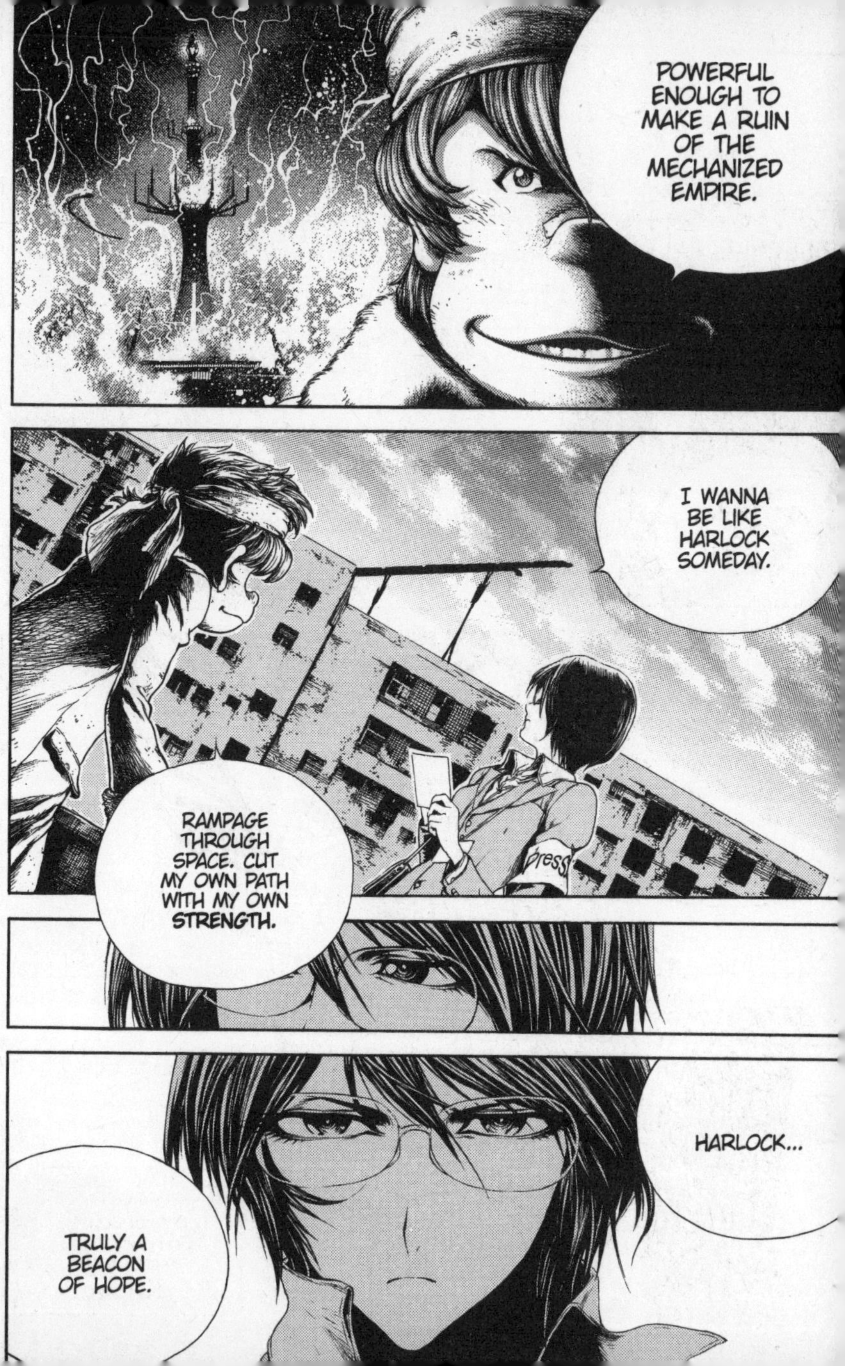
POWERFUL ENOUGH TO MAKE A RUIN OF THE MECHANIZED EMPIRE.
I WANNA BE LIKE HARLOCK SOMEDAY.
RAMPAGE THROUGH SPACE. CUT MY OWN PATH WITH MY OWN STRENGTH.
HARLOCK...
TRULY A BEACON OF HOPE.

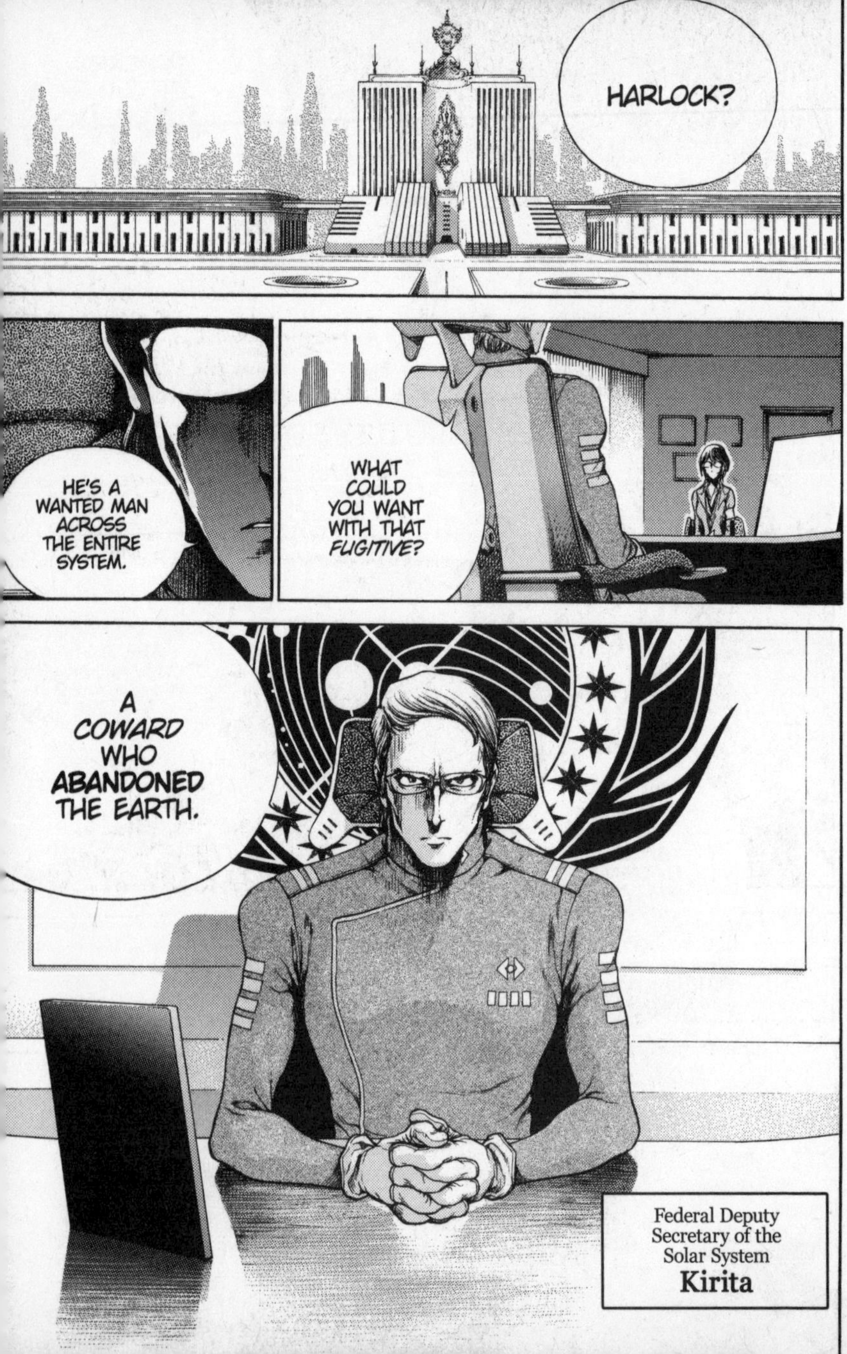
HARLOCK?
WHAT COULD YOU WANT WITH THAT FUGITIVE?
HE'S A WANTED MAN ACROSS THE ENTIRE SYSTEM.
A COWARD WHO ABANDONED THE EARTH.
Federal Deputy Secretary of the Solar System
Kirita

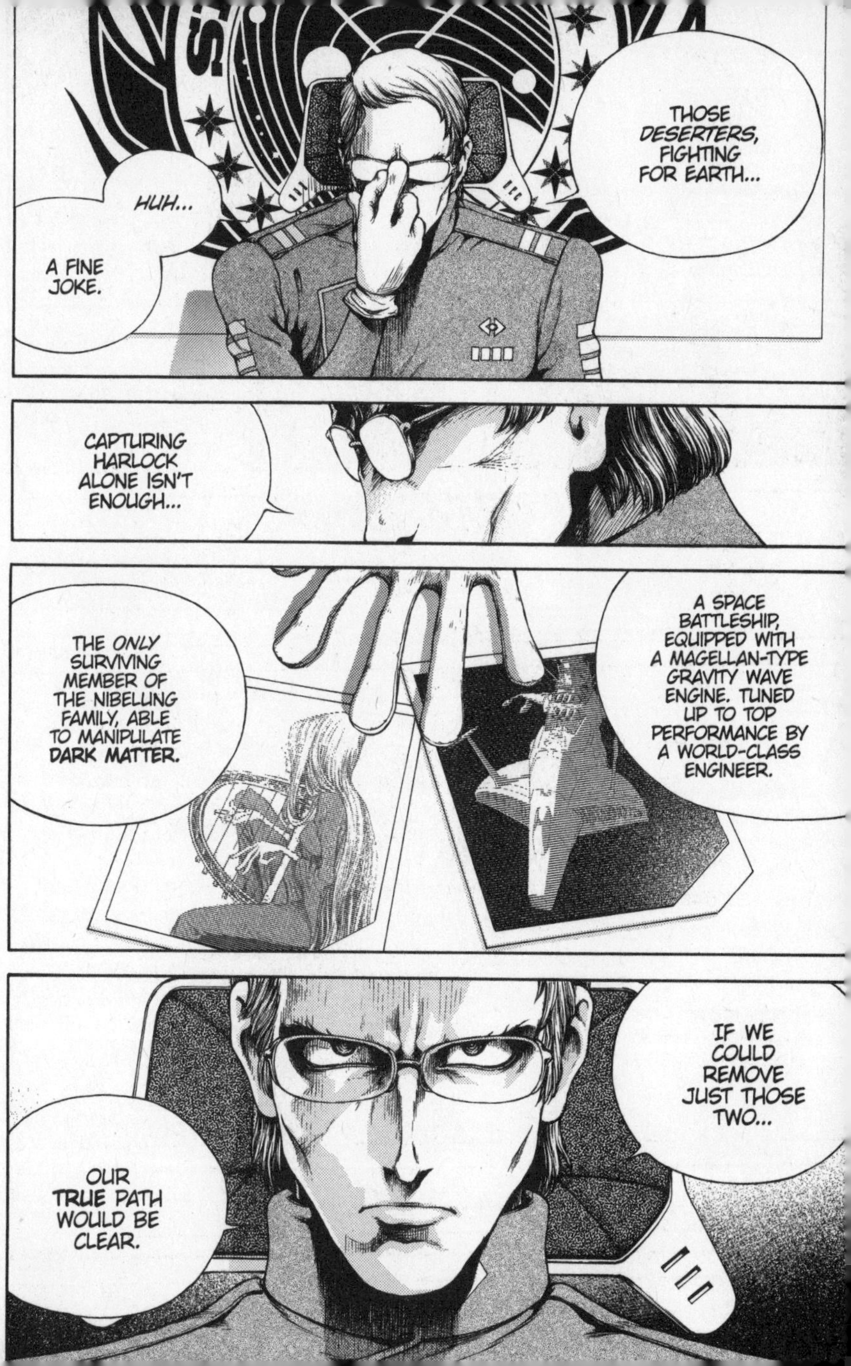
THOSE DESERTERS, FIGHTING FOR EARTH...
HUH...
A FINE JOKE.
CAPTURING HARLOCK ALONE ISN'T ENOUGH...
A SPACE BATTLESHIP, EQUIPPED WITH A MAGELLAN-TYPE GRAVITY WAVE ENGINE. TUNED UP TO TOP PERFORMANCE BY A WORLD-CLASS ENGINEER.
THE *ONLY* SURVIVING MEMBER OF THE NIBELUNG FAMILY, ABLE TO MANIPULATE **DARK MATTER**.
IF WE COULD REMOVE JUST THOSE TWO...
OUR TRUE PATH WOULD BE CLEAR.

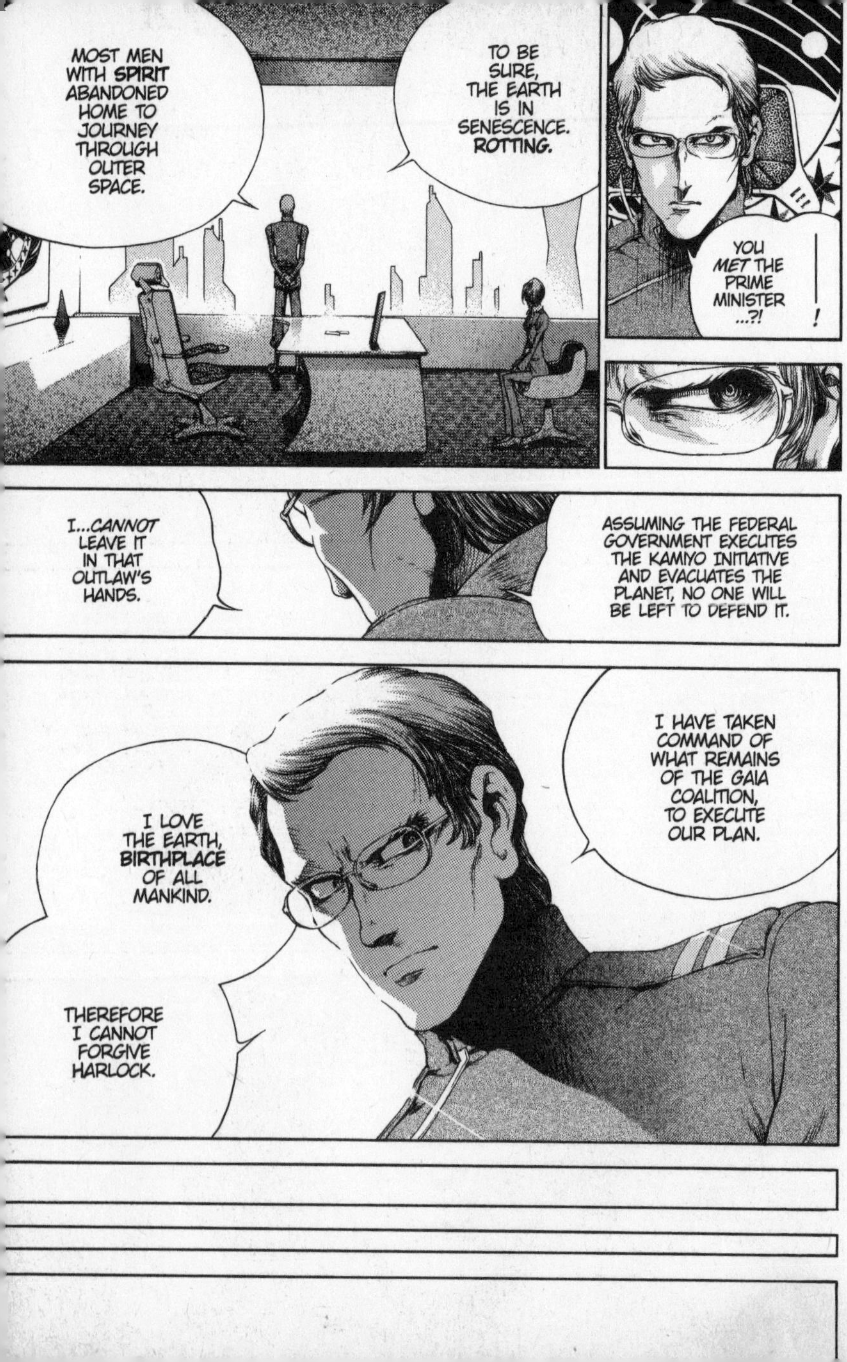
YOU MET THE PRIME MINISTER ...?!
!
TO BE SURE, THE EARTH IS IN SENESCENCE. ROTTING.
MOST MEN WITH SPIRIT ABANDONED HOME TO JOURNEY THROUGH OUTER SPACE.
ASSUMING THE FEDERAL GOVERNMENT EXECUTES THE KAMIYO INITIATIVE AND EVACUATES THE PLANET, NO ONE WILL BE LEFT TO DEFEND IT.
I...CANNOT LEAVE IT IN THAT OUTLAW'S HANDS.
I HAVE TAKEN COMMAND OF WHAT REMAINS OF THE GAIA COALITION, TO EXECUTE OUR PLAN.
I LOVE THE EARTH, BIRTHPLACE OF ALL MANKIND.
THEREFORE I CANNOT FORGIVE HARLOCK.

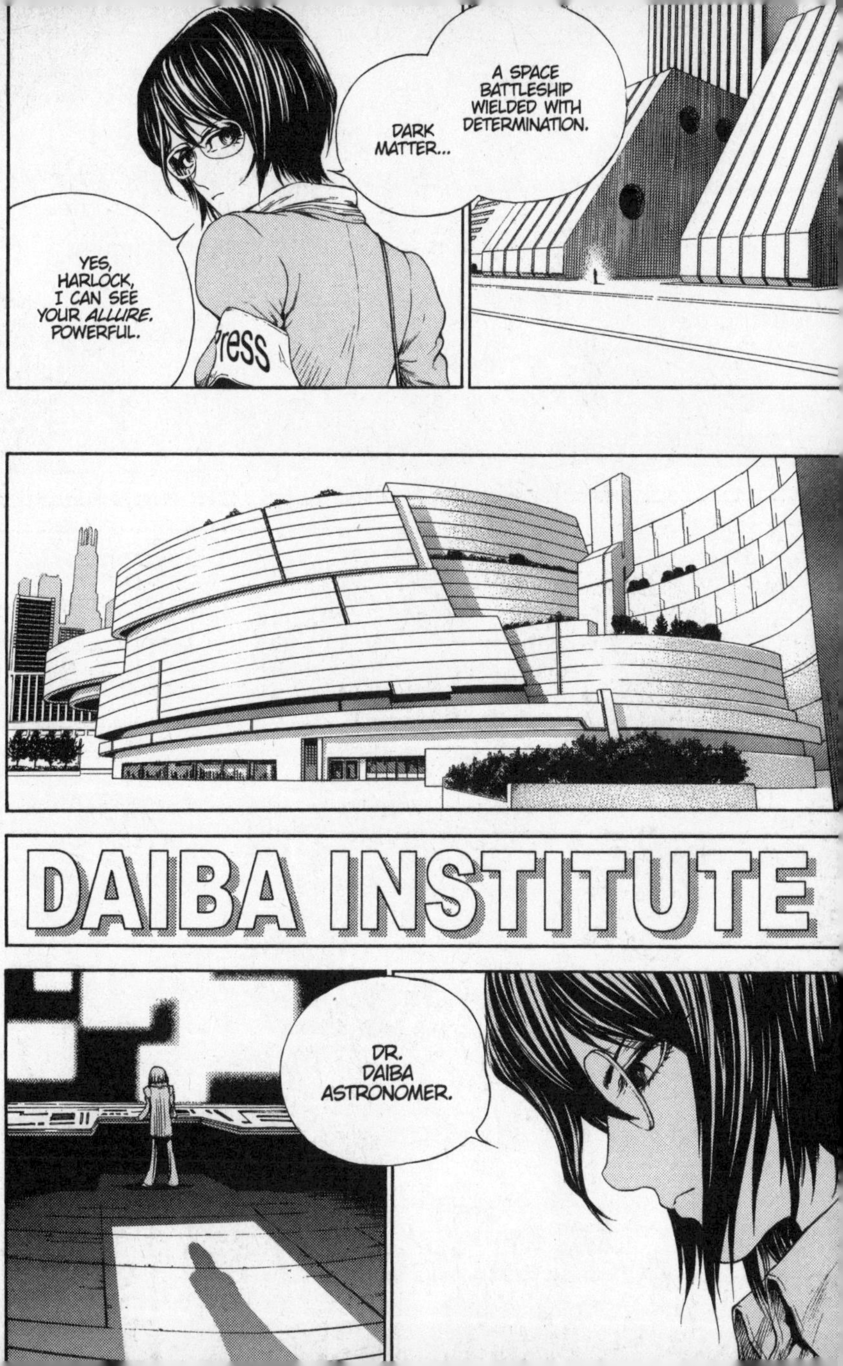
A SPACE BATTLESHIP WIELDED WITH DETERMINATION.
DARK MATTER...
YES, HARLOCK, I CAN SEE YOUR *ALLURE*. POWERFUL.
Press
DAIBA INSTITUTE
DR. DAIBA ASTRONOMER.

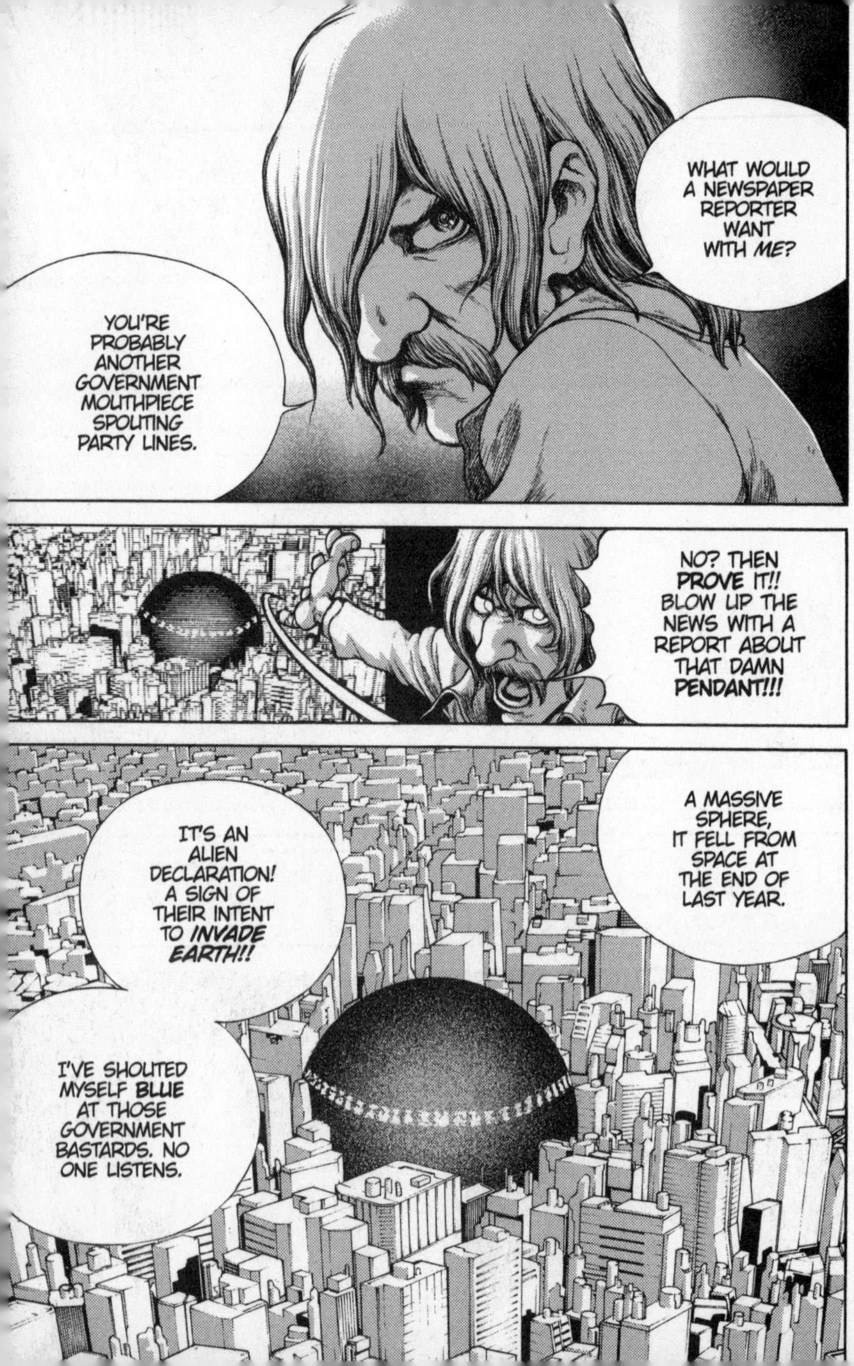
WHAT WOULD A NEWSPAPER REPORTER WANT WITH *ME*?
YOU'RE PROBABLY ANOTHER GOVERNMENT MOUTHPIECE SPOUTING PARTY LINES.
NO? THEN **PROVE** IT!! BLOW UP THE NEWS WITH A REPORT ABOUT THAT DAMN **PENDANT**!!!
A MASSIVE SPHERE, IT FELL FROM SPACE AT THE END OF LAST YEAR.
IT'S AN ALIEN DECLARATION! A SIGN OF THEIR INTENT TO ***INVADE EARTH***!!
I'VE SHOUTED MYSELF **BLUE** AT THOSE GOVERNMENT BASTARDS. NO ONE LISTENS.

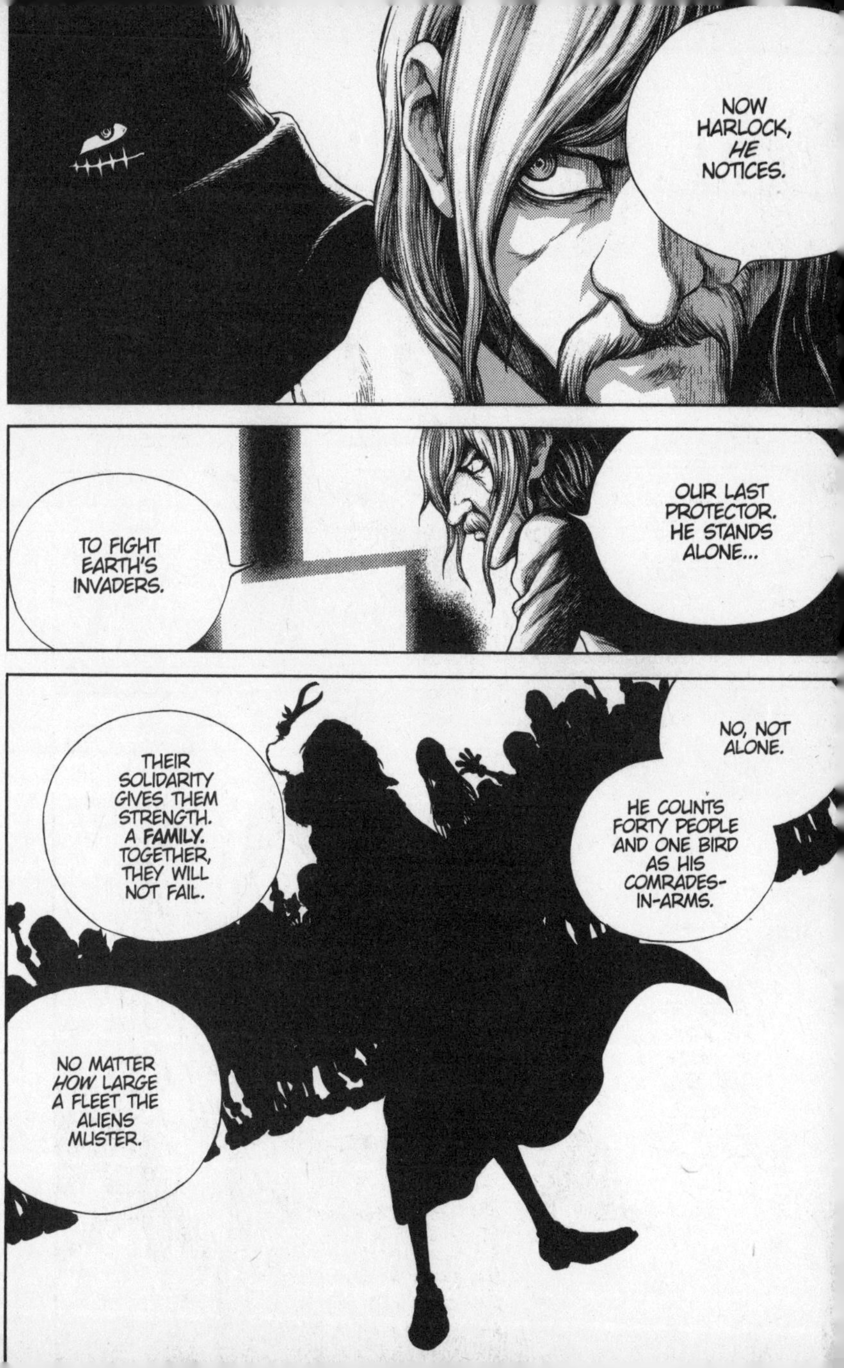
NOW HARLOCK, *HE* NOTICES.
OUR LAST PROTECTOR. HE STANDS ALONE...
TO FIGHT EARTH'S INVADERS.
NO, NOT ALONE.
HE COUNTS FORTY PEOPLE AND ONE BIRD AS HIS COMRADES-IN-ARMS.
THEIR SOLIDARITY GIVES THEM STRENGTH. A **FAMILY**. TOGETHER, THEY WILL NOT FAIL.
NO MATTER *HOW* LARGE A FLEET THE ALIENS MUSTER.

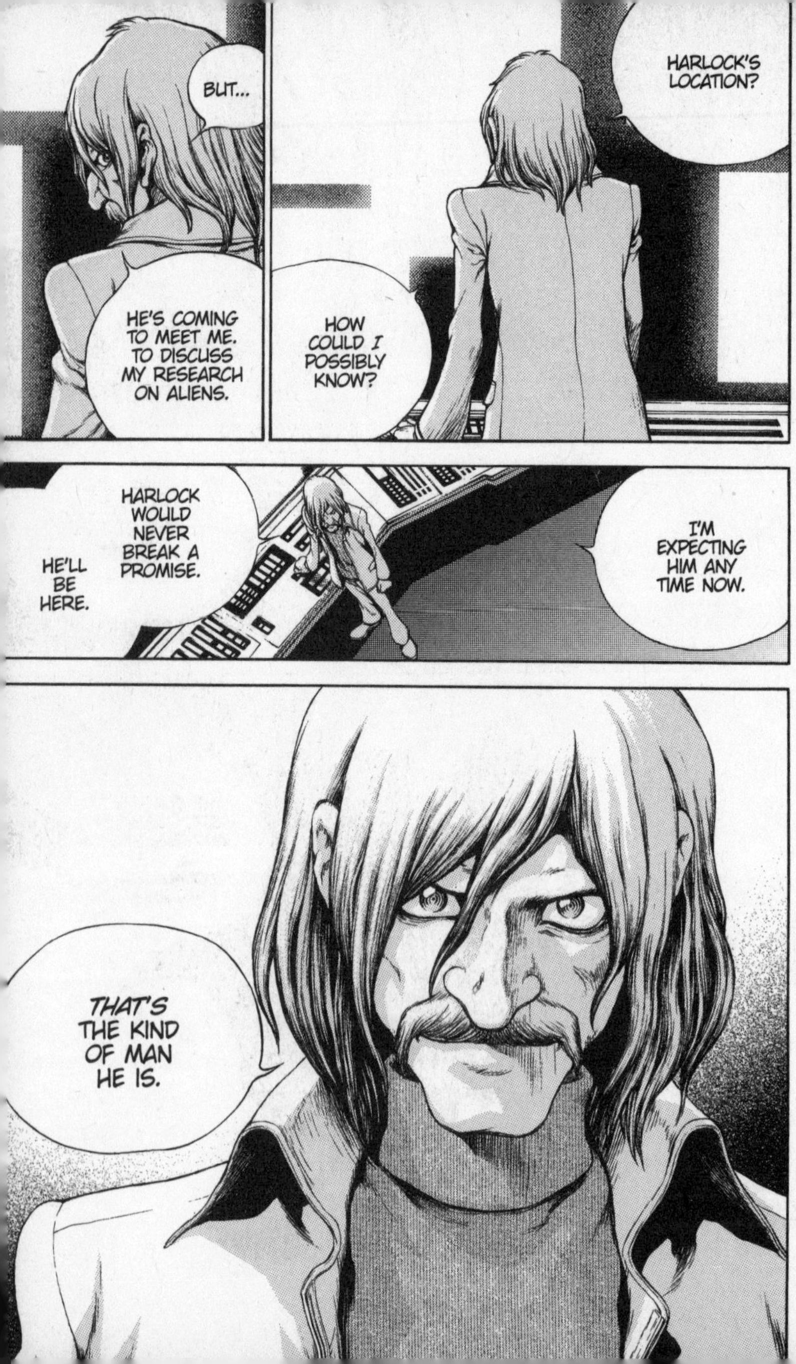
HARLOCK'S LOCATION?
HOW COULD I POSSIBLY KNOW?
BUT...
HE'S COMING TO MEET ME. TO DISCUSS MY RESEARCH ON ALIENS.
I'M EXPECTING HIM ANY TIME NOW.
HARLOCK WOULD NEVER BREAK A PROMISE.
HE'LL BE HERE.
THAT'S THE KIND OF MAN HE IS.

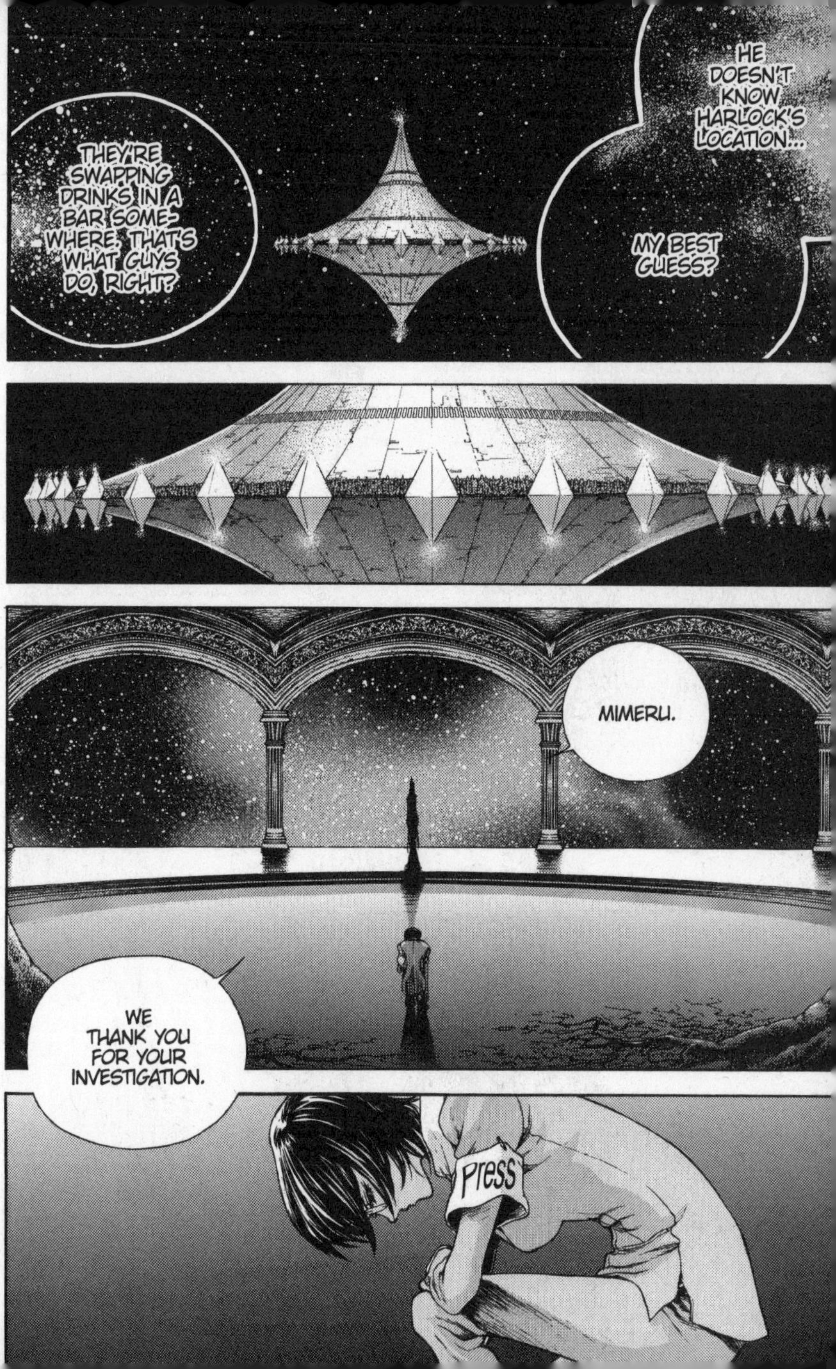
HE DOESN'T KNOW HARLOCK'S LOCATION...
MY BEST GUESS?
THEY'RE SWAPPING DRINKS IN A BAR SOME-WHERE. THAT'S WHAT GUYS DO, RIGHT?
MIMERU.
WE THANK YOU FOR YOUR INVESTIGATION.
Press

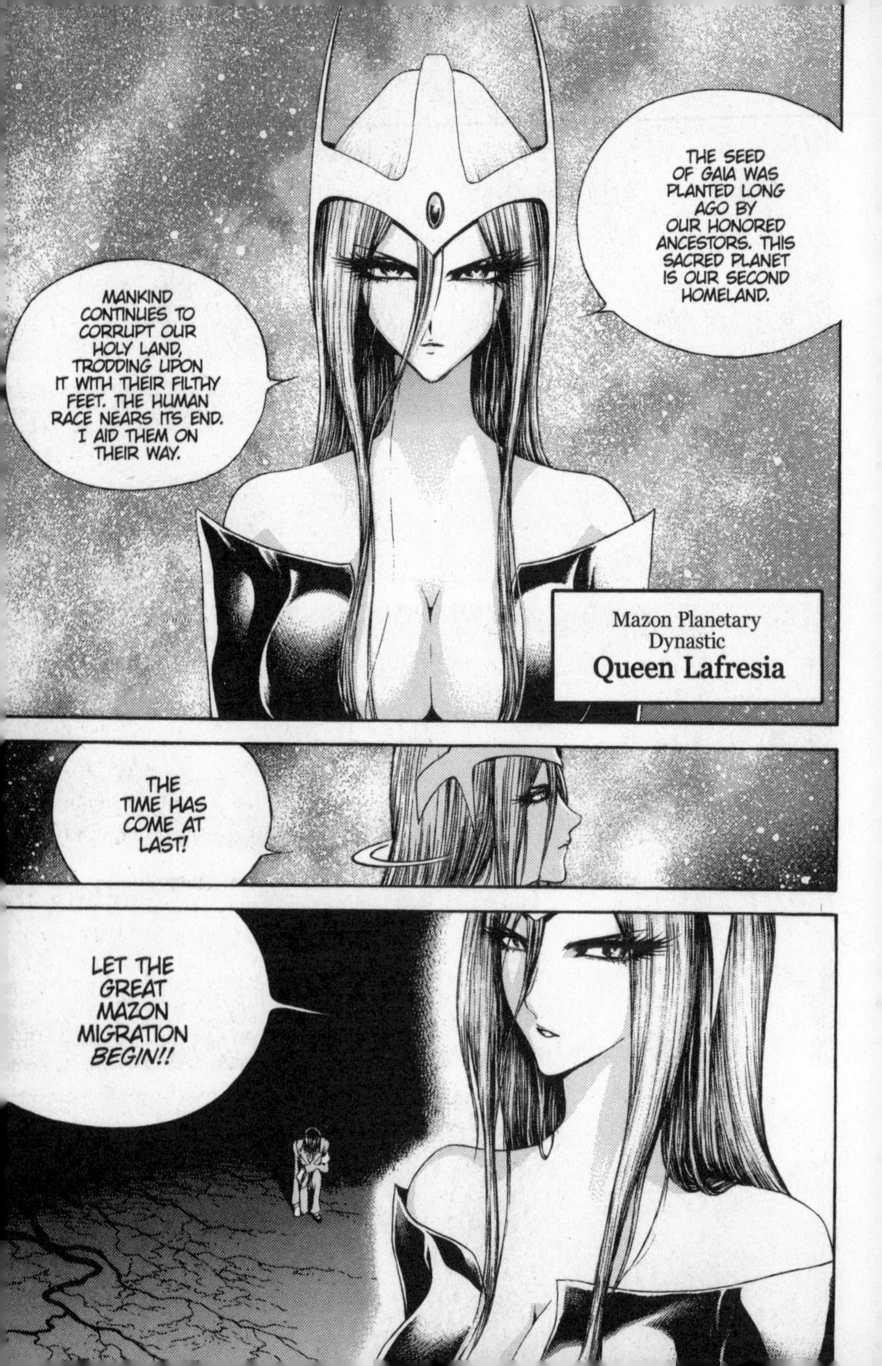
THE SEED OF GAIA WAS PLANTED LONG AGO BY OUR HONORED ANCESTORS. THIS SACRED PLANET IS OUR SECOND HOMELAND.
MANKIND CONTINUES TO CORRUPT OUR HOLY LAND, TRODDING UPON IT WITH THEIR FILTHY FEET. THE HUMAN RACE NEARS ITS END. I AID THEM ON THEIR WAY.
Mazon Planetary Dynastic
Queen Lafresia
THE TIME HAS COME AT LAST!
LET THE GREAT MAZON MIGRATION *BEGIN!!*

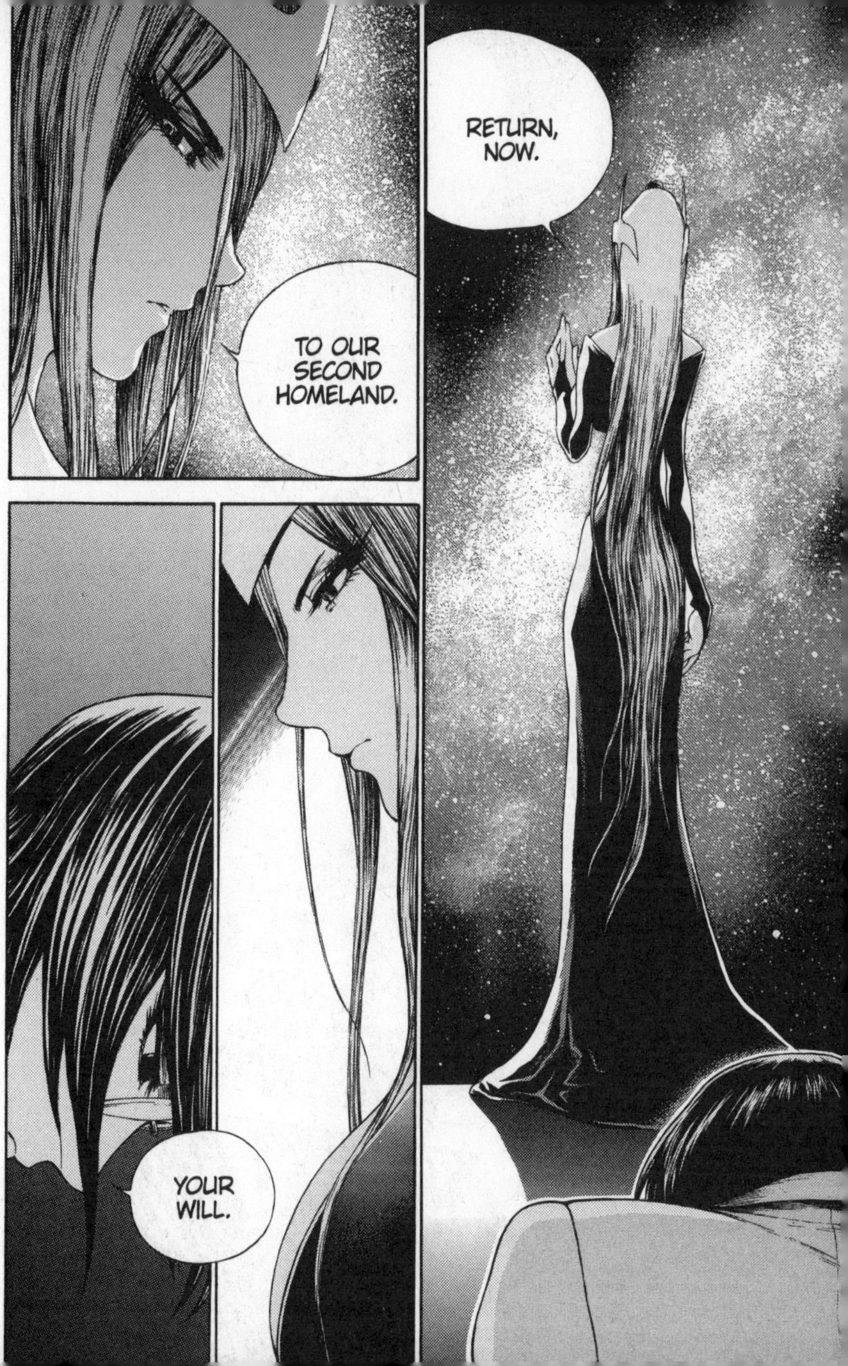
RETURN, NOW.
TO OUR SECOND HOMELAND.
YOUR WILL.

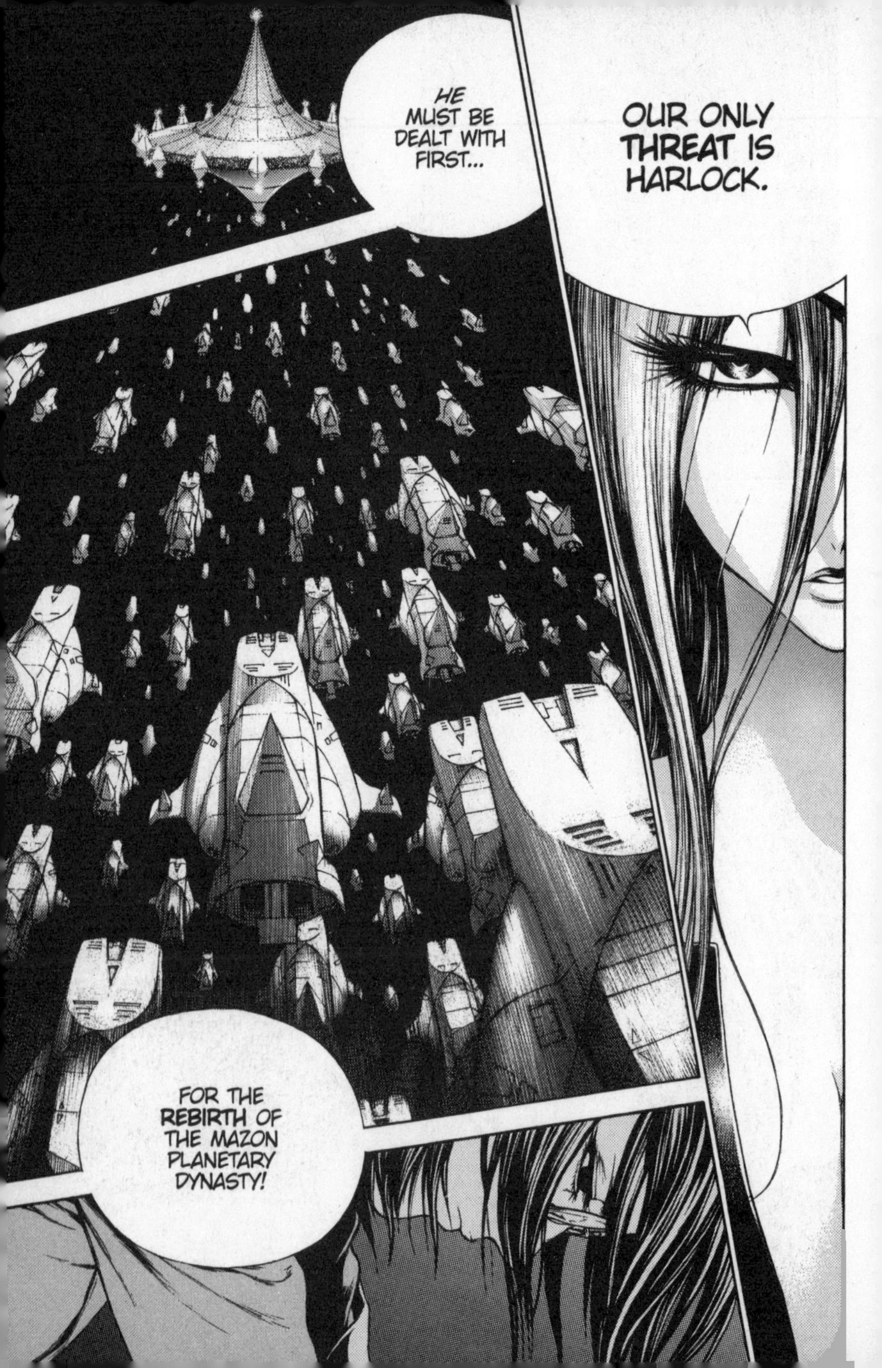
OUR ONLY THREAT IS HARLOCK.
HE MUST BE DEALT WITH FIRST...
FOR THE REBIRTH OF THE MAZON PLANETARY DYNASTY!

Crreeak...

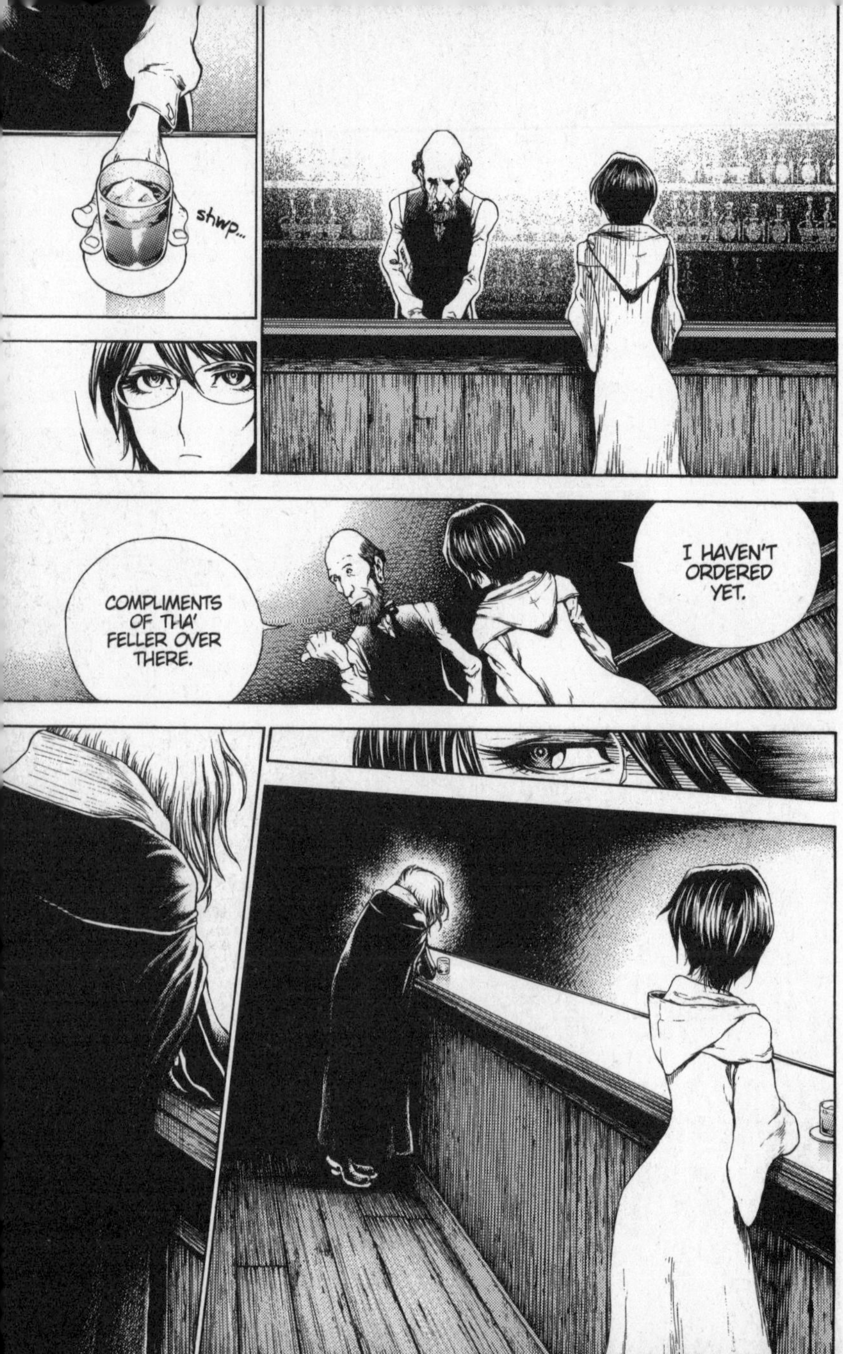
shwp...
I HAVEN'T ORDERED YET.
COMPLIMENTS OF THA' FELLER OVER THERE.

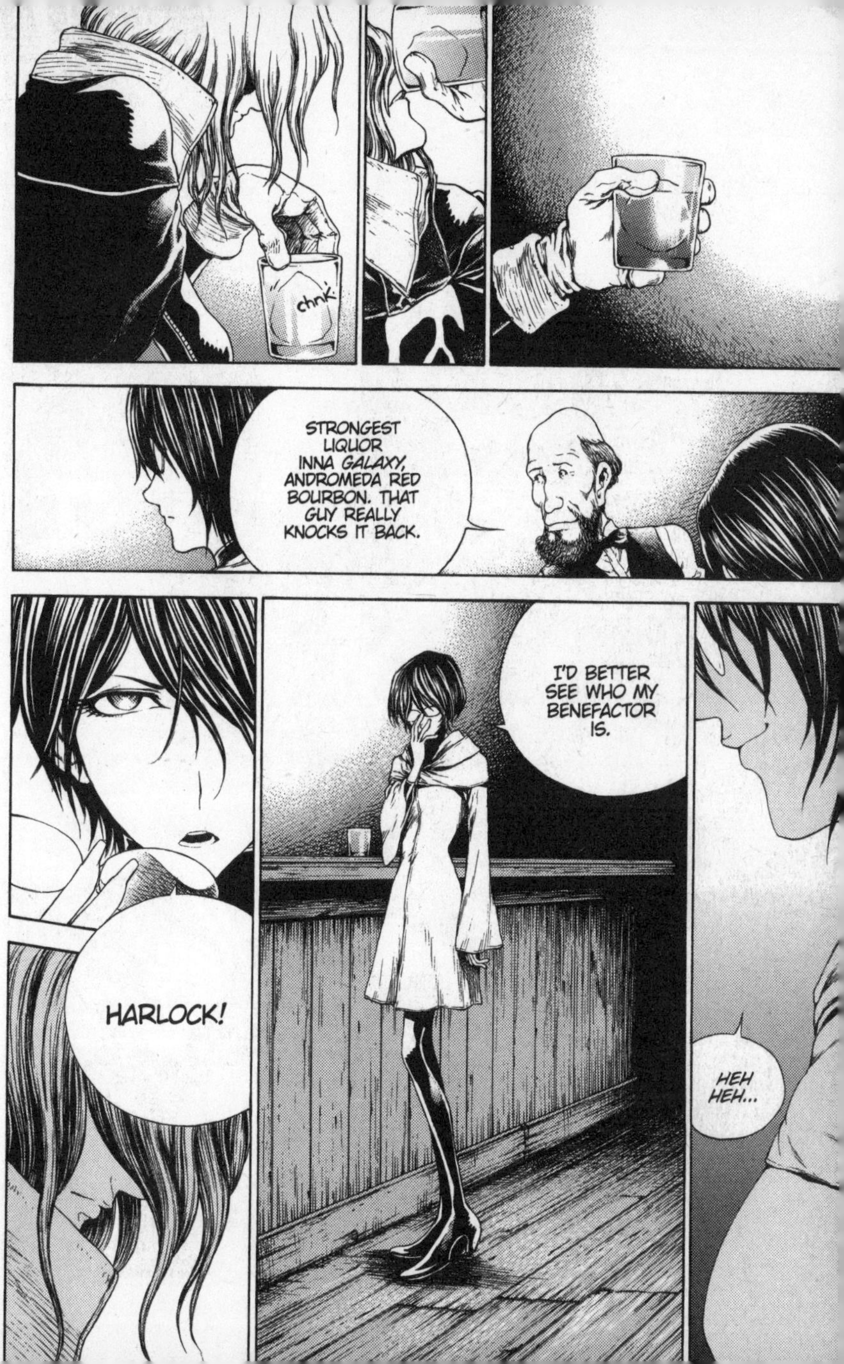
chnk
STRONGEST LIQUOR INNA *GALAXY*, ANDROMEDA RED BOURBON. THAT GUY REALLY KNOCKS IT BACK.
HEH HEH...
I'D BETTER SEE WHO MY BENEFACTOR IS.
HARLOCK!

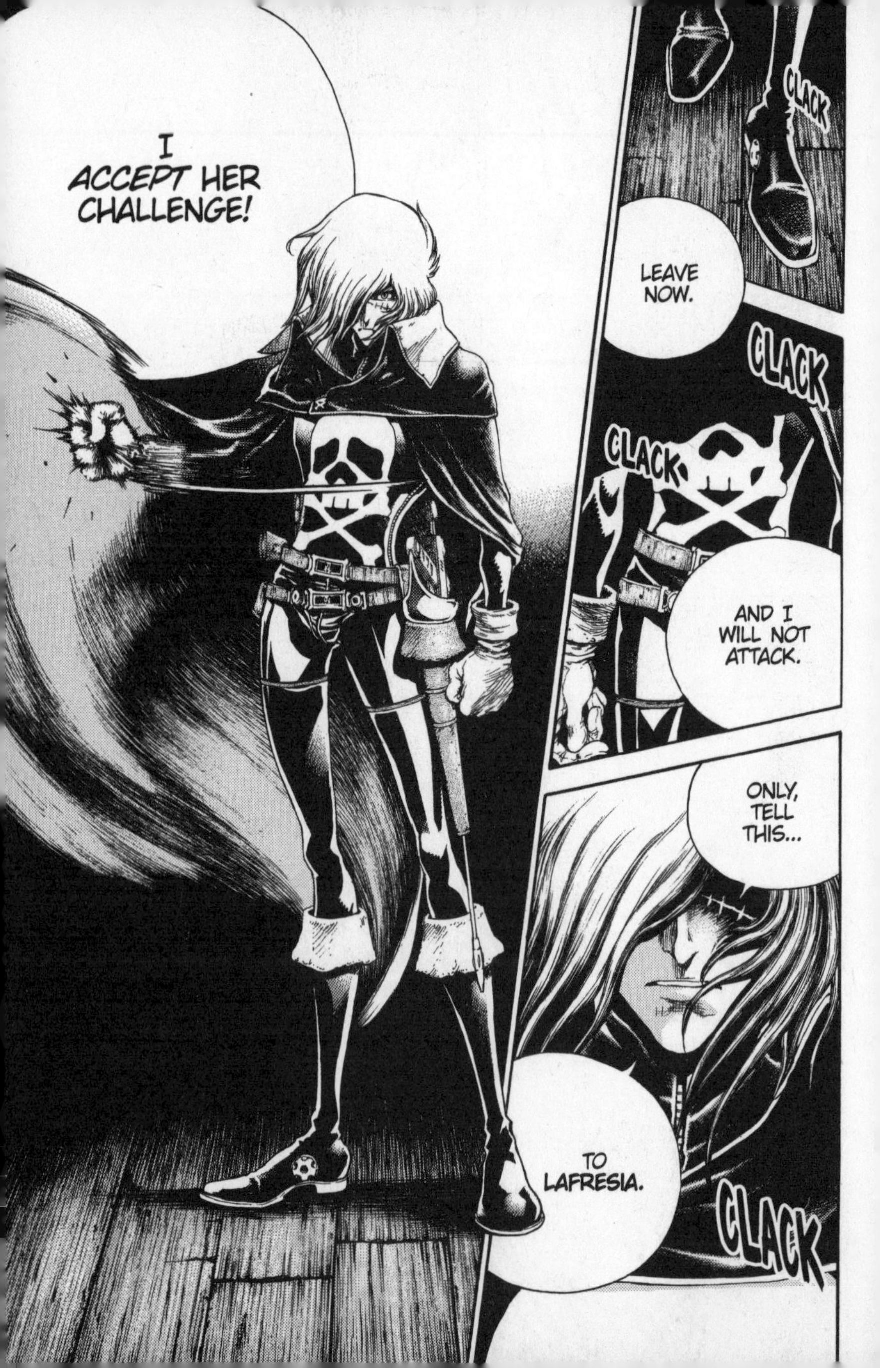
CLACK
LEAVE NOW.
CLACK
CLACK
AND I WILL NOT ATTACK.
ONLY, TELL THIS...
TO LAFRESIA.
CLACK
I *ACCEPT* HER CHALLENGE!

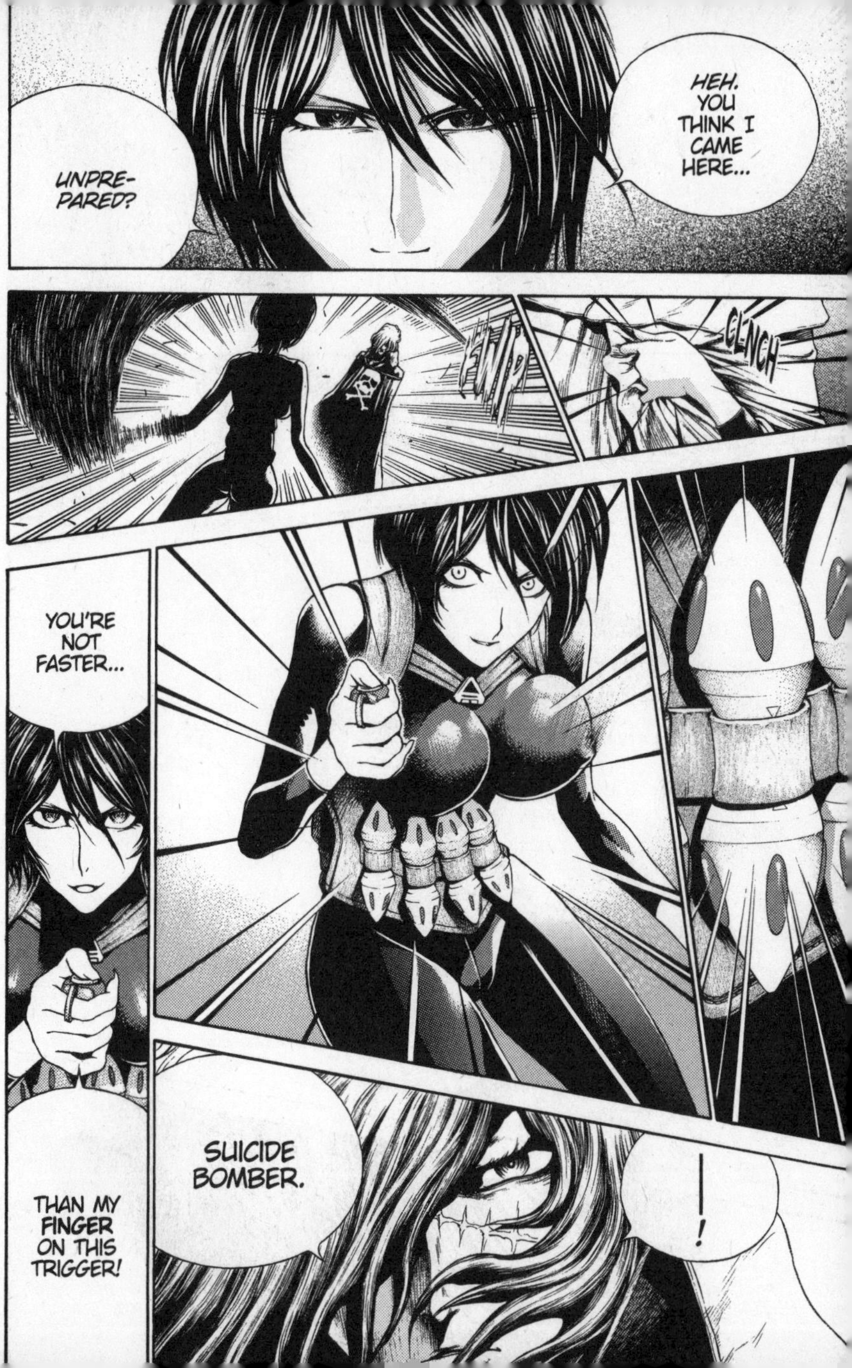
HEH. YOU THINK I CAME HERE...
UNPRE-PARED?
CLINCH
FWIP
!
SUICIDE BOMBER.
YOU'RE NOT FASTER...
THAN MY FINGER ON THIS TRIGGER!

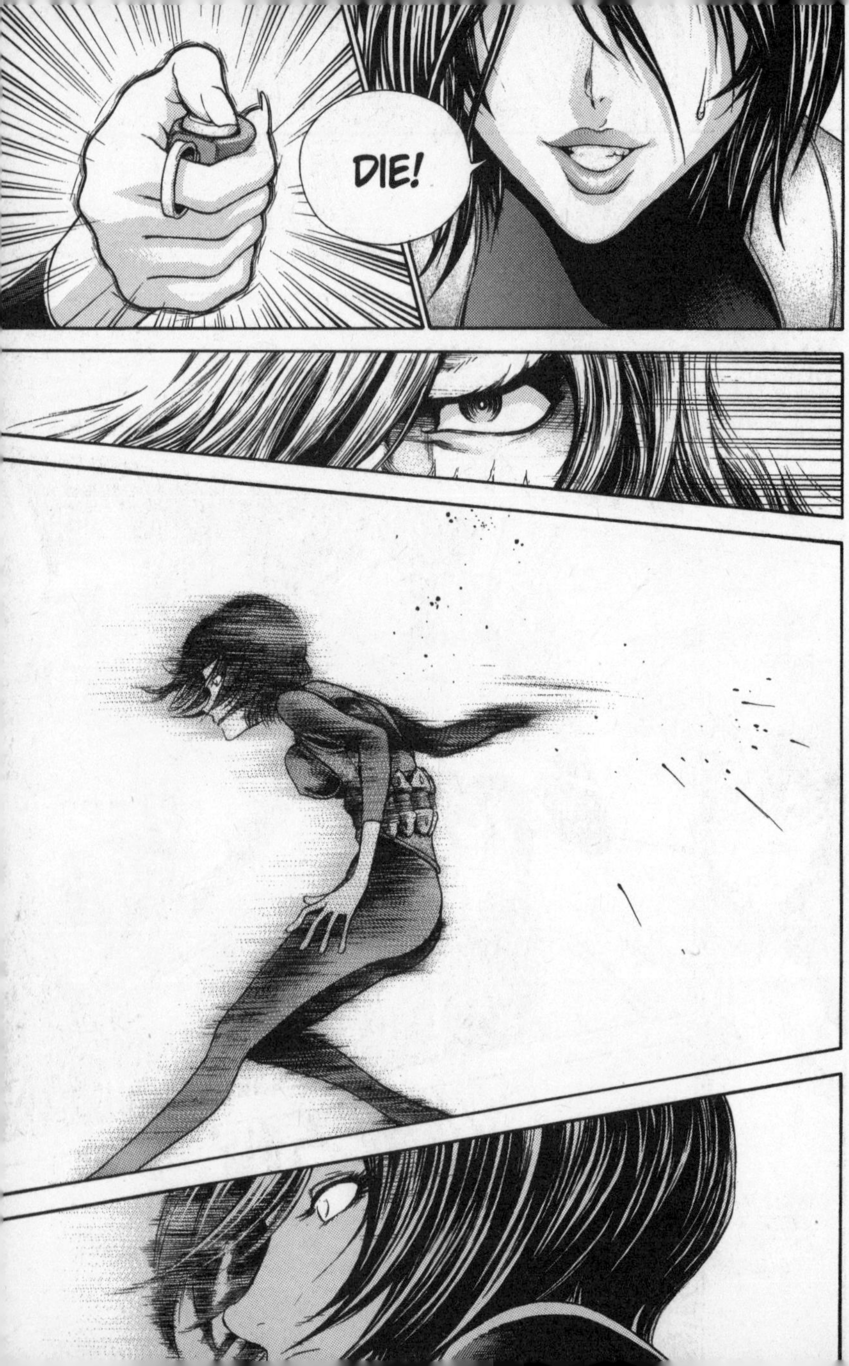
DIE!

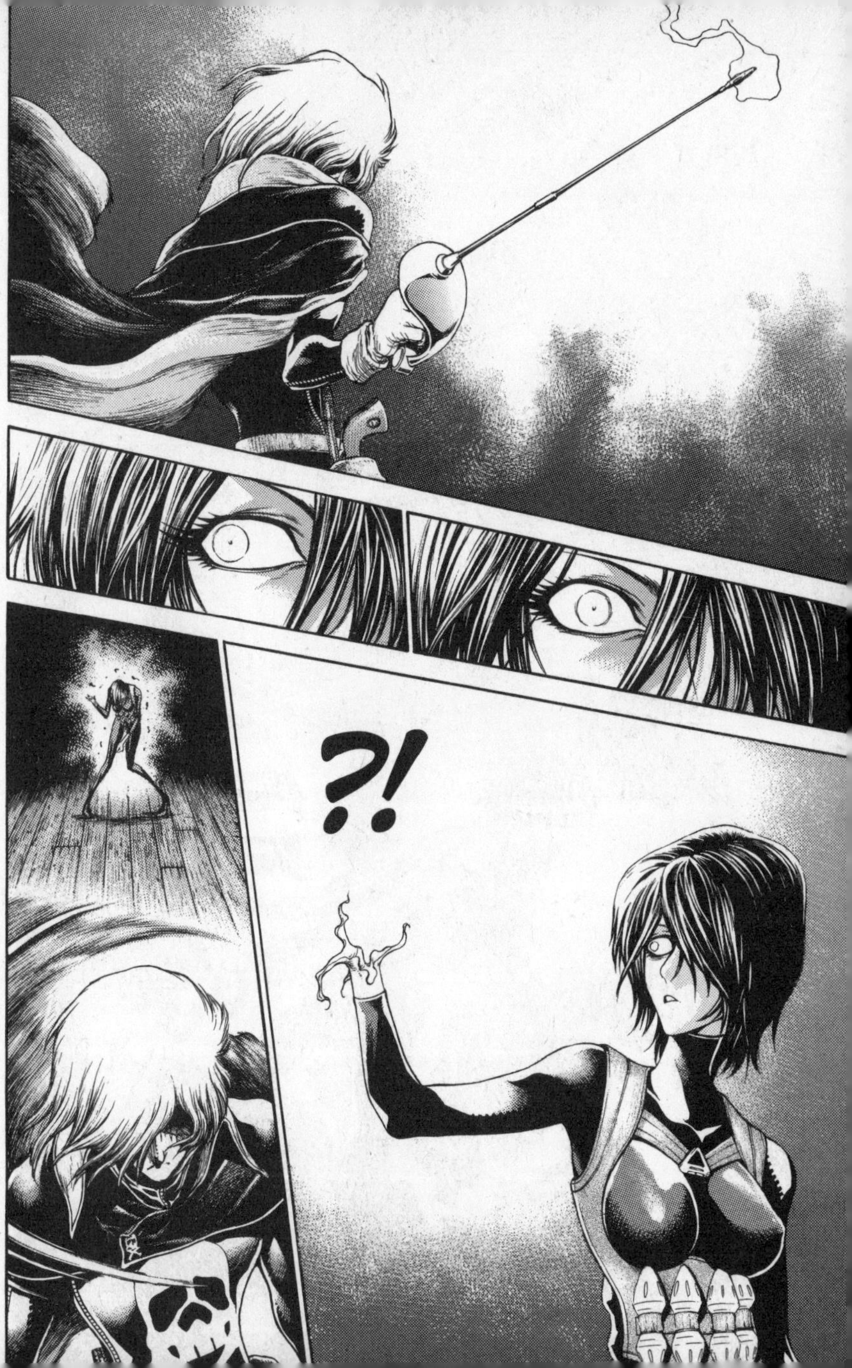
?!

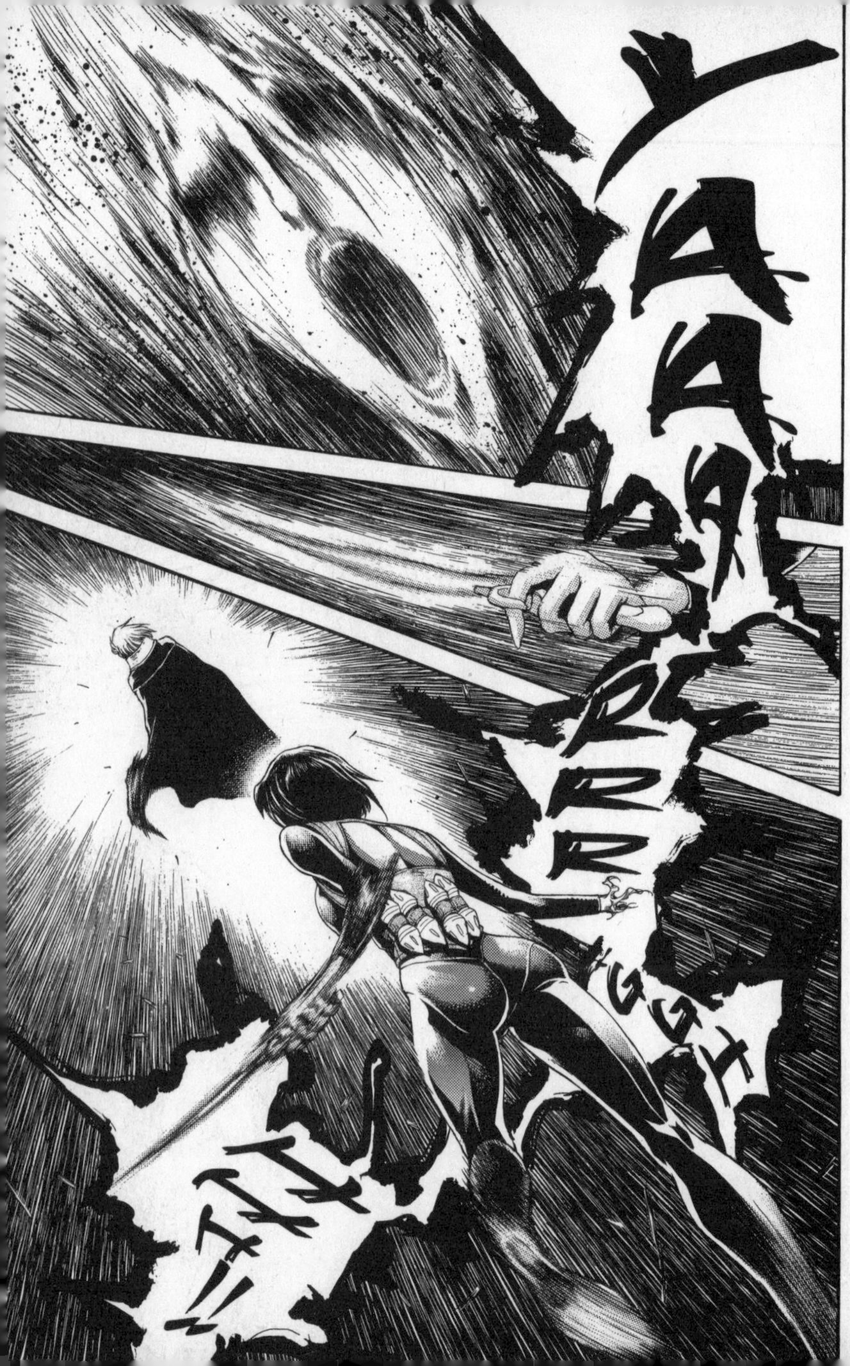
YAAARRRRRGGH

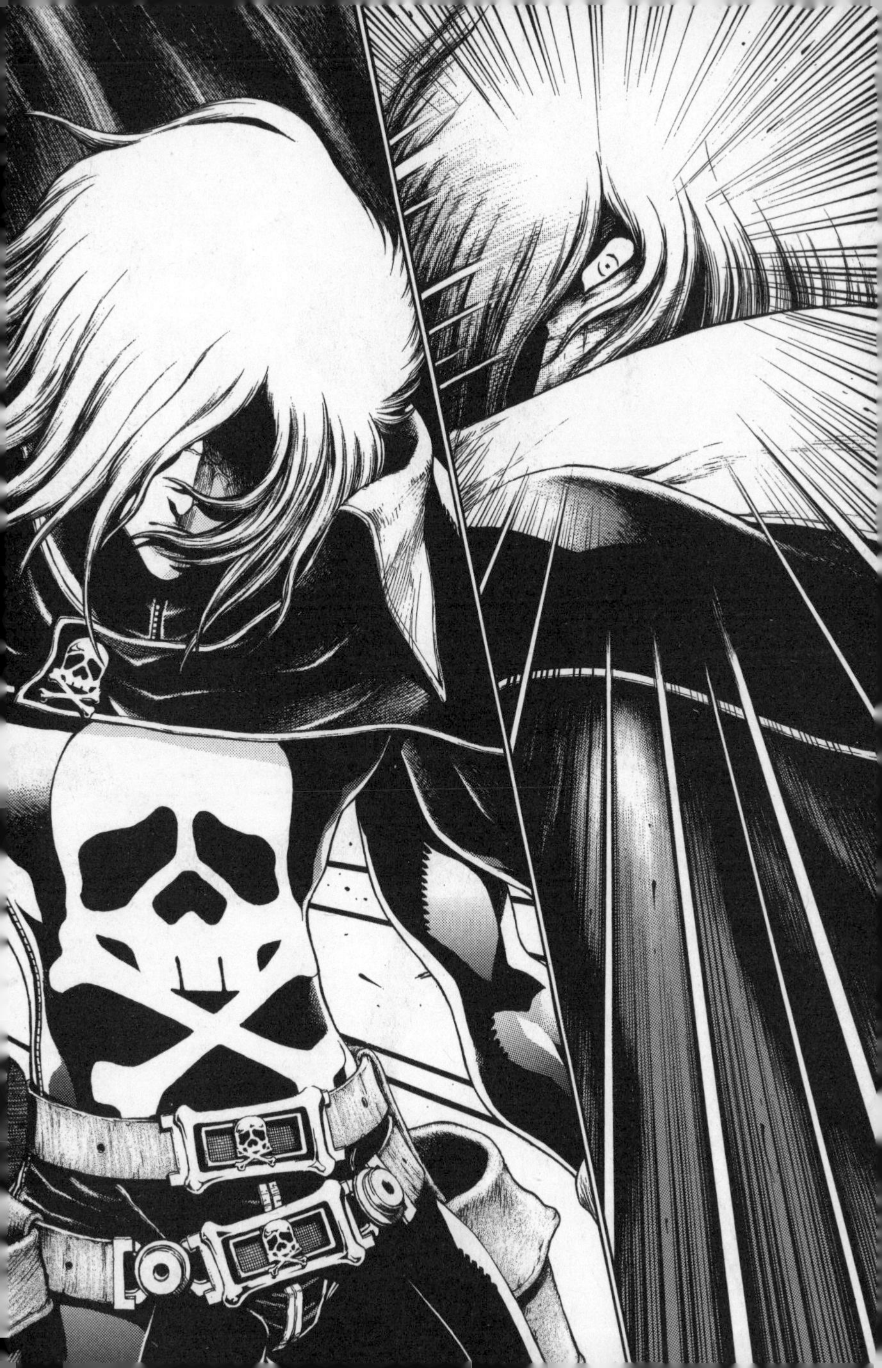

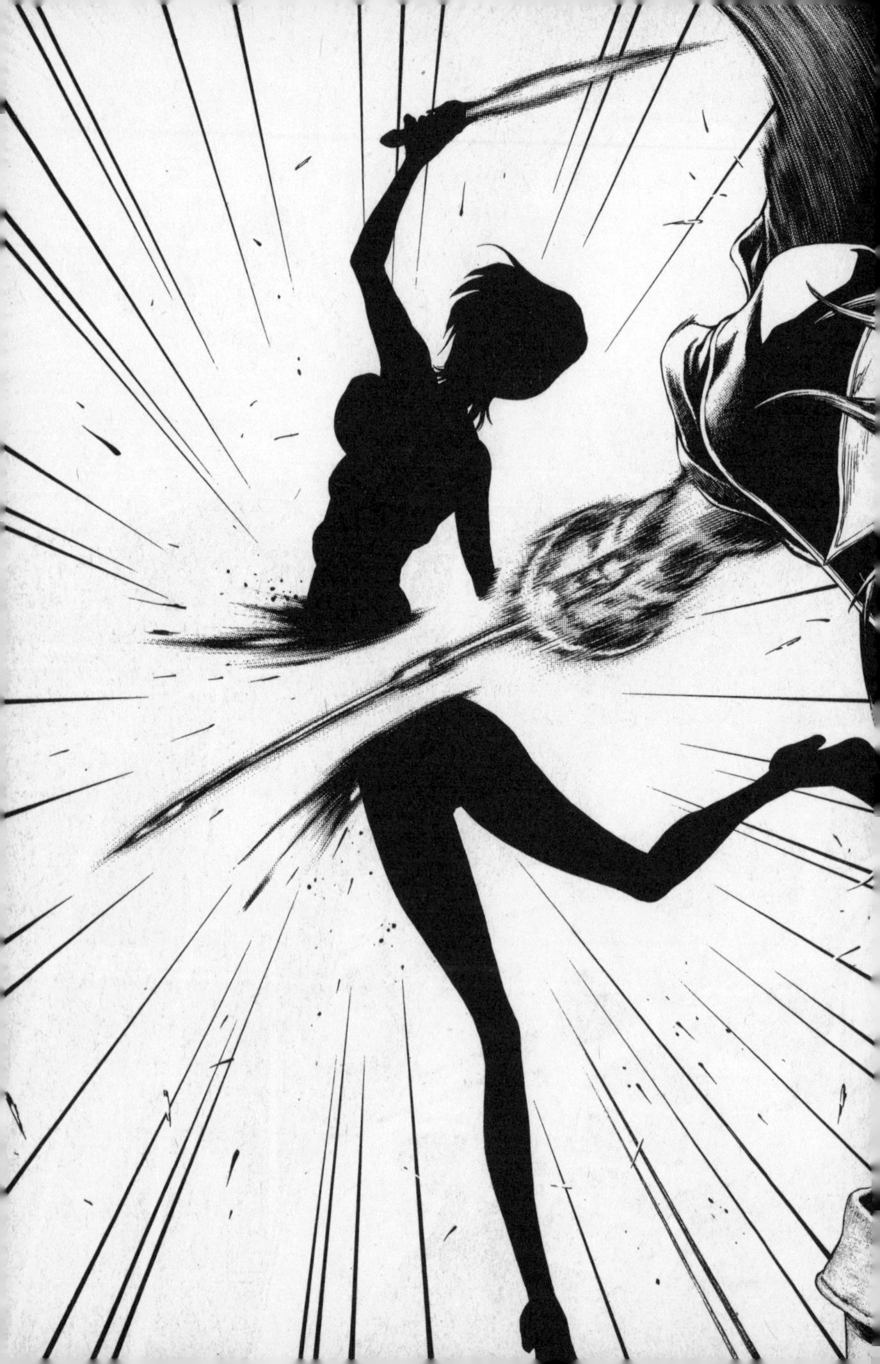

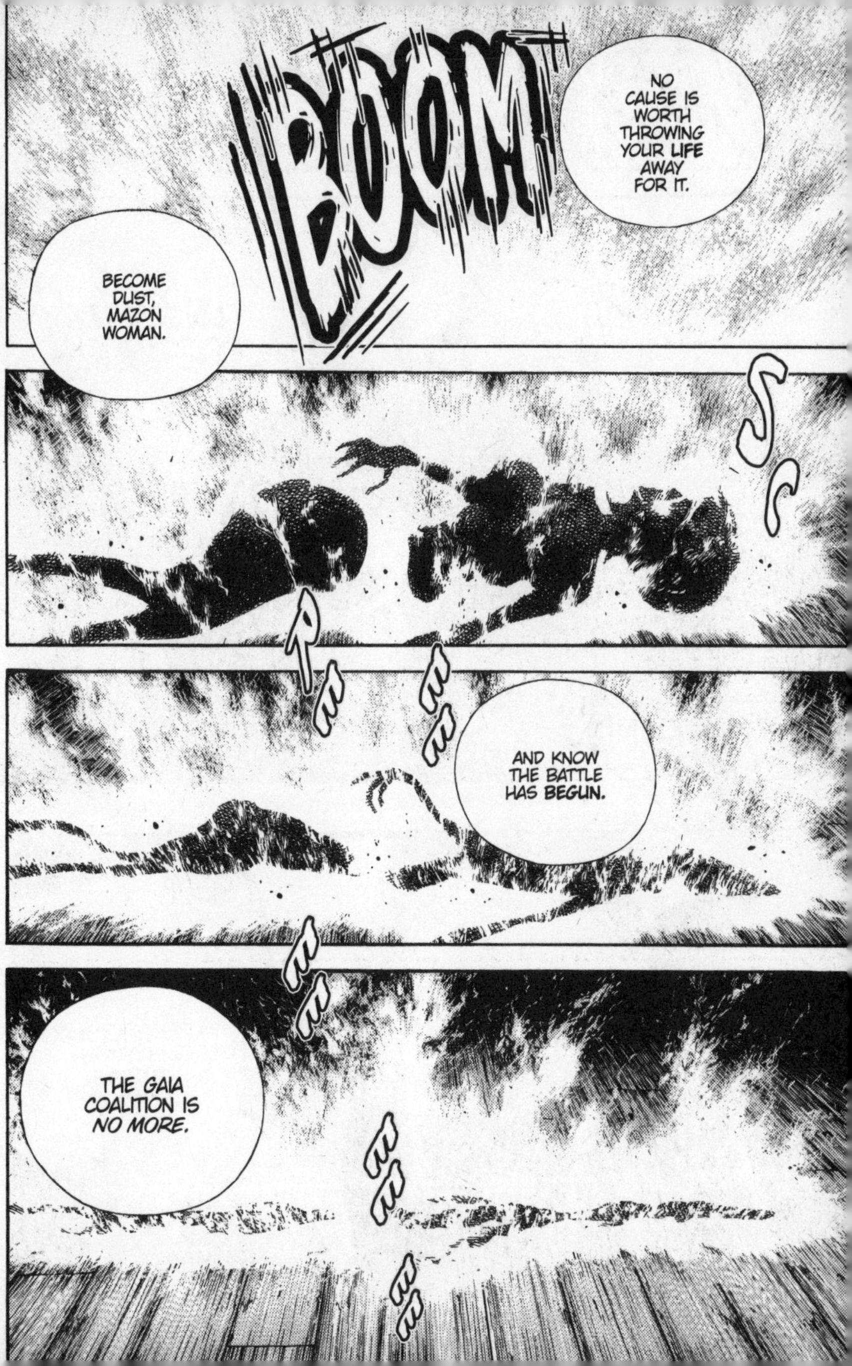
NO CAUSE IS WORTH THROWING YOUR LIFE AWAY FOR IT.
BOOM
BECOME DUST, MAZON WOMAN.
AND KNOW THE BATTLE HAS BEGUN.
THE GAIA COALITION IS NO MORE.

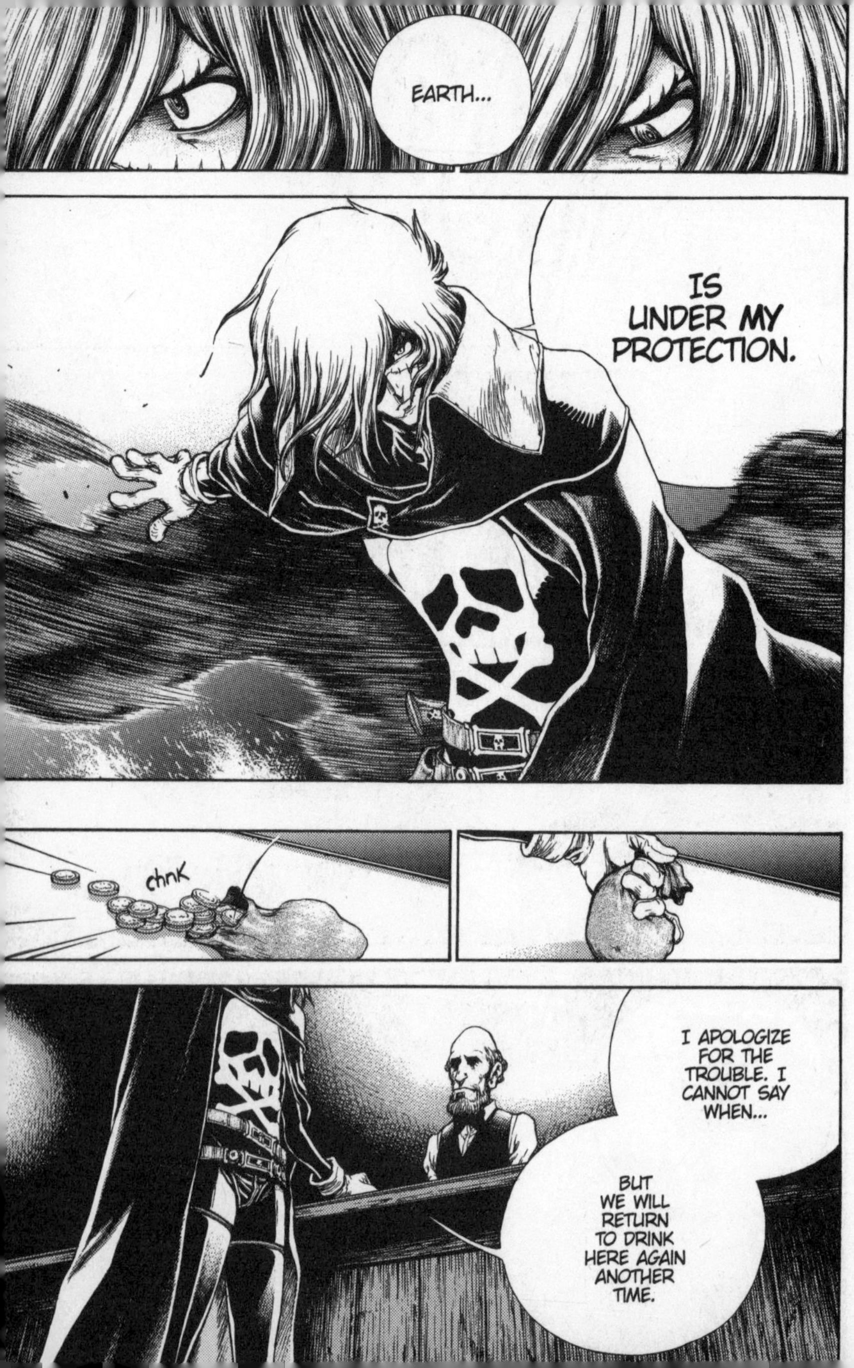
EARTH...
IS UNDER MY PROTECTION.
chnk
I APOLOGIZE FOR THE TROUBLE. I CANNOT SAY WHEN...
BUT WE WILL RETURN TO DRINK HERE AGAIN ANOTHER TIME.

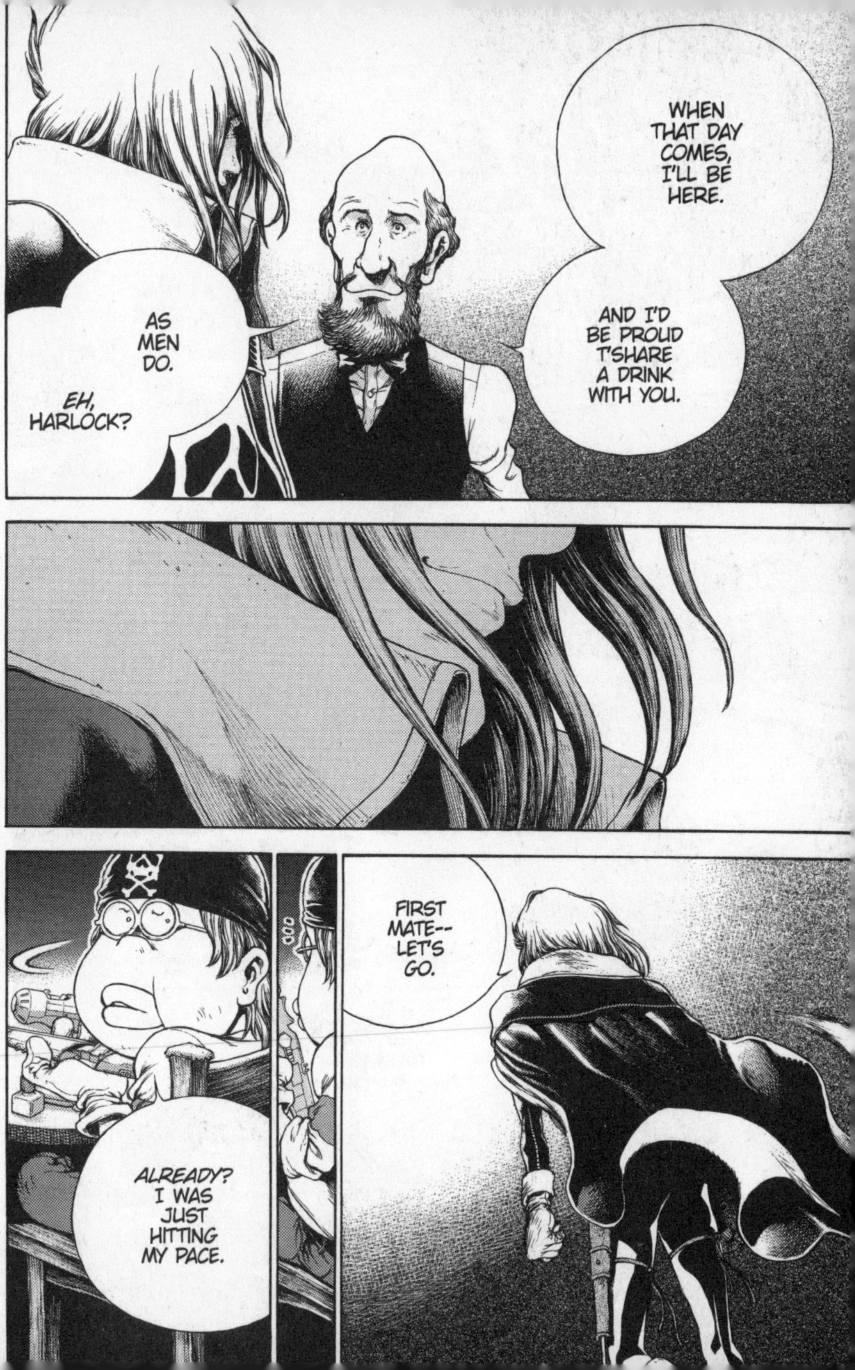
WHEN THAT DAY COMES, I'LL BE HERE.
AND I'D BE PROUD T'SHARE A DRINK WITH YOU.
AS MEN DO.
EH, HARLOCK?
FIRST MATE-- LET'S GO.
ALREADY? I WAS JUST HITTING MY PACE.

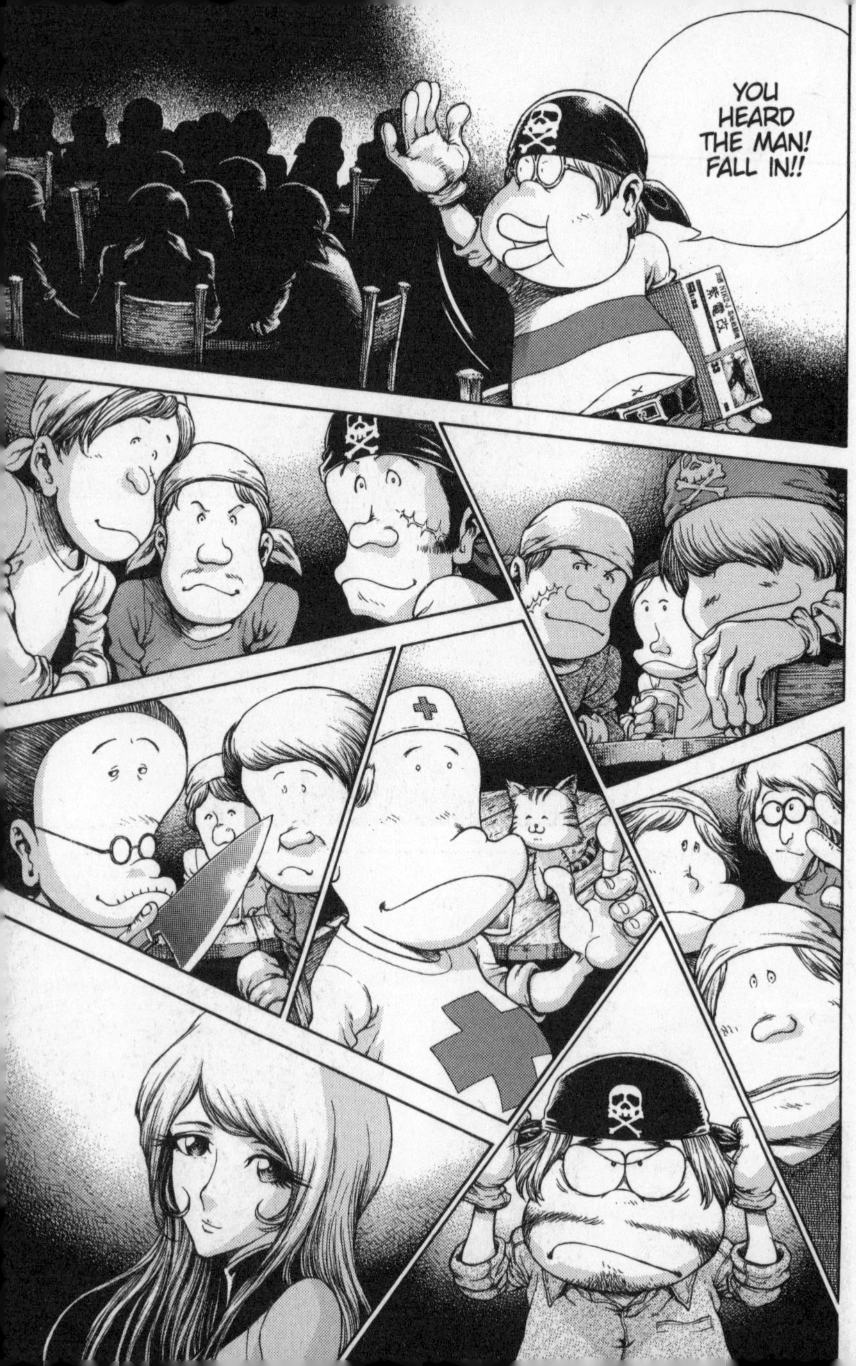
YOU HEARD THE MAN! FALL IN!!

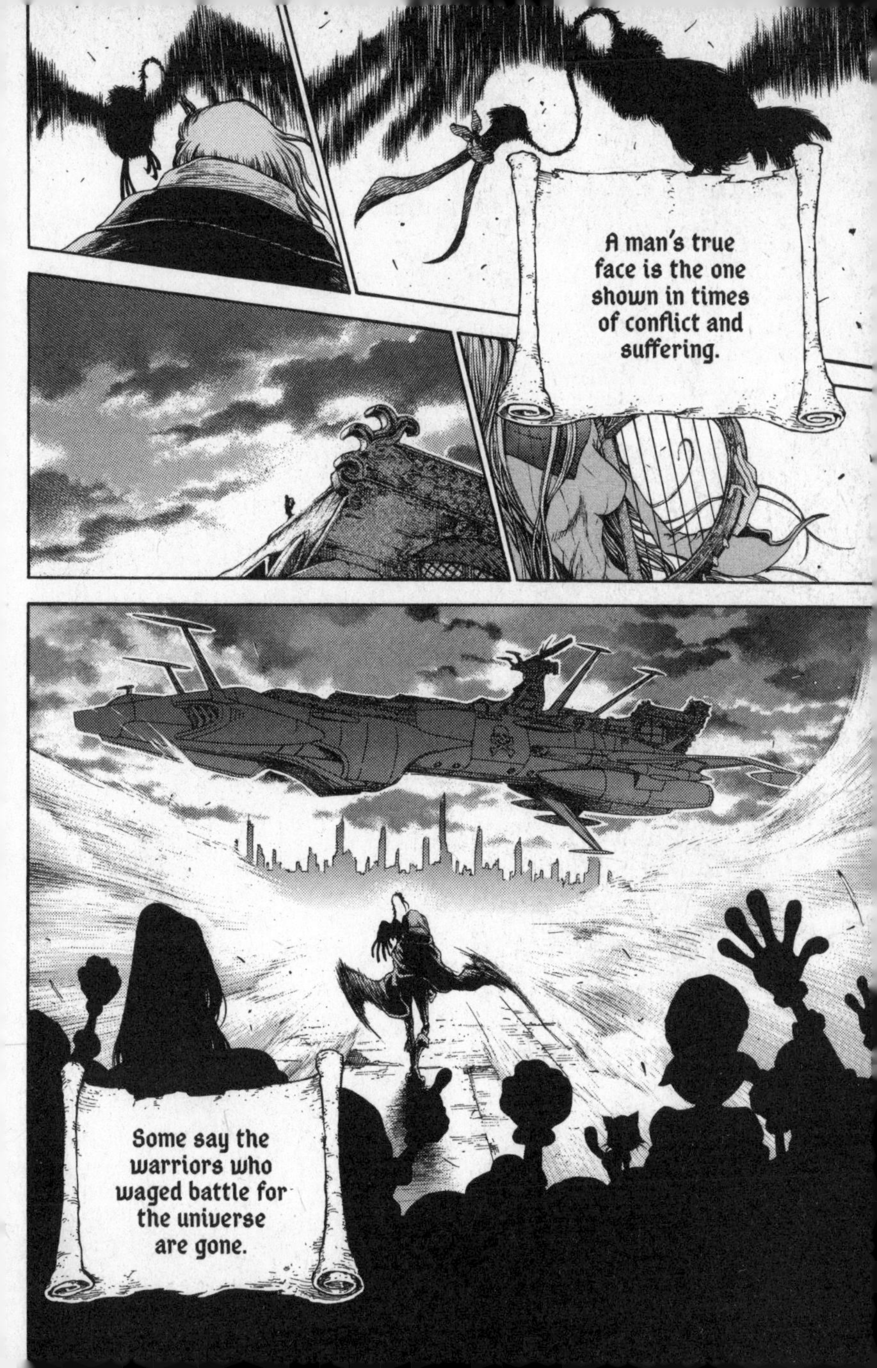
A man's true face is the one shown in times of conflict and suffering.
Some say the warriors who waged battle for the universe are gone.

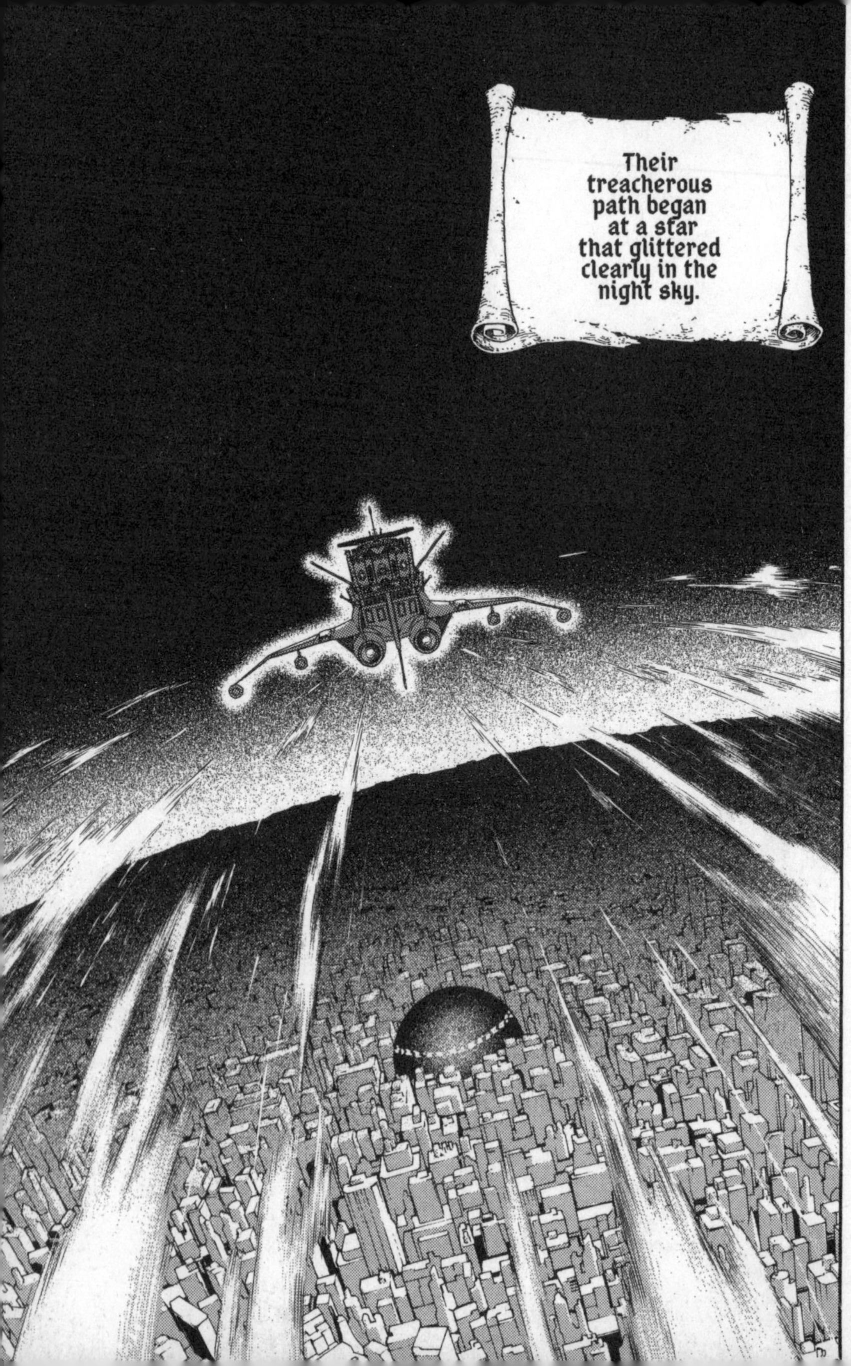
Their treacherous path began at a star that glittered clearly in the night sky.

CAPTAIN HARLOCK **1**
SPACE PIRATE DIMENSIONAL VOYAGE

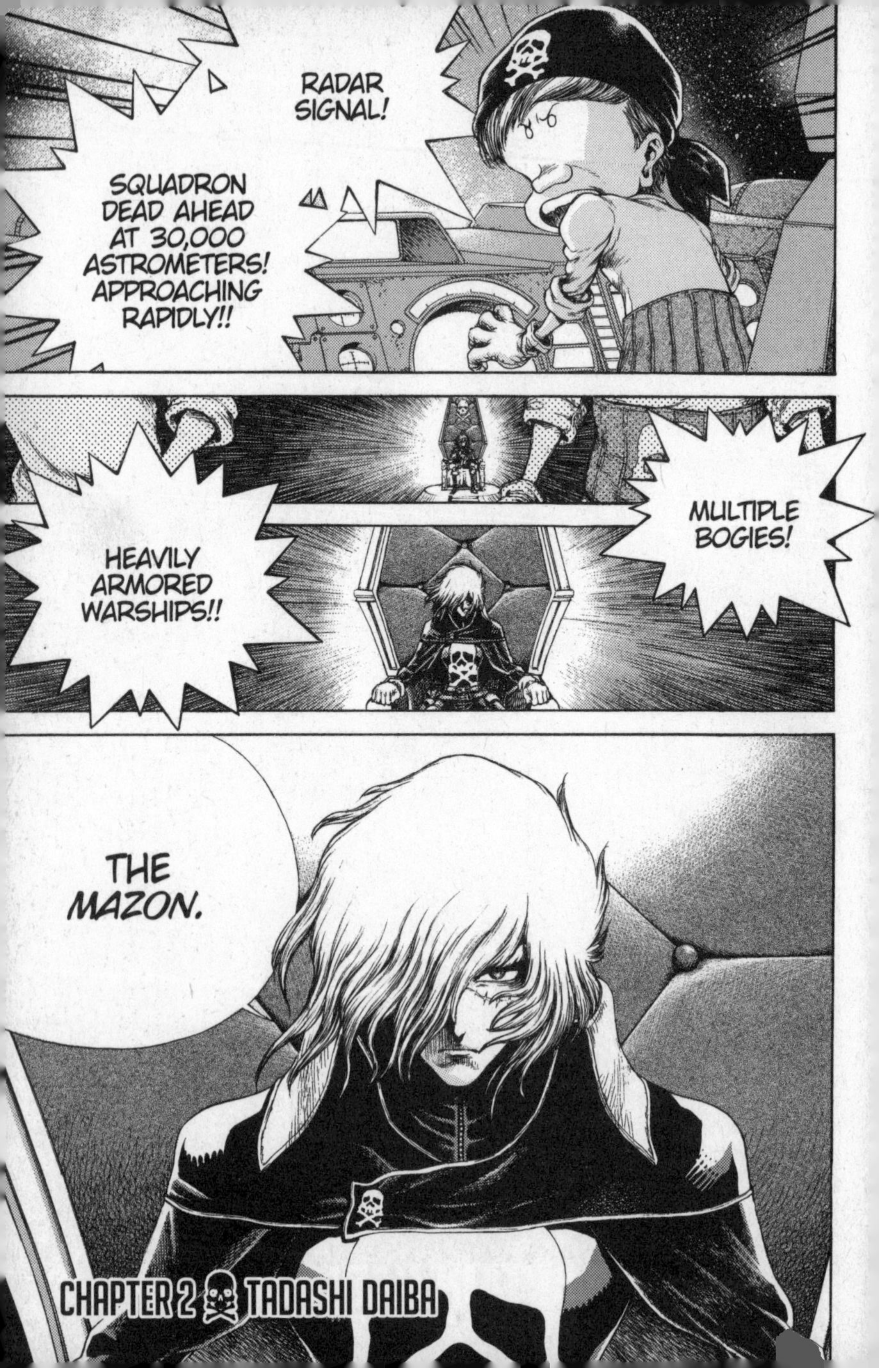
RADAR SIGNAL!
SQUADRON DEAD AHEAD AT 30,000 ASTROMETERS! APPROACHING RAPIDLY!!
MULTIPLE BOGIES!
HEAVILY ARMORED WARSHIPS!!
THE MAZON.

CHAPTER 2 ☠ TADASHI DAIBA

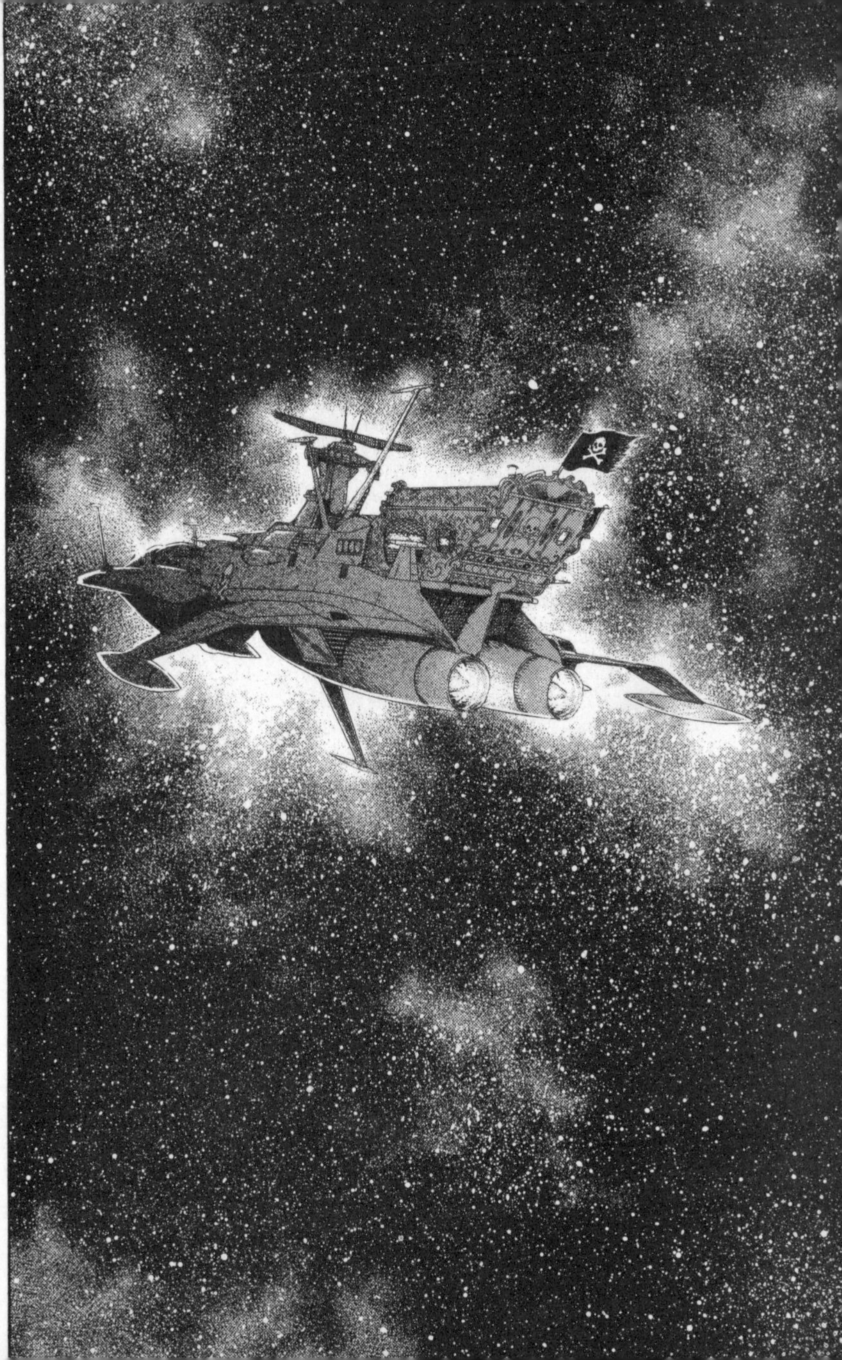

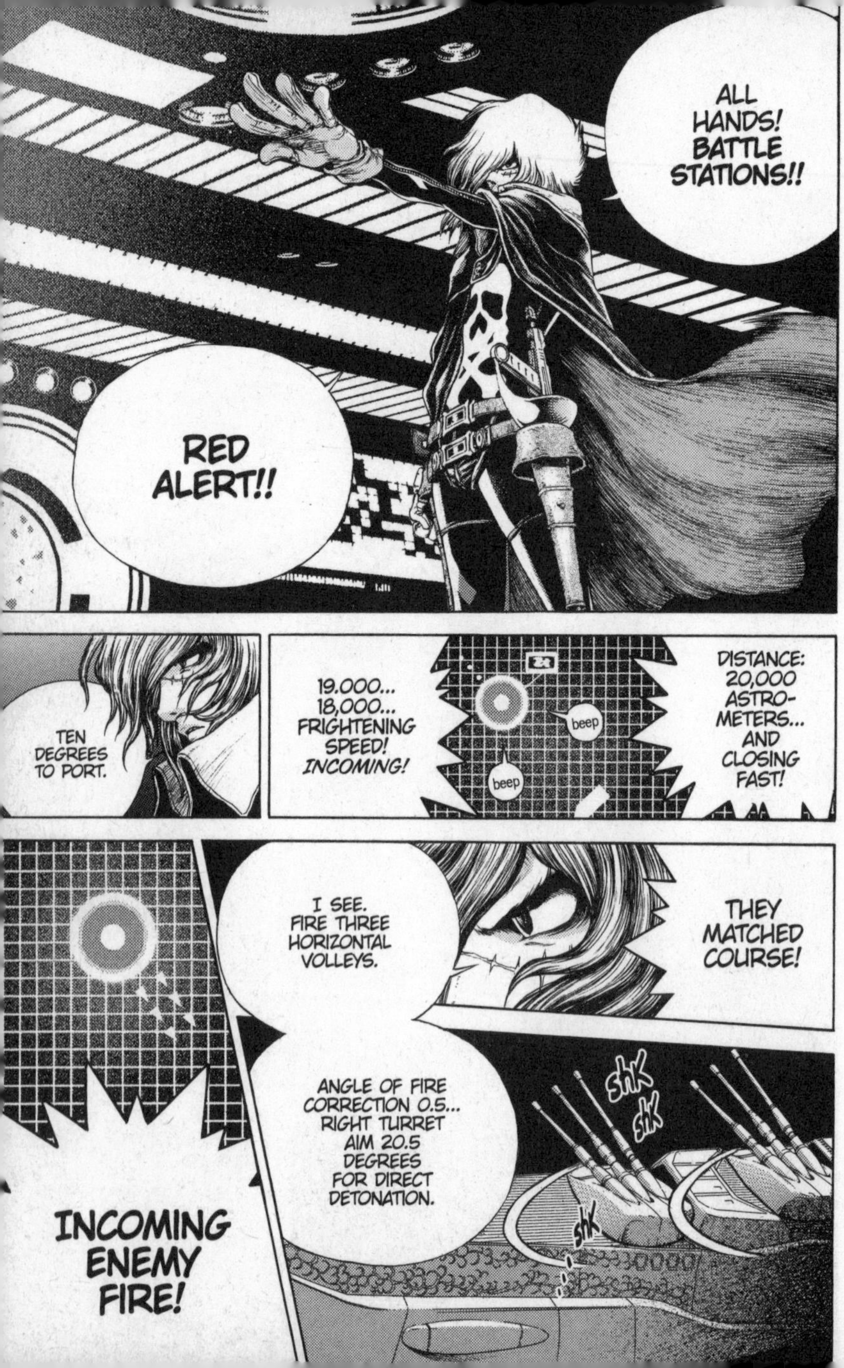
ALL HANDS! BATTLE STATIONS!!
RED ALERT!!
DISTANCE: 20,000 ASTRO-METERS... AND CLOSING FAST!
beep
beep
19.000... 18,000... FRIGHTENING SPEED! INCOMING!
TEN DEGREES TO PORT.
THEY MATCHED COURSE!
I SEE. FIRE THREE HORIZONTAL VOLLEYS.
shK
shK
ANGLE OF FIRE CORRECTION 0.5... RIGHT TURRET AIM 20.5 DEGREES FOR DIRECT DETONATION.
shK
INCOMING ENEMY FIRE!

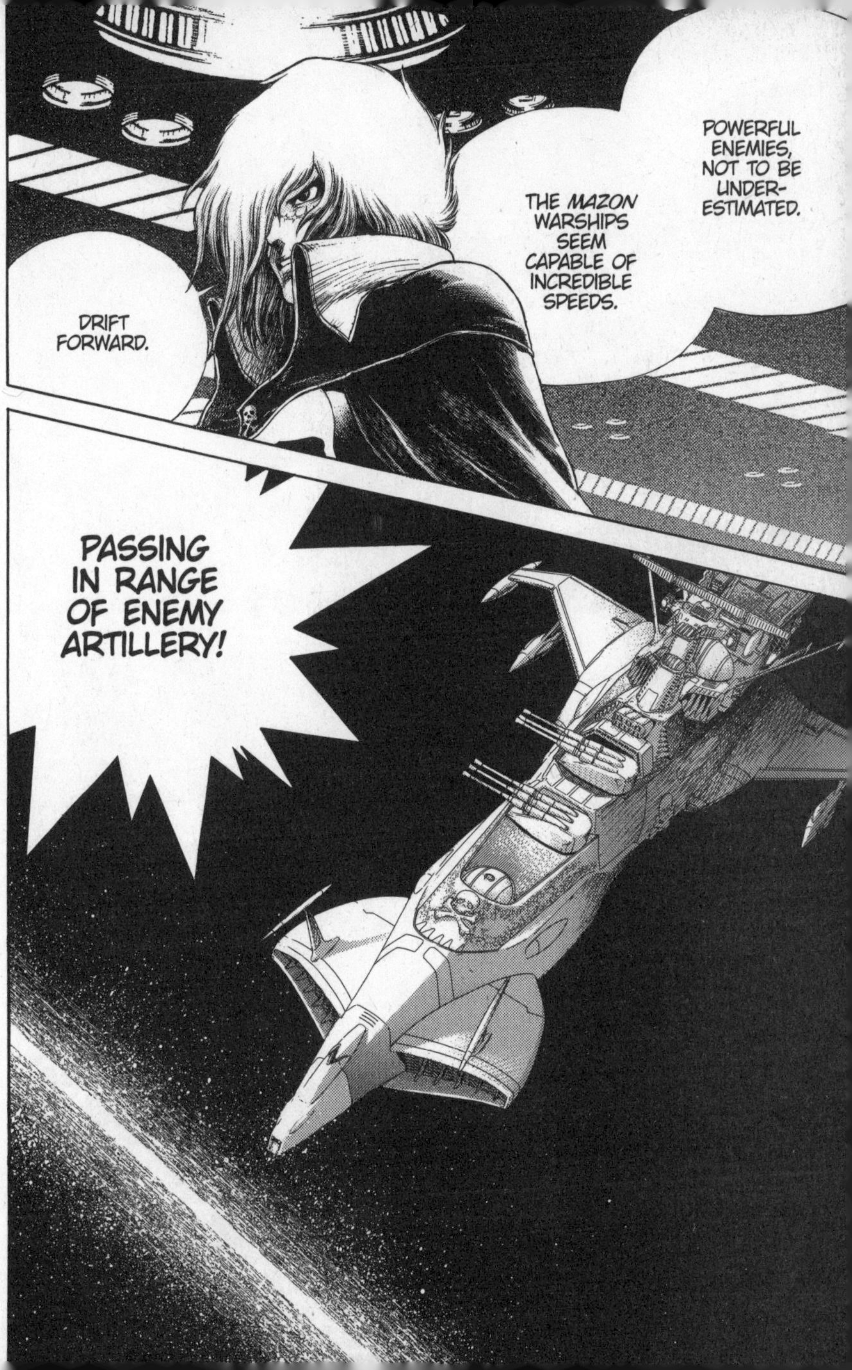
POWERFUL ENEMIES, NOT TO BE UNDER-ESTIMATED.
THE *MAZON* WARSHIPS SEEM CAPABLE OF INCREDIBLE SPEEDS.
DRIFT FORWARD.
PASSING IN RANGE OF ENEMY ARTILLERY!

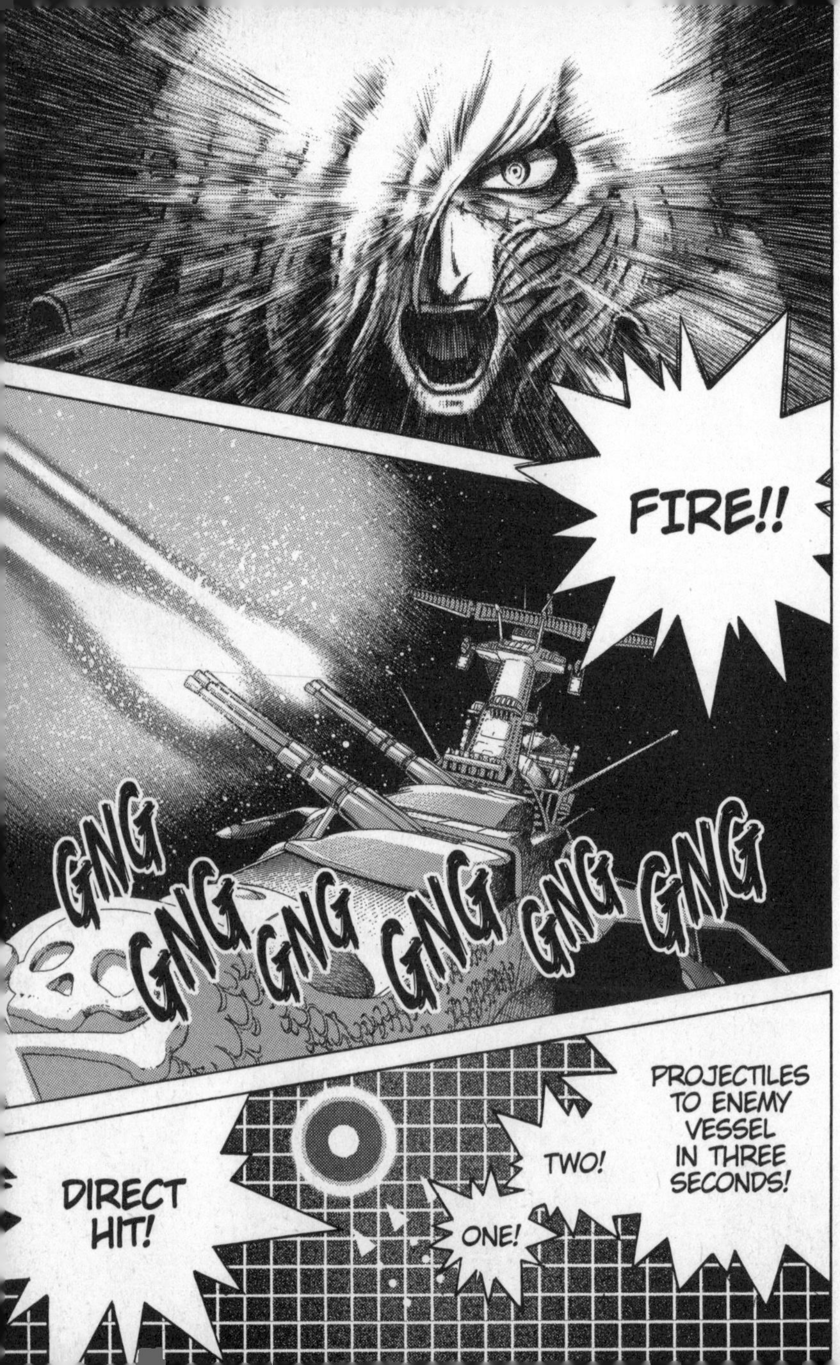
FIRE!!
GNG GNG GNG GNG GNG GNG
PROJECTILES TO ENEMY VESSEL IN THREE SECONDS!
TWO!
ONE!
DIRECT HIT!

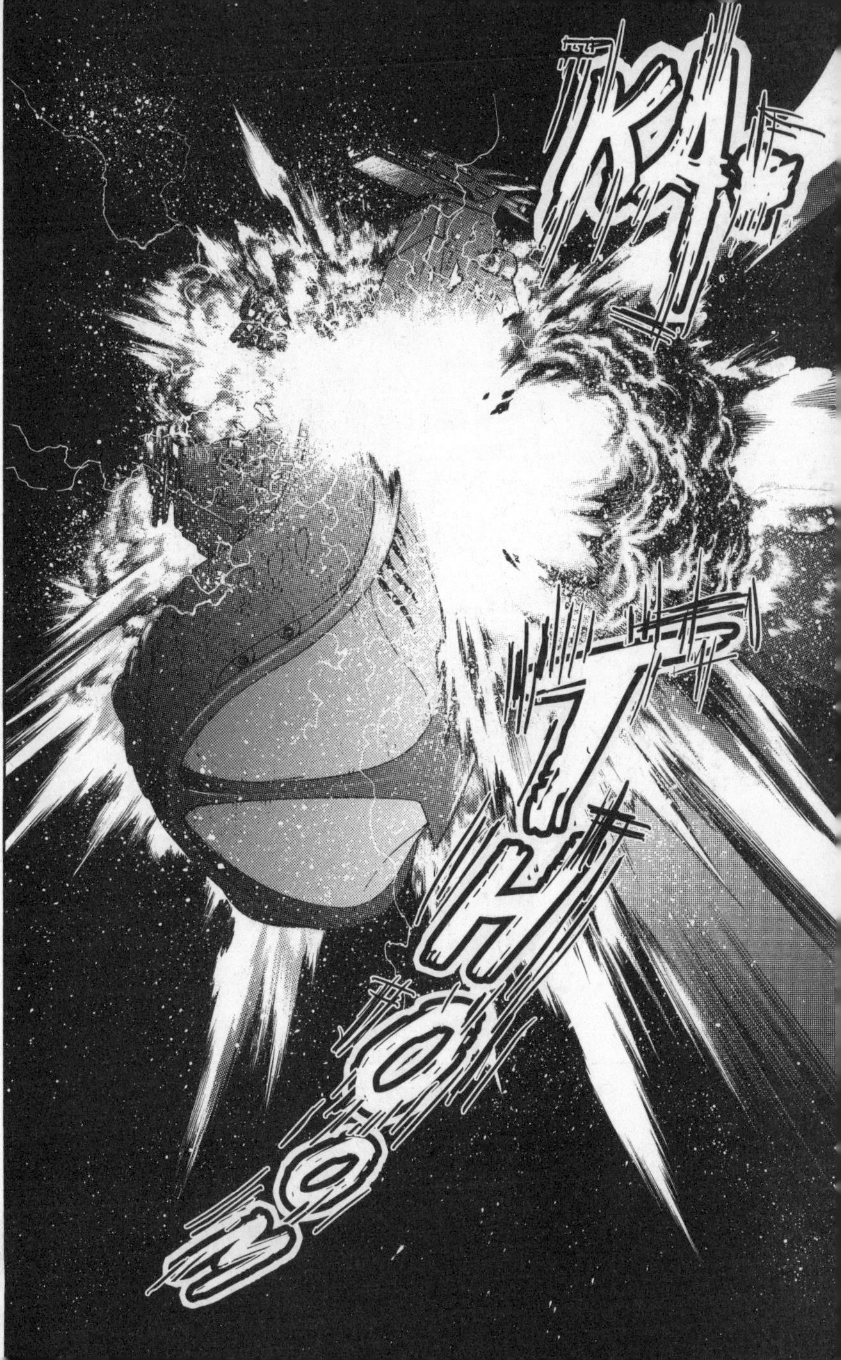
KA-THOOM

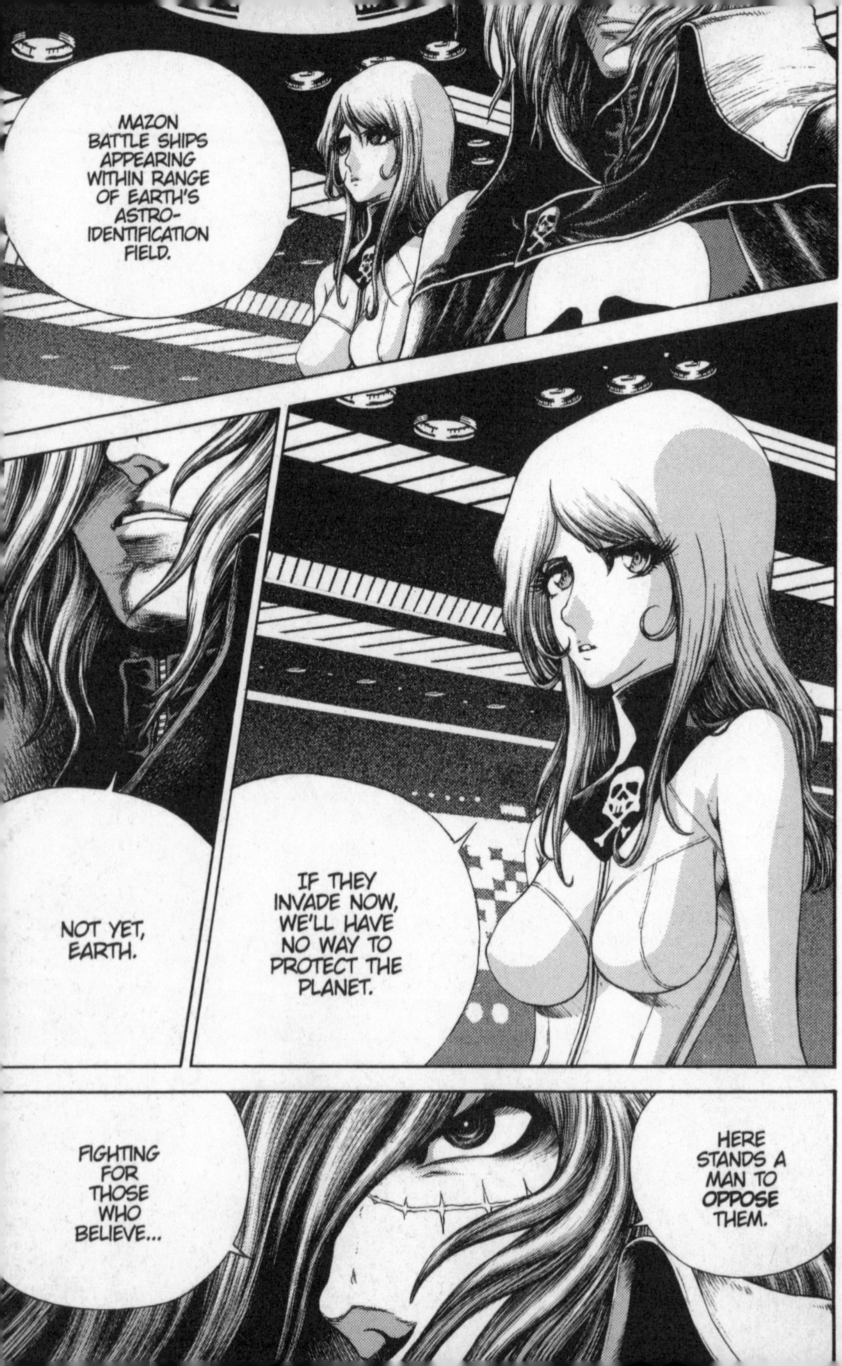
MAZON BATTLE SHIPS APPEARING WITHIN RANGE OF EARTH'S ASTRO-IDENTIFICATION FIELD.
IF THEY INVADE NOW, WE'LL HAVE NO WAY TO PROTECT THE PLANET.
NOT YET, EARTH.
HERE STANDS A MAN TO OPPOSE THEM.
FIGHTING FOR THOSE WHO BELIEVE...

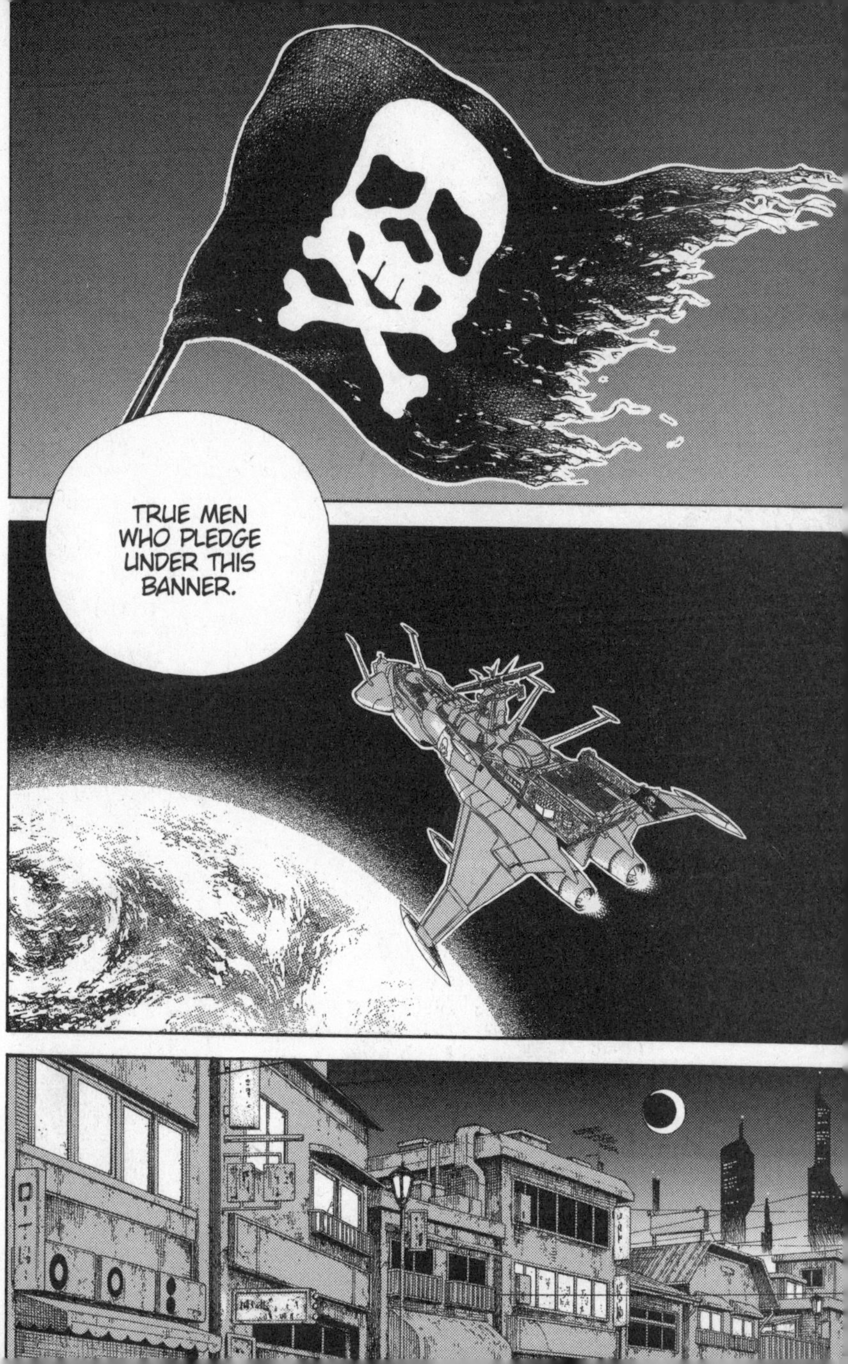
TRUE MEN WHO PLEDGE UNDER THIS BANNER.

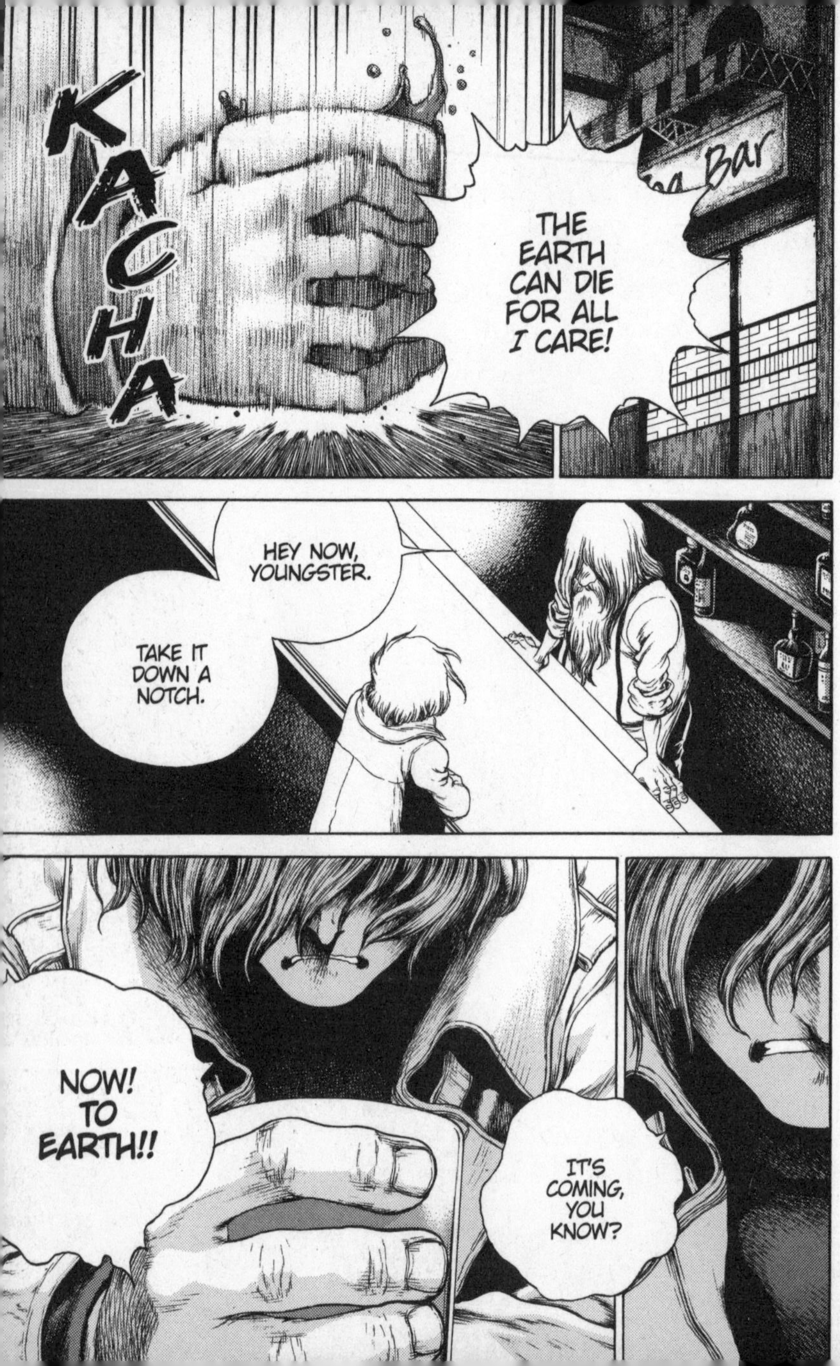
Bar
THE EARTH CAN DIE FOR ALL I CARE!
KACHA
HEY NOW, YOUNGSTER.
TAKE IT DOWN A NOTCH.
IT'S COMING, YOU KNOW?
NOW! TO EARTH!!

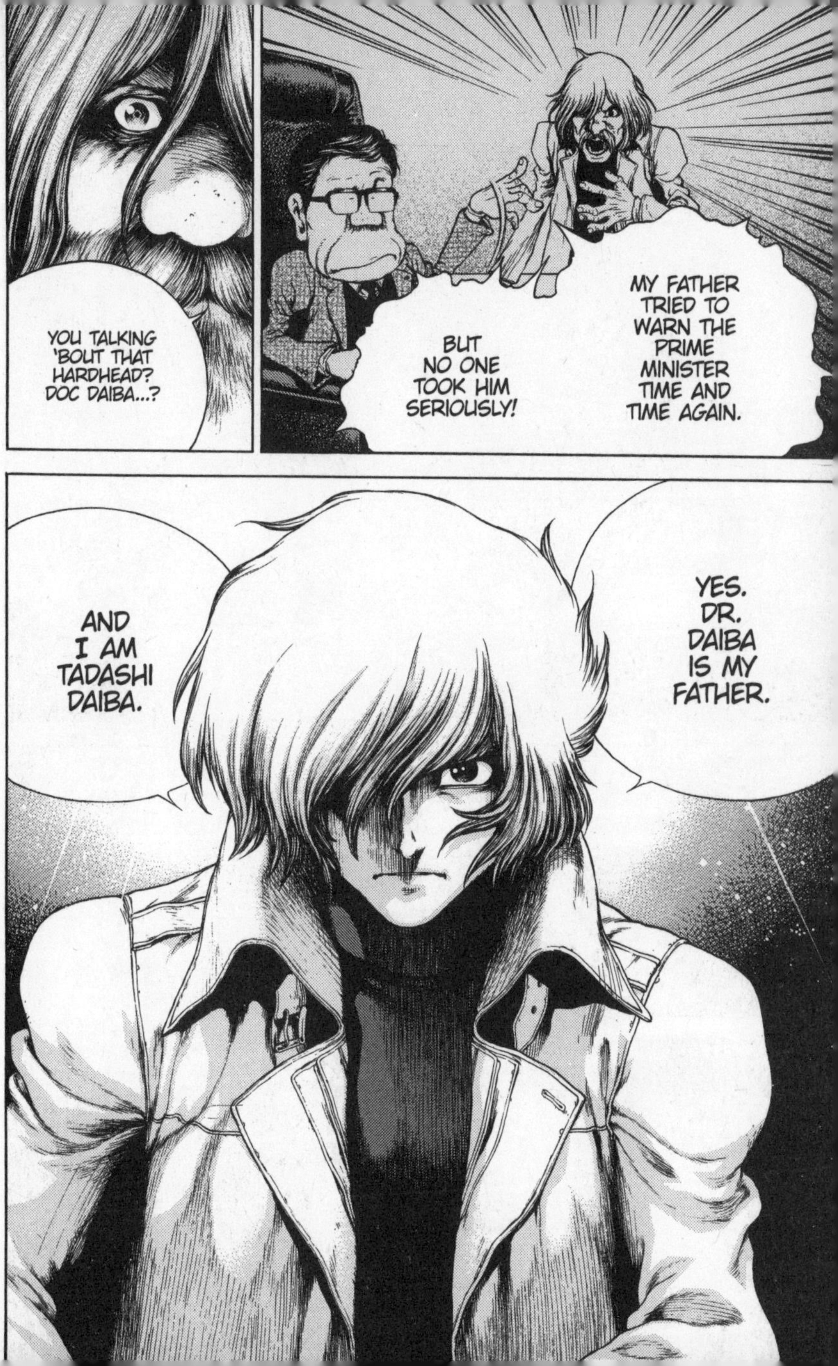
MY FATHER TRIED TO WARN THE PRIME MINISTER TIME AND TIME AGAIN.
BUT NO ONE TOOK HIM SERIOUSLY!
YOU TALKING 'BOUT THAT HARDHEAD? DOC DAIBA...?
YES. DR. DAIBA IS MY FATHER.
AND I AM TADASHI DAIBA.

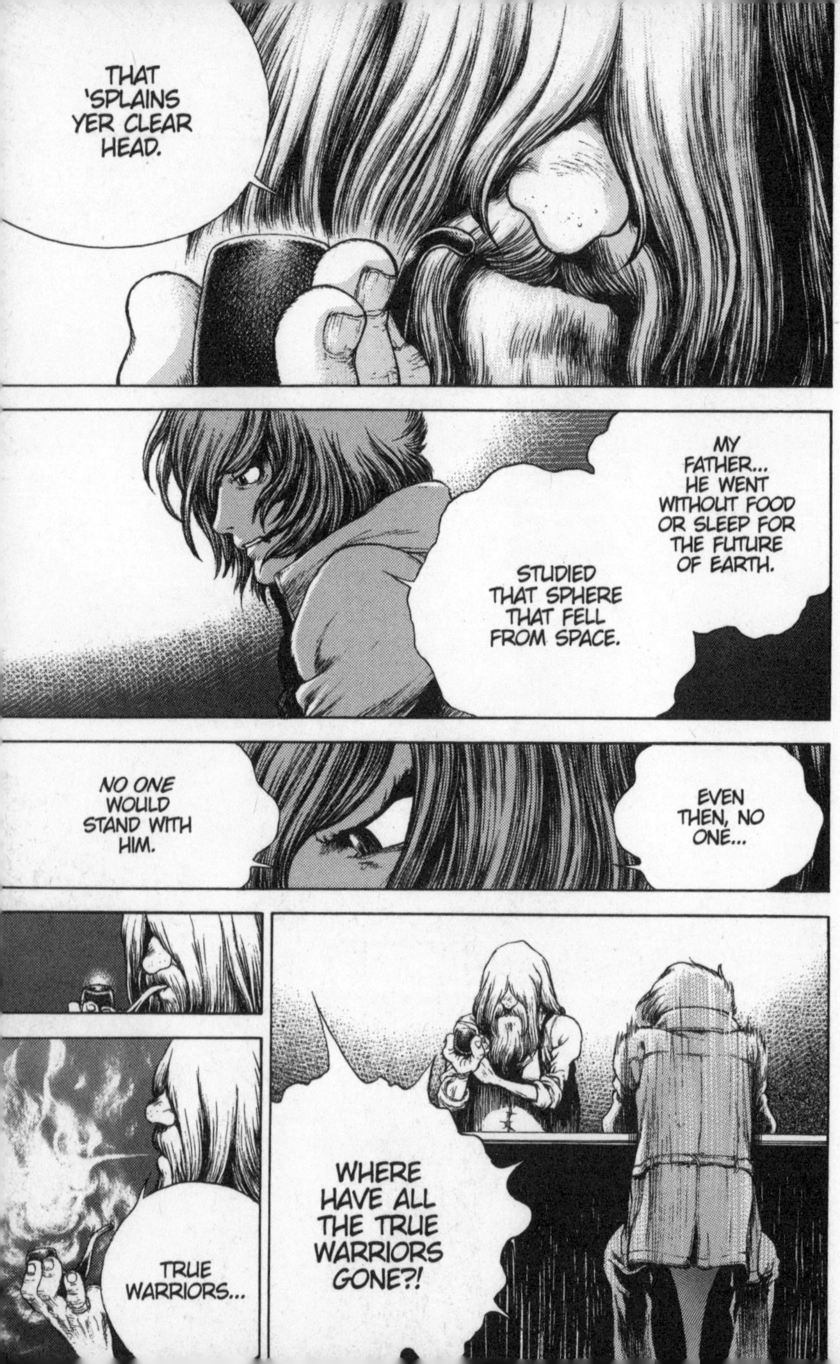
THAT 'SPLAINS YER CLEAR HEAD.
MY FATHER... HE WENT WITHOUT FOOD OR SLEEP FOR THE FUTURE OF EARTH.
STUDIED THAT SPHERE THAT FELL FROM SPACE.
EVEN THEN, NO ONE...
NO ONE WOULD STAND WITH HIM.
WHERE HAVE ALL THE TRUE WARRIORS GONE?!
TRUE WARRIORS...

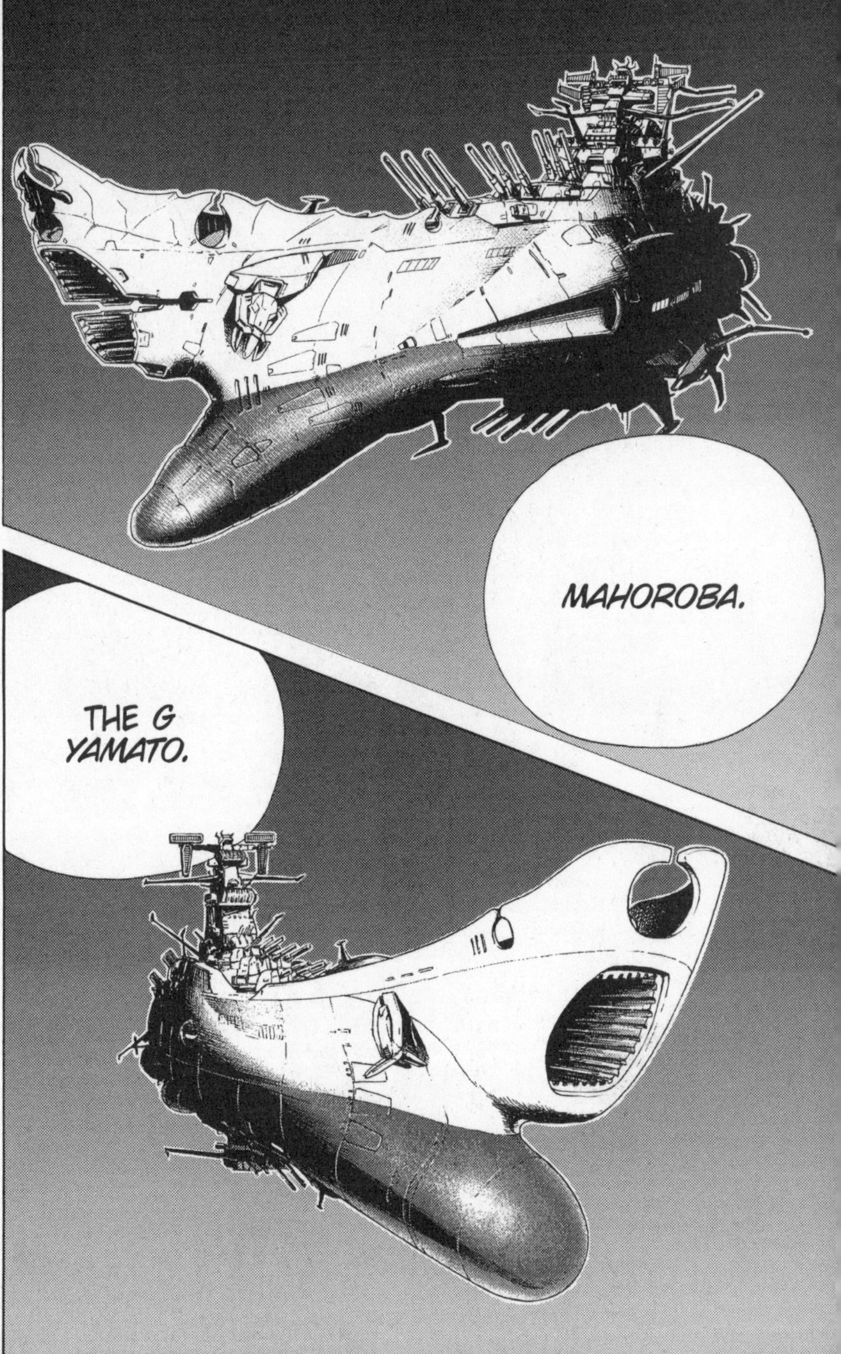
MAHOROBA.
THE G YAMATO.

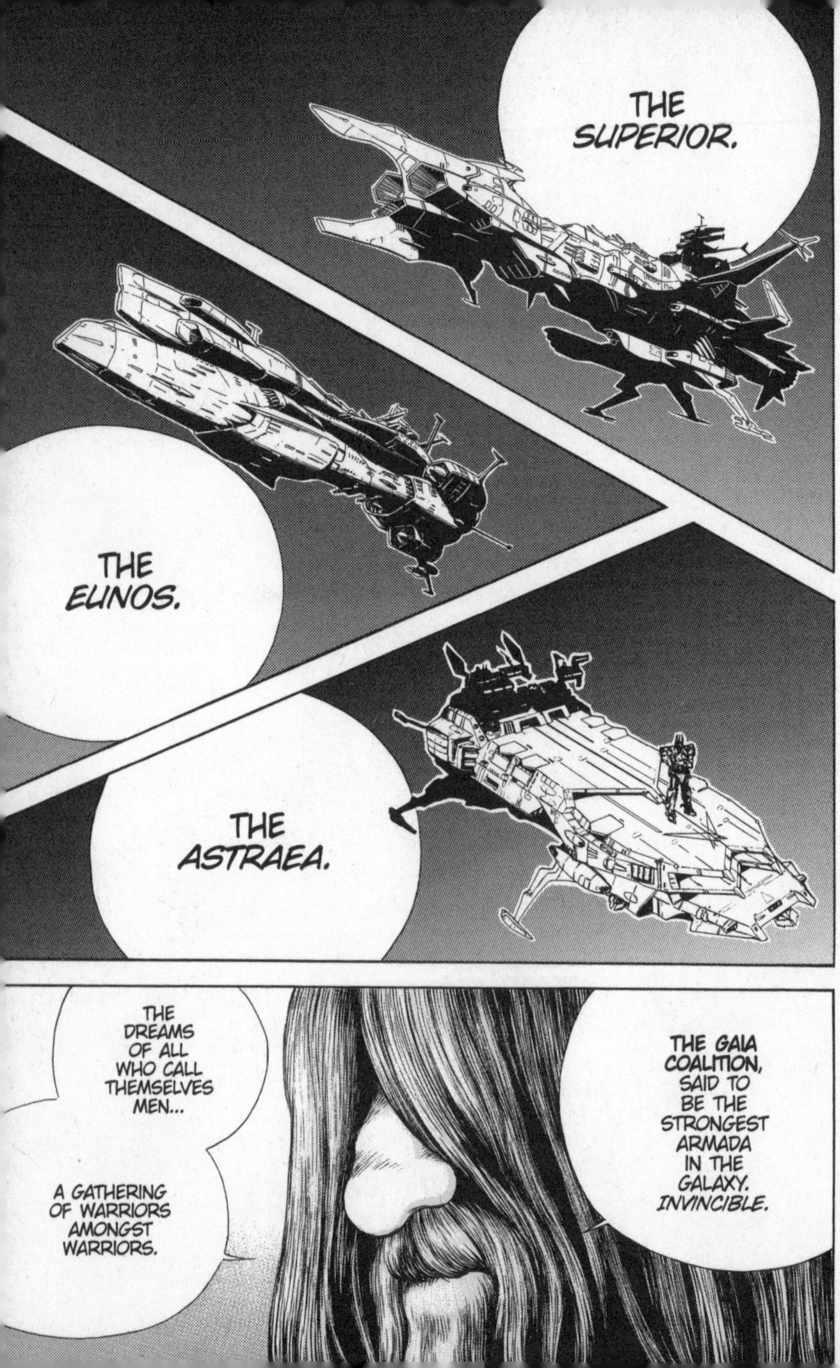
THE SUPERIOR.
THE EUNOS.
THE ASTRAEA.
THE GAIA COALITION, SAID TO BE THE STRONGEST ARMADA IN THE GALAXY. INVINCIBLE.
THE DREAMS OF ALL WHO CALL THEMSELVES MEN...
A GATHERING OF WARRIORS AMONGST WARRIORS.

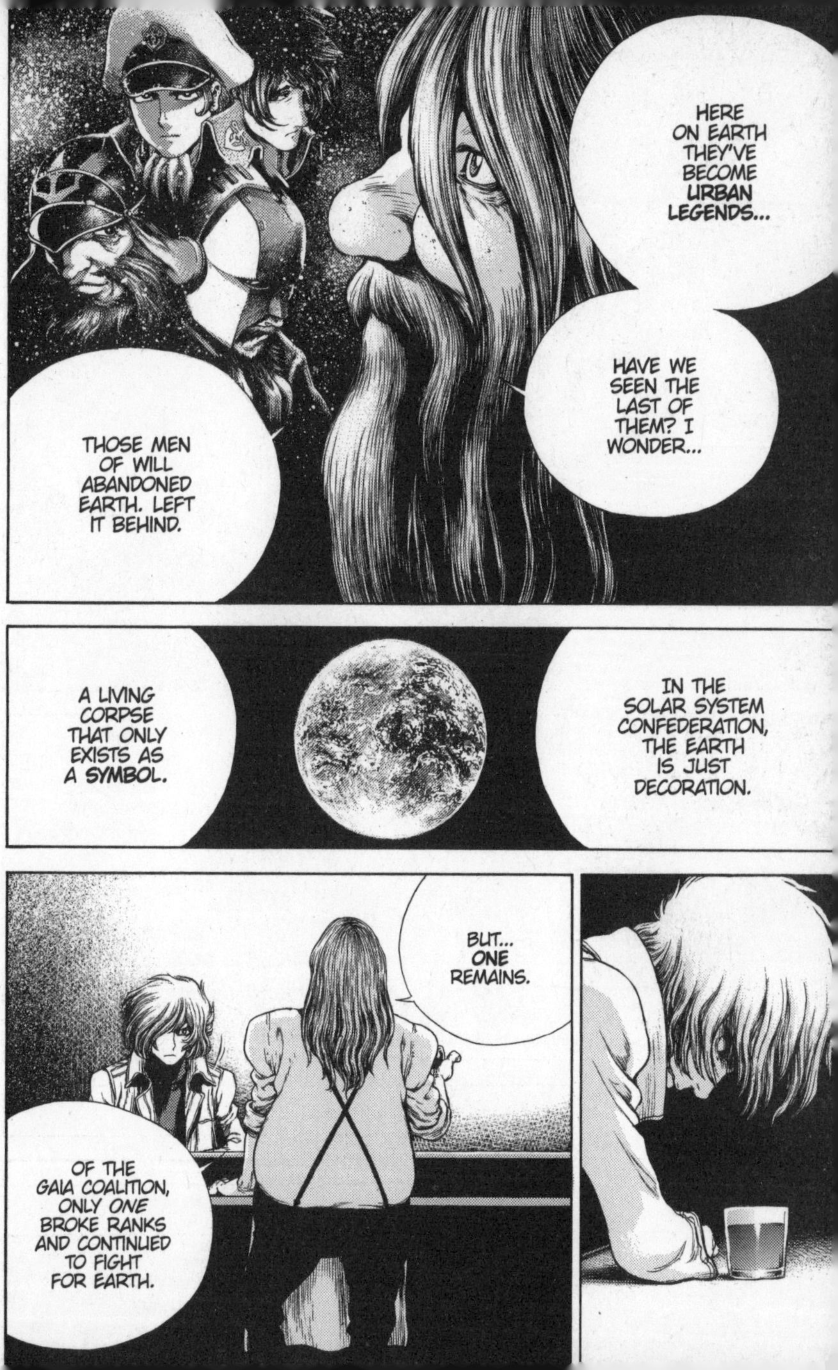
HERE ON EARTH THEY'VE BECOME URBAN LEGENDS...
HAVE WE SEEN THE LAST OF THEM? I WONDER...
THOSE MEN OF WILL ABANDONED EARTH. LEFT IT BEHIND.
IN THE SOLAR SYSTEM CONFEDERATION, THE EARTH IS JUST DECORATION.
A LIVING CORPSE THAT ONLY EXISTS AS A SYMBOL.
BUT... ONE REMAINS.
OF THE GAIA COALITION, ONLY *ONE* BROKE RANKS AND CONTINUED TO FIGHT FOR EARTH.

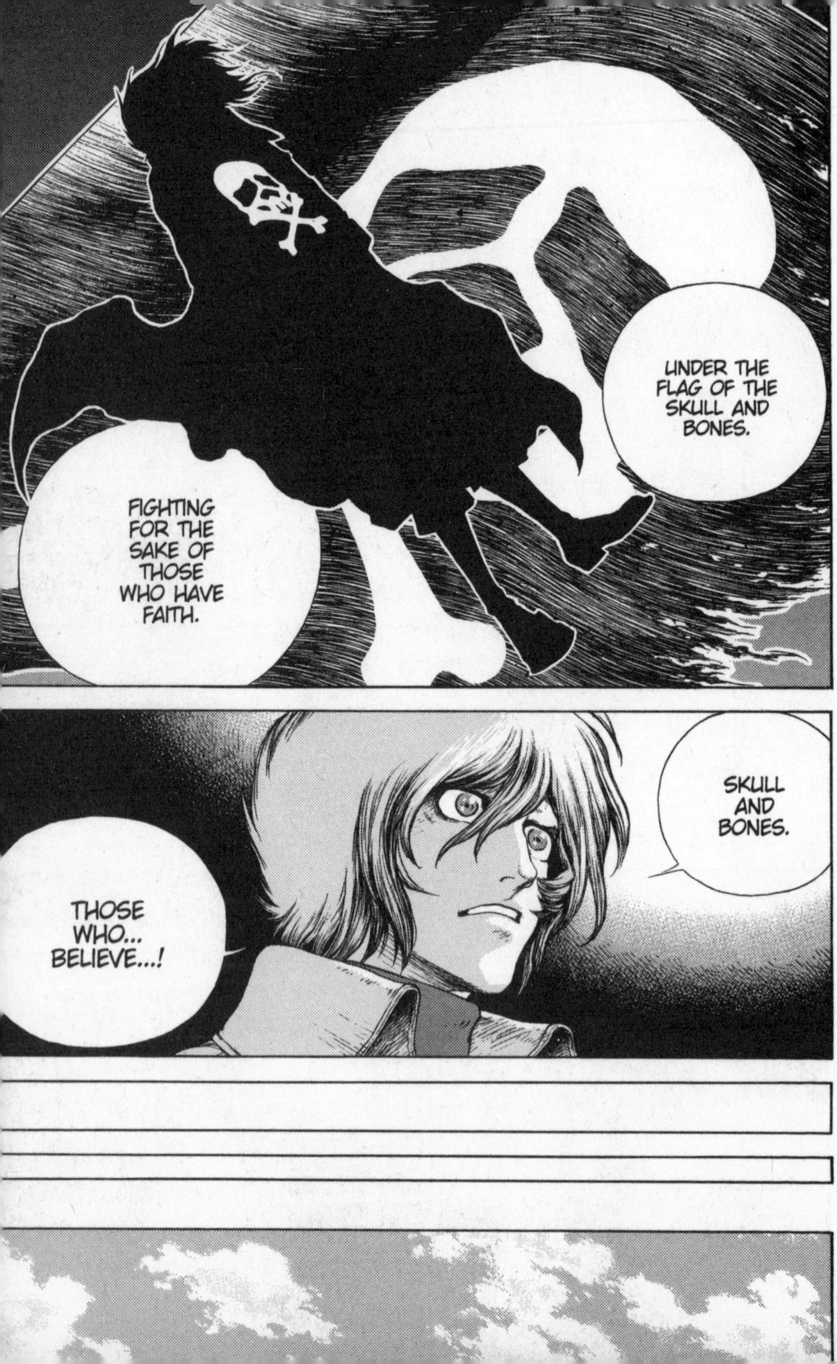
UNDER THE FLAG OF THE SKULL AND BONES.
FIGHTING FOR THE SAKE OF THOSE WHO HAVE FAITH.
SKULL AND BONES.
THOSE WHO... BELIEVE...!

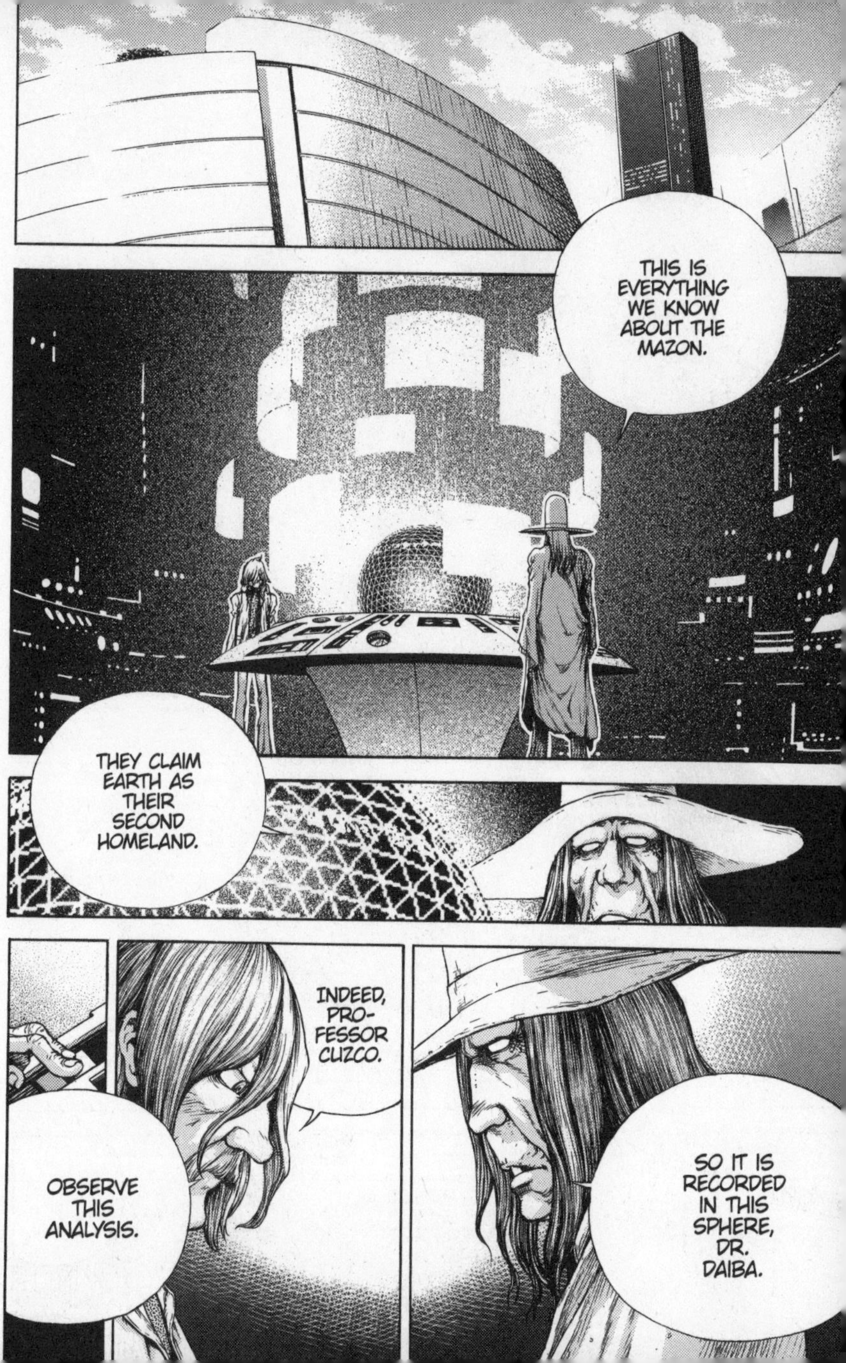
THIS IS EVERYTHING WE KNOW ABOUT THE MAZON.
THEY CLAIM EARTH AS THEIR SECOND HOMELAND.
SO IT IS RECORDED IN THIS SPHERE, DR. DAIBA.
INDEED, PRO-FESSOR CUZCO.
OBSERVE THIS ANALYSIS.

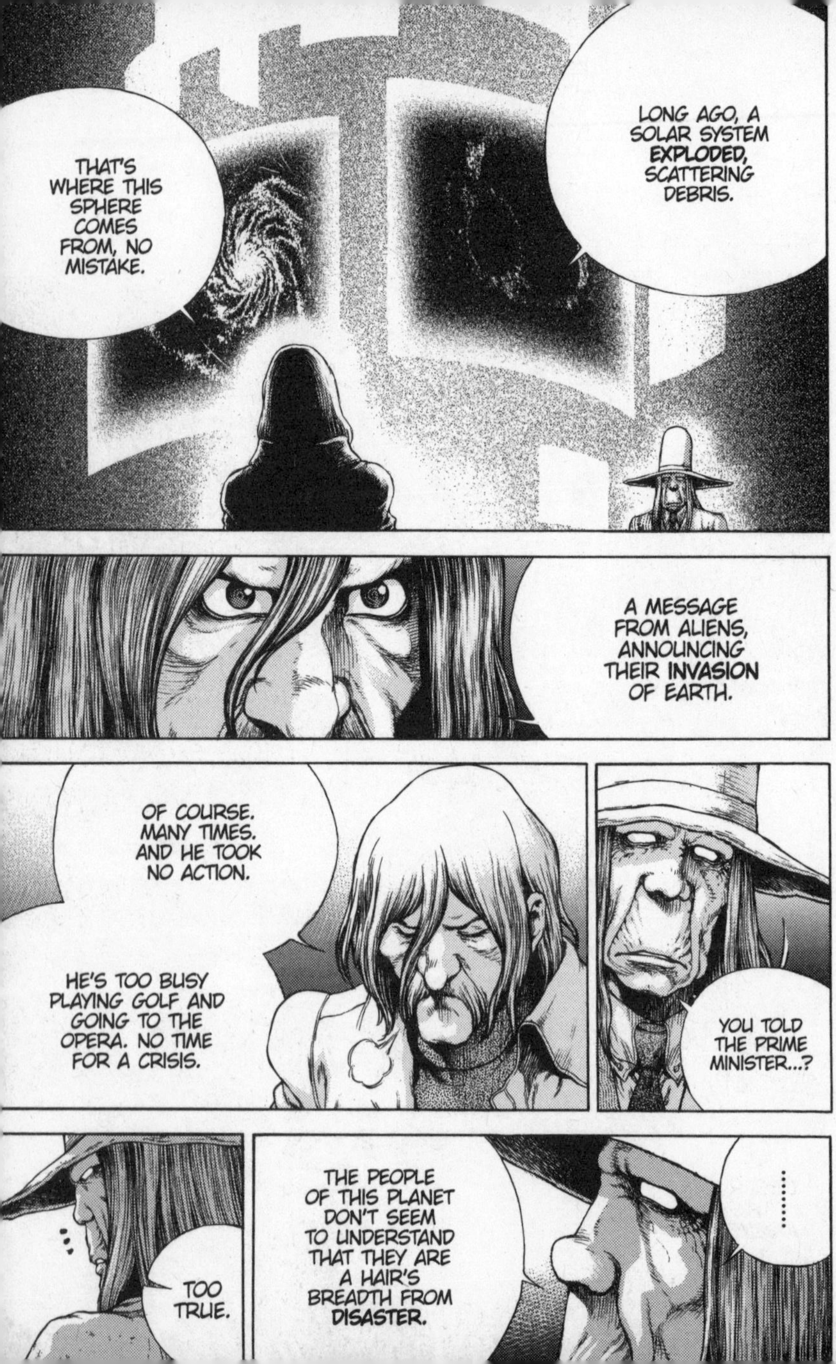
LONG AGO, A SOLAR SYSTEM **EXPLODED,** SCATTERING DEBRIS.
THAT'S WHERE THIS SPHERE COMES FROM, NO MISTAKE.
A MESSAGE FROM ALIENS, ANNOUNCING THEIR **INVASION** OF EARTH.
YOU TOLD THE PRIME MINISTER...?
OF COURSE. MANY TIMES. AND HE TOOK NO ACTION.
HE'S TOO BUSY PLAYING GOLF AND GOING TO THE OPERA. NO TIME FOR A CRISIS.
......
THE PEOPLE OF THIS PLANET DON'T SEEM TO UNDERSTAND THAT THEY ARE A HAIR'S BREADTH FROM **DISASTER.**
...
TOO TRUE.

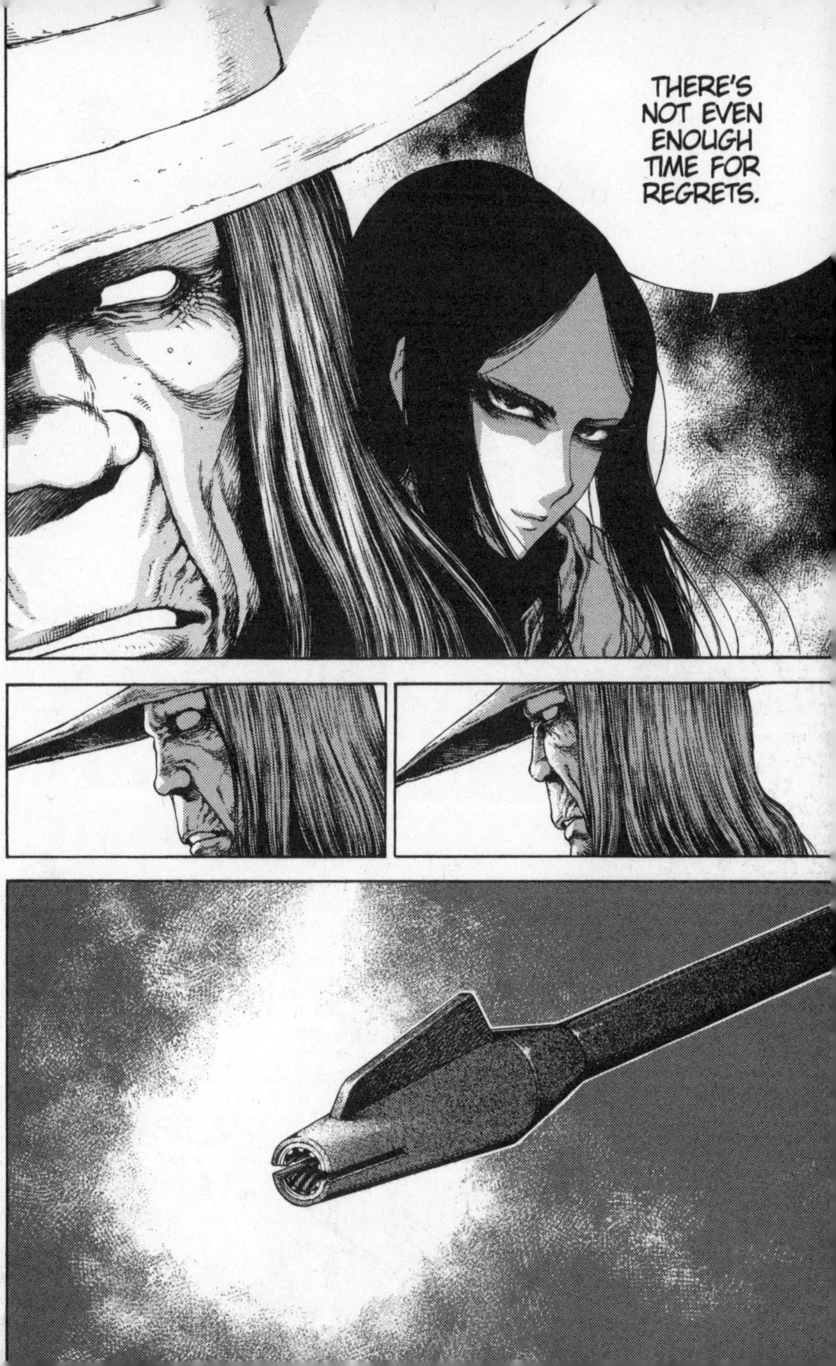
THERE'S NOT EVEN ENOUGH TIME FOR REGRETS.

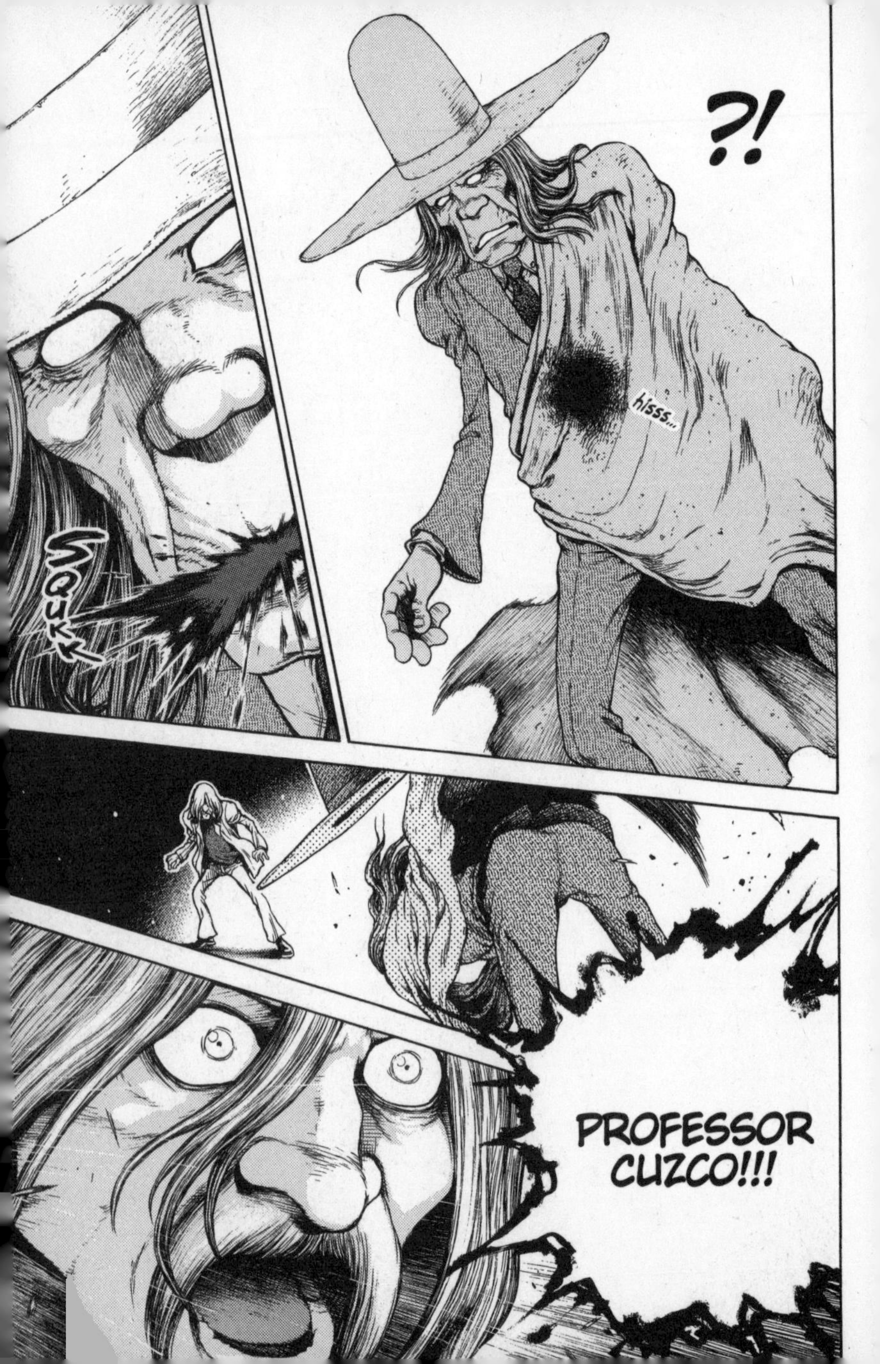
?!
hisss...
SQUKK
PROFESSOR CUZCO!!!

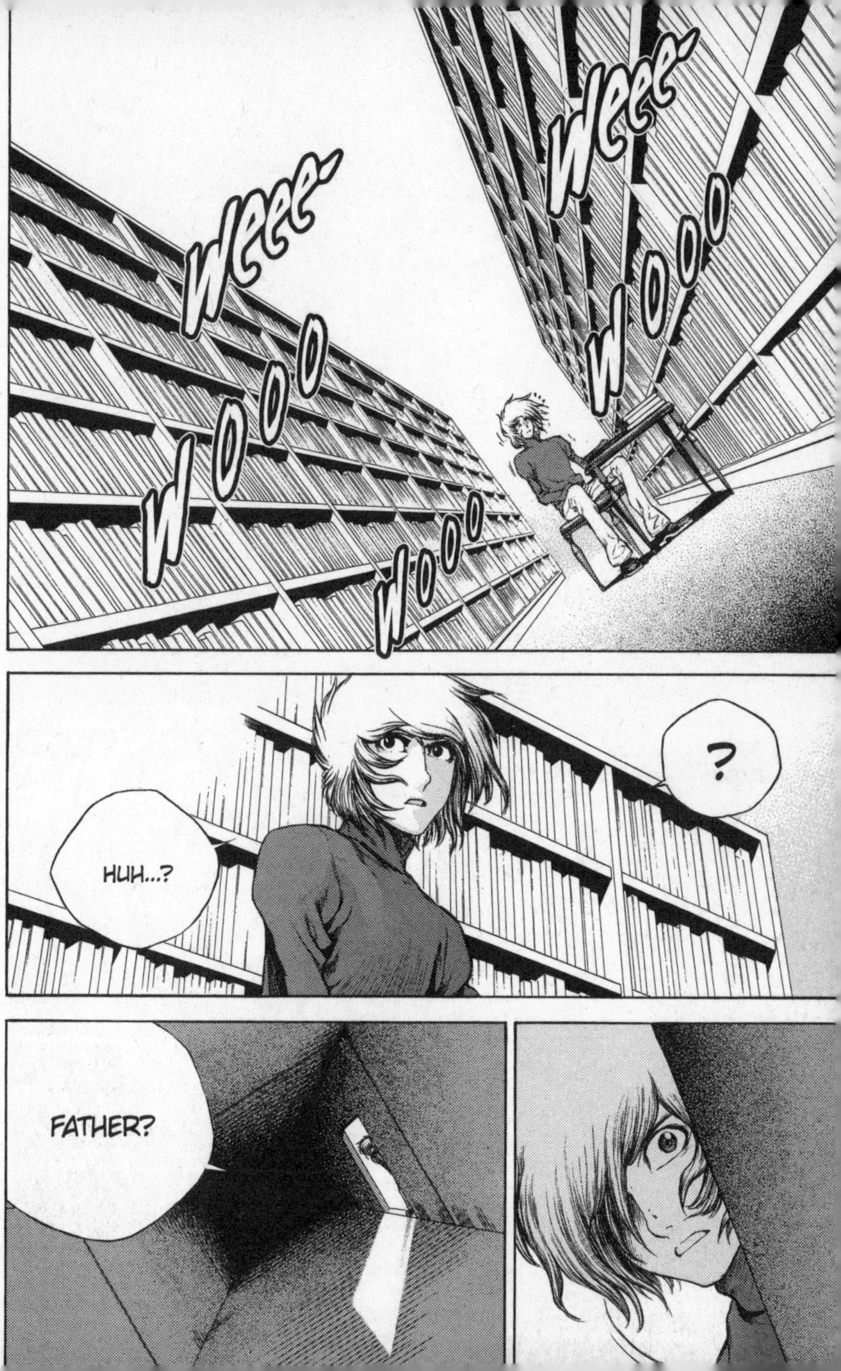
WEEE-WOOO
WEEE-WOOO
WOOO
?
HUH...?
FATHER?

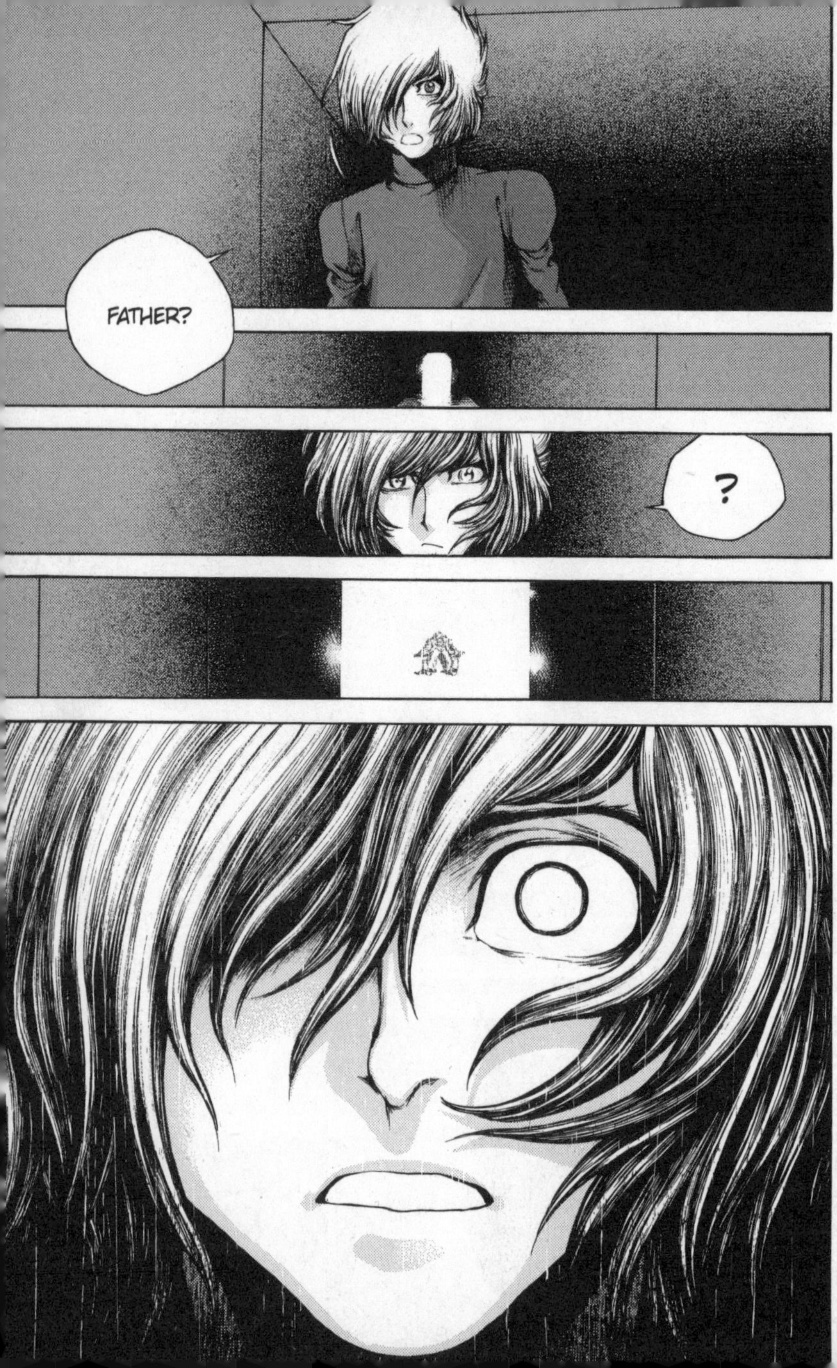
FATHER?
?

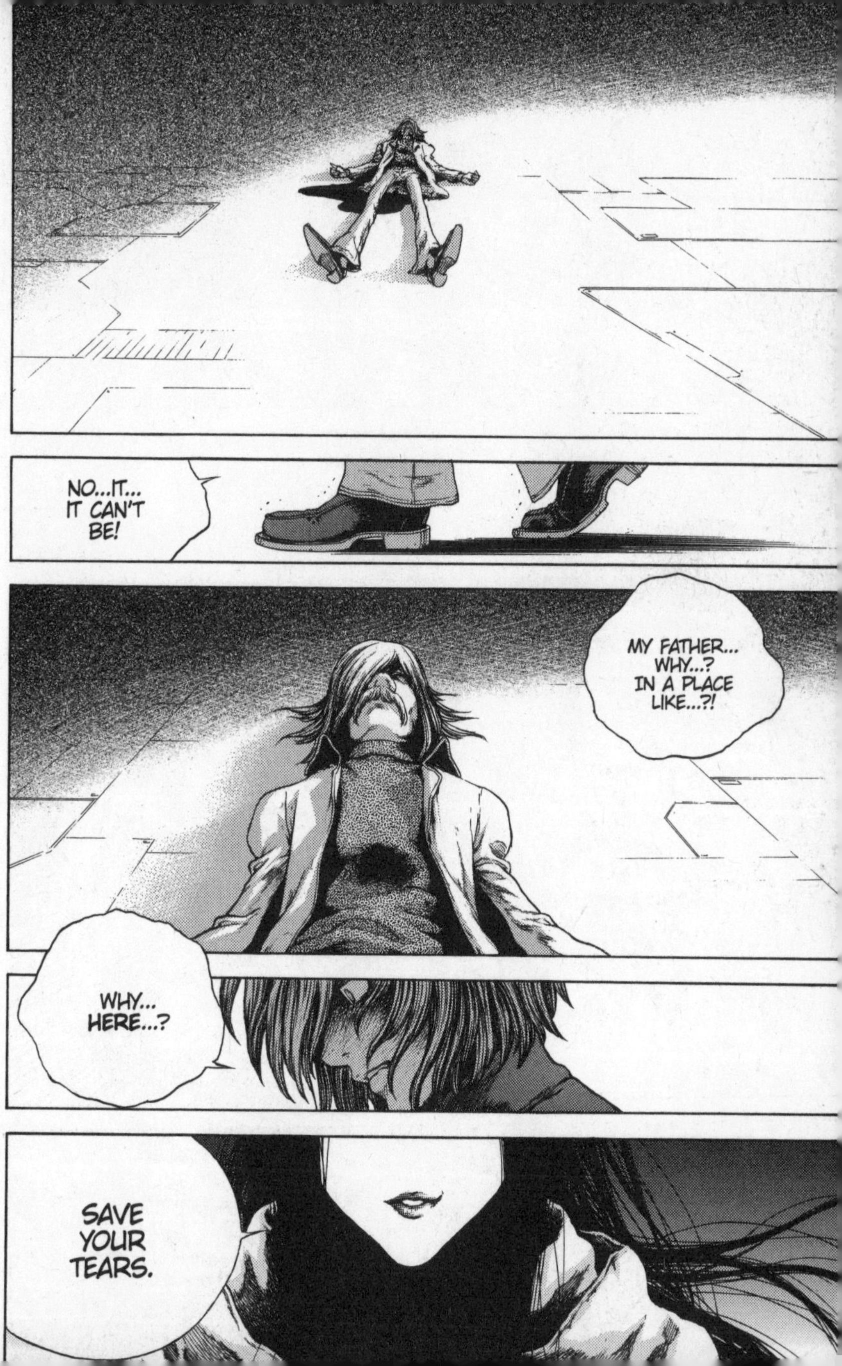
NO...IT... IT CAN'T BE!
MY FATHER... WHY...? IN A PLACE LIKE...?!
WHY... HERE...?
SAVE YOUR TEARS.

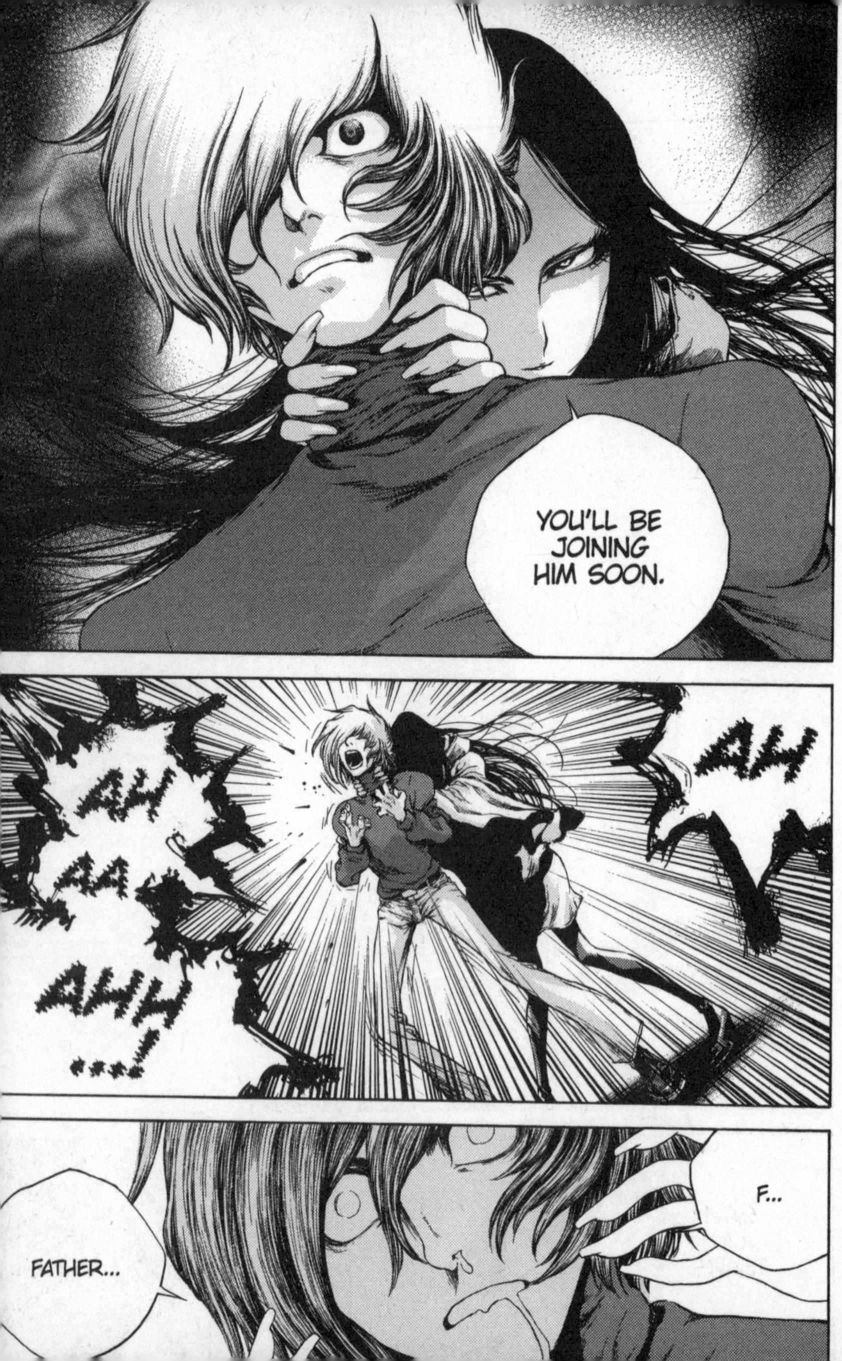
YOU'LL BE JOINING HIM SOON.
AH
AH AA AHH...!
F...
FATHER...

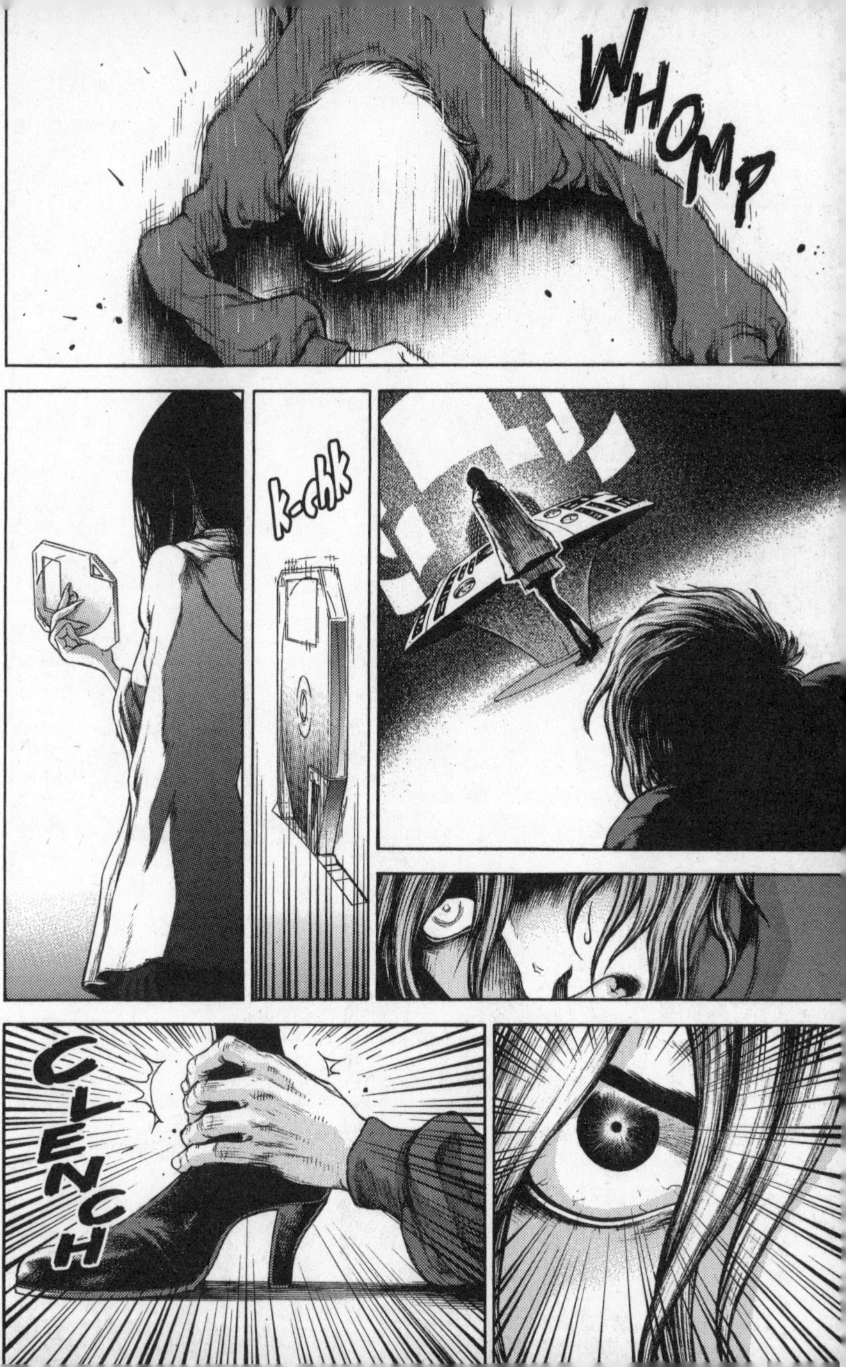
WHOMP
k-chk
CLENCH

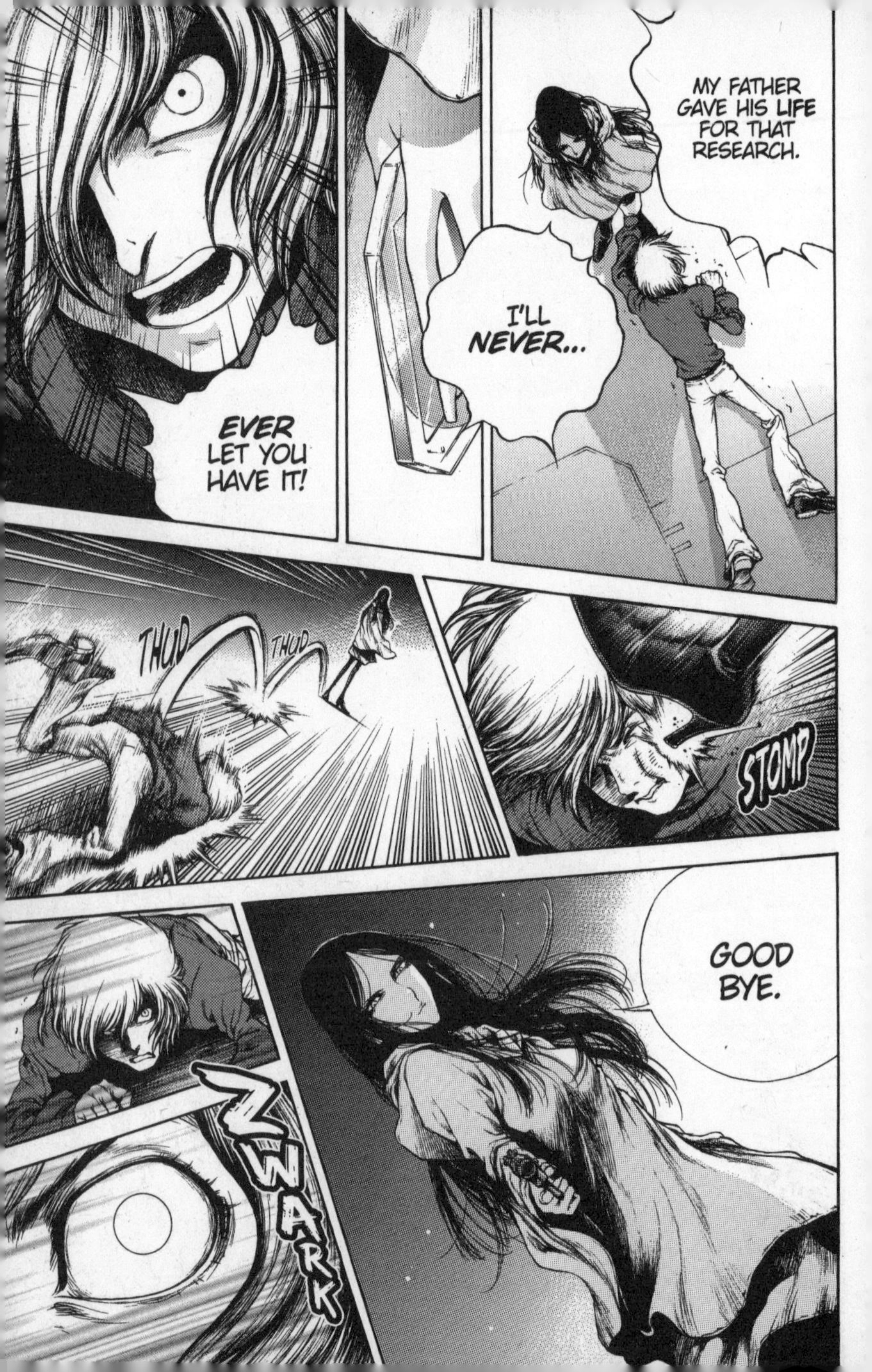
MY FATHER GAVE HIS LIFE FOR THAT RESEARCH.
I'LL NEVER...
EVER LET YOU HAVE IT!
STOMP
THUD
THUD
GOOD BYE.
ZWARK

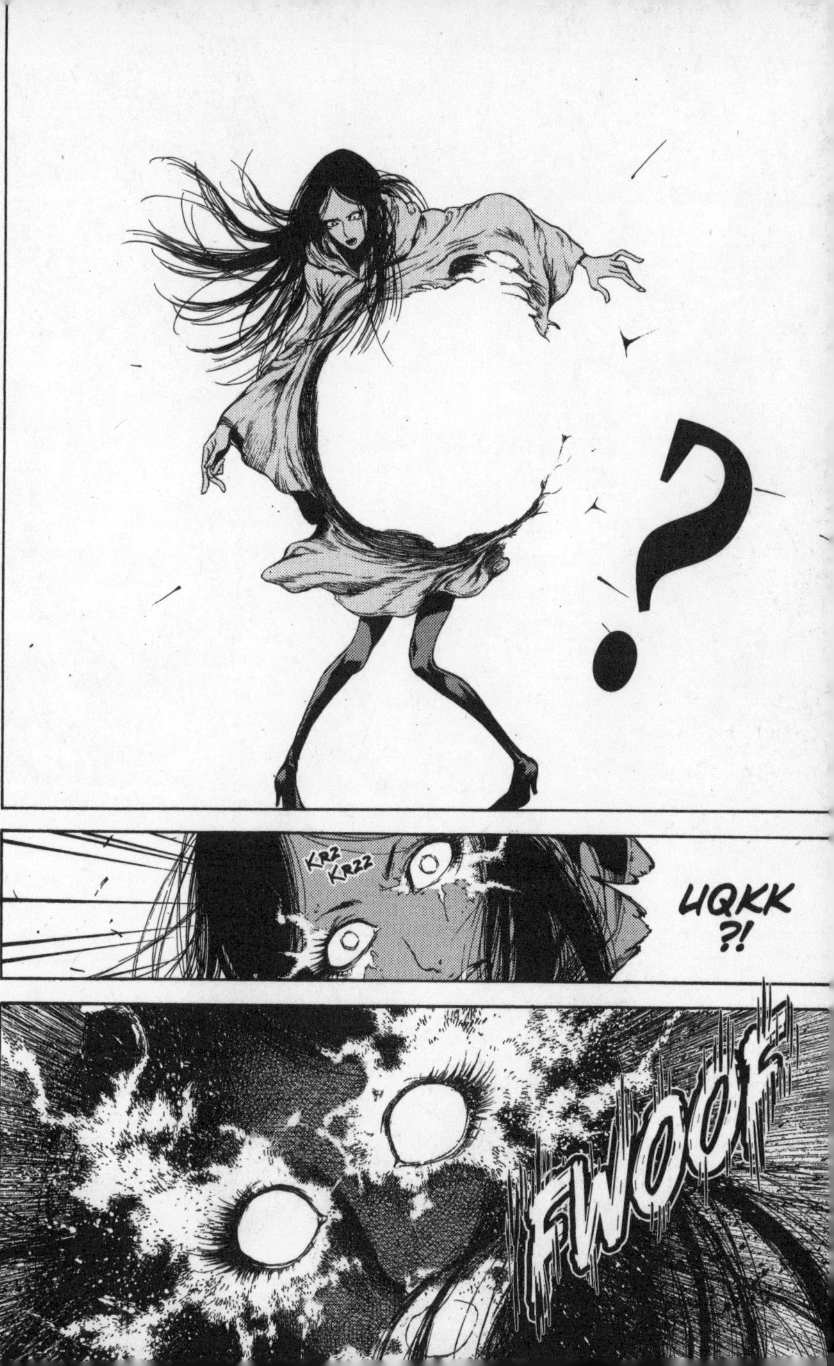
?
UQKK ?!
KRZ
KRZZ
FWOOF

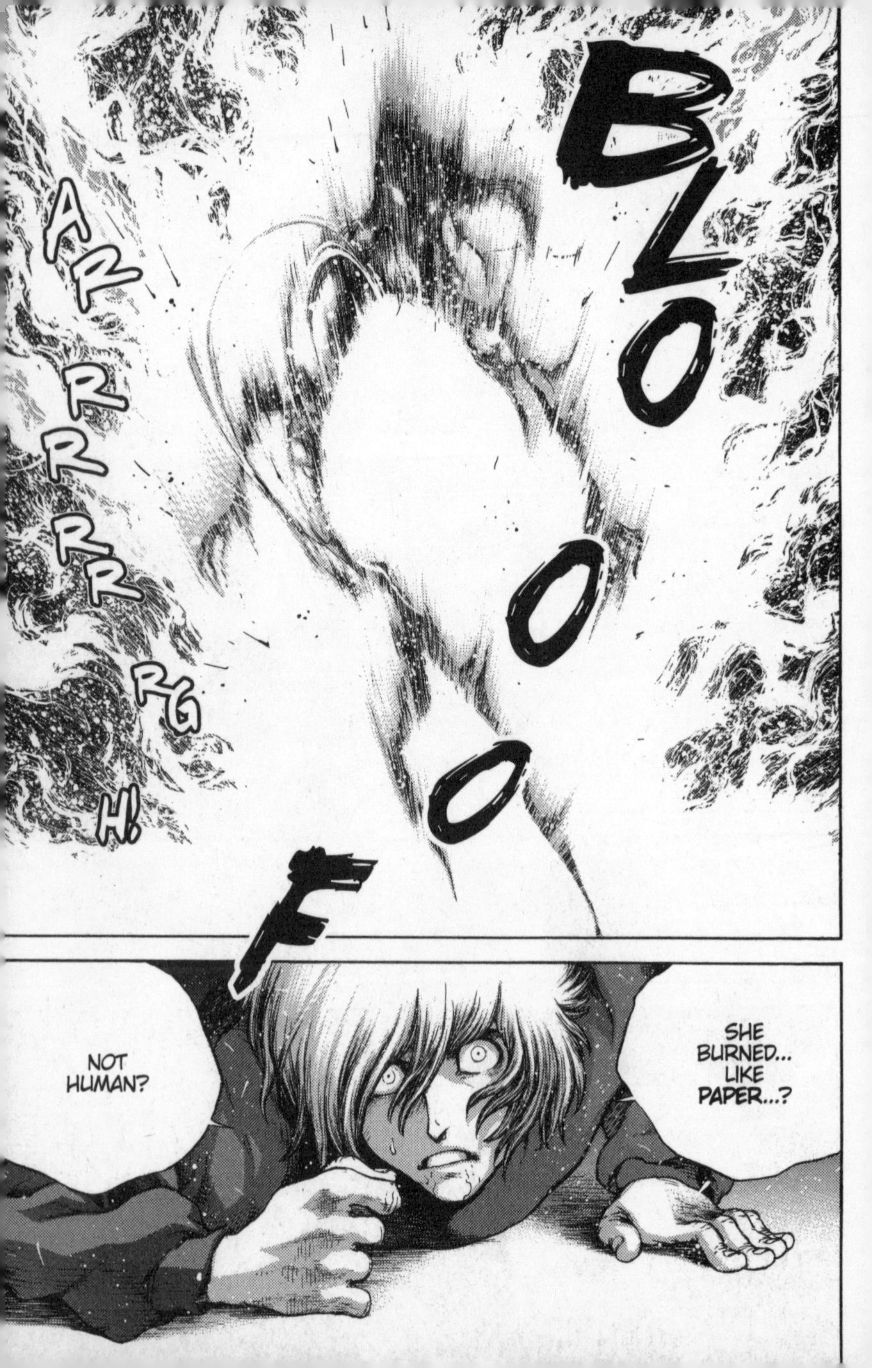
BLOOOF
ARRRRRRGH!
SHE BURNED... LIKE PAPER...?
NOT HUMAN?

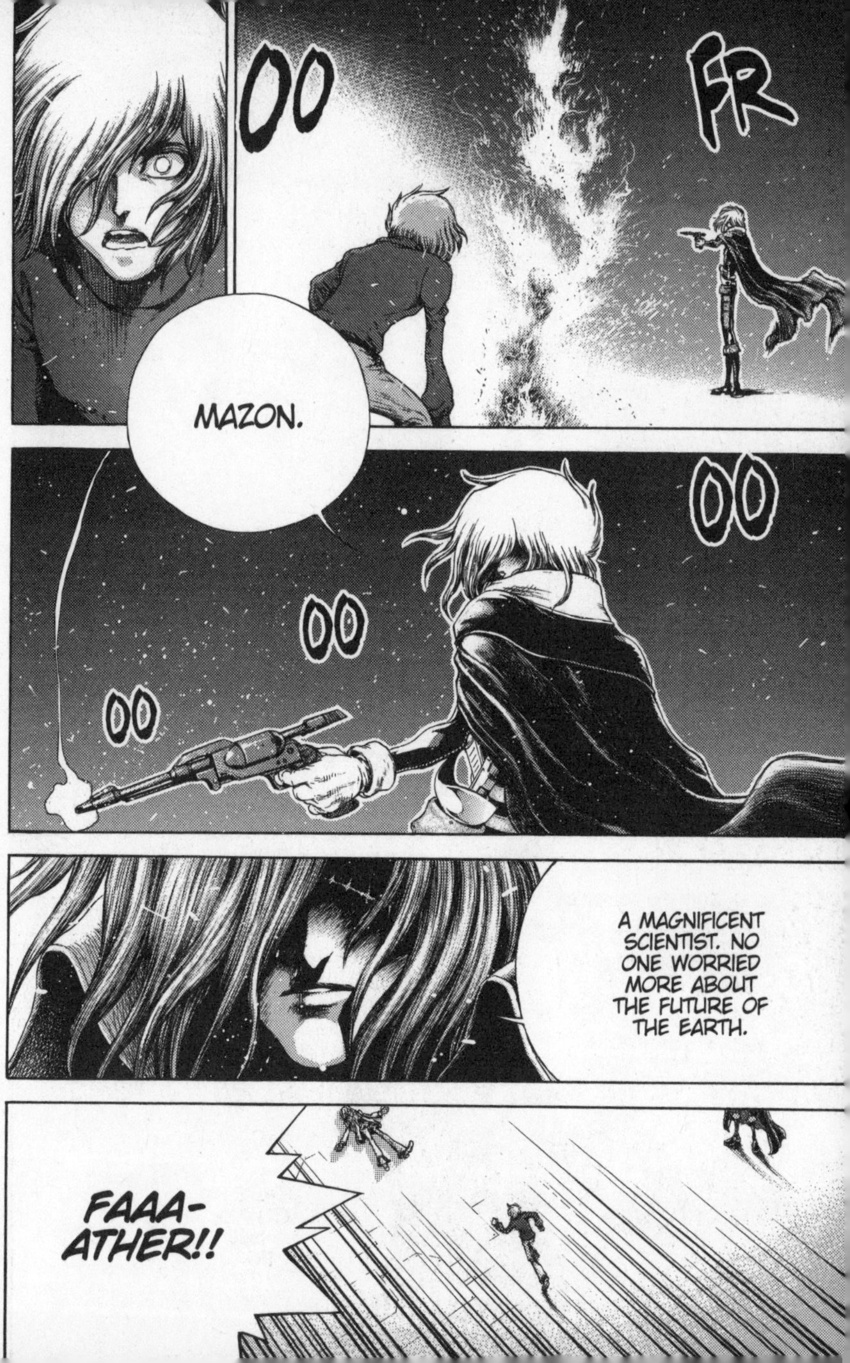
FR
OO
MAZON.
OO
OO
OO
A MAGNIFICENT SCIENTIST. NO ONE WORRIED MORE ABOUT THE FUTURE OF THE EARTH.
FAAA-ATHER!!

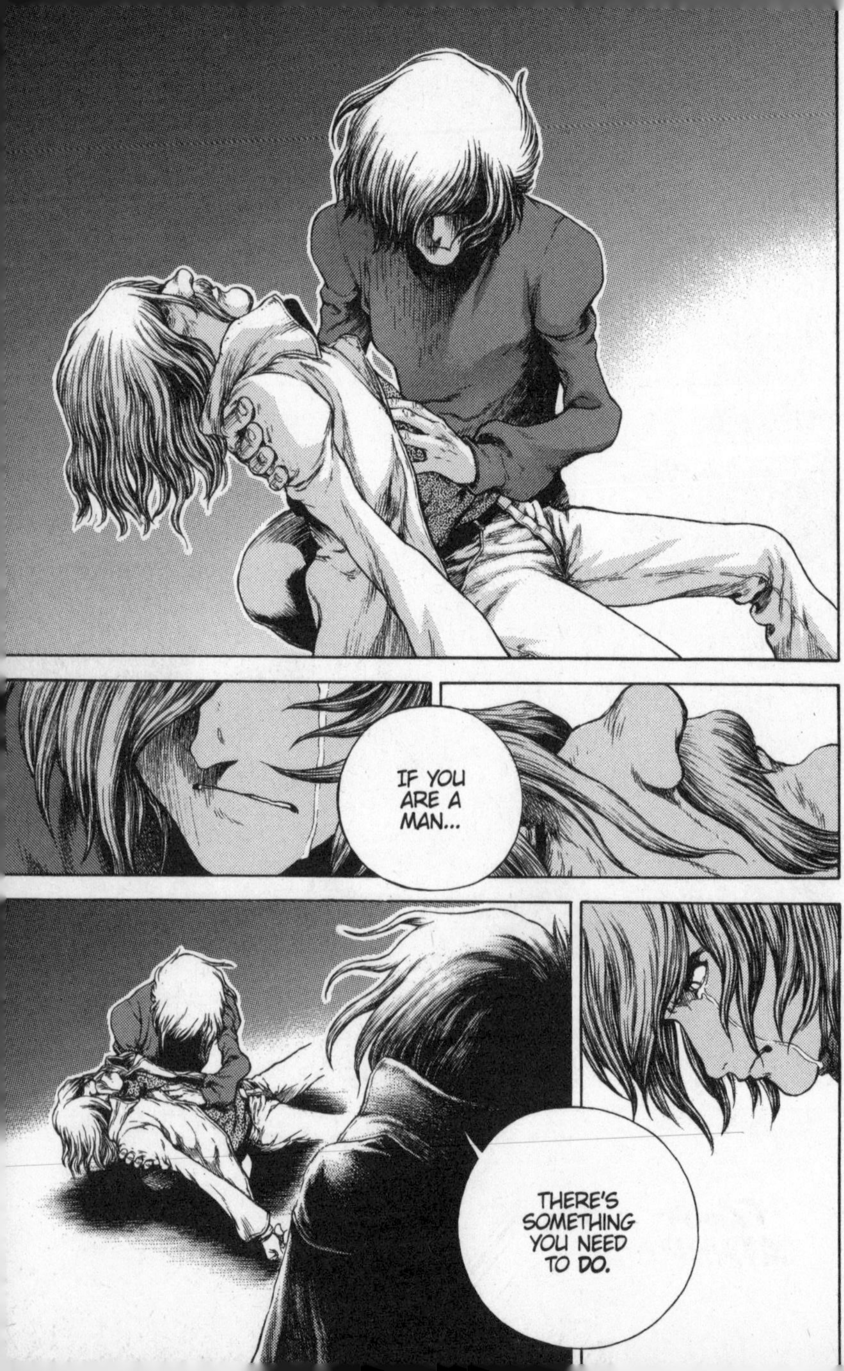
IF YOU ARE A MAN...
THERE'S SOMETHING YOU NEED TO DO.

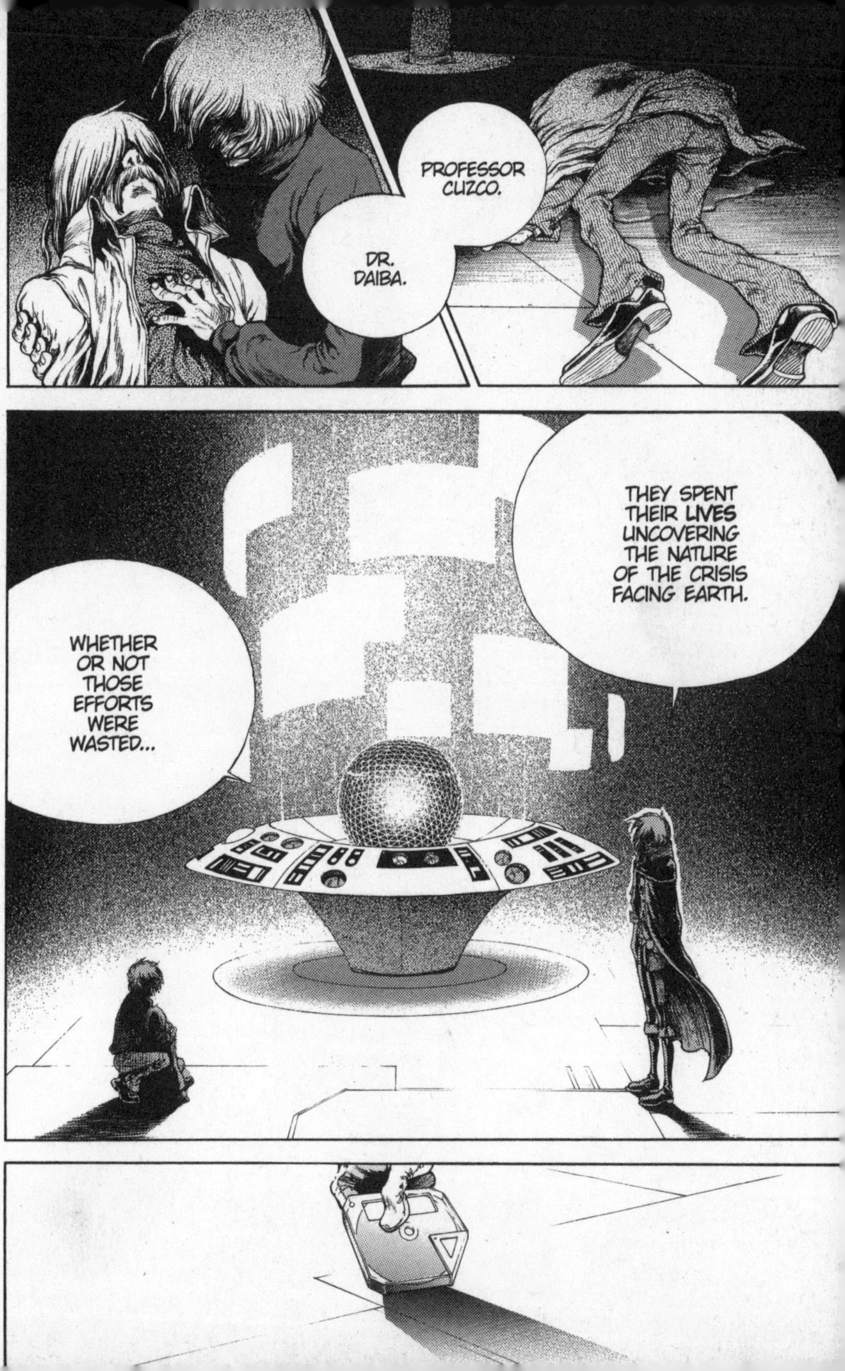
PROFESSOR CUZCO.
DR. DAIBA.
THEY SPENT THEIR LIVES UNCOVERING THE NATURE OF THE CRISIS FACING EARTH.
WHETHER OR NOT THOSE EFFORTS WERE WASTED...

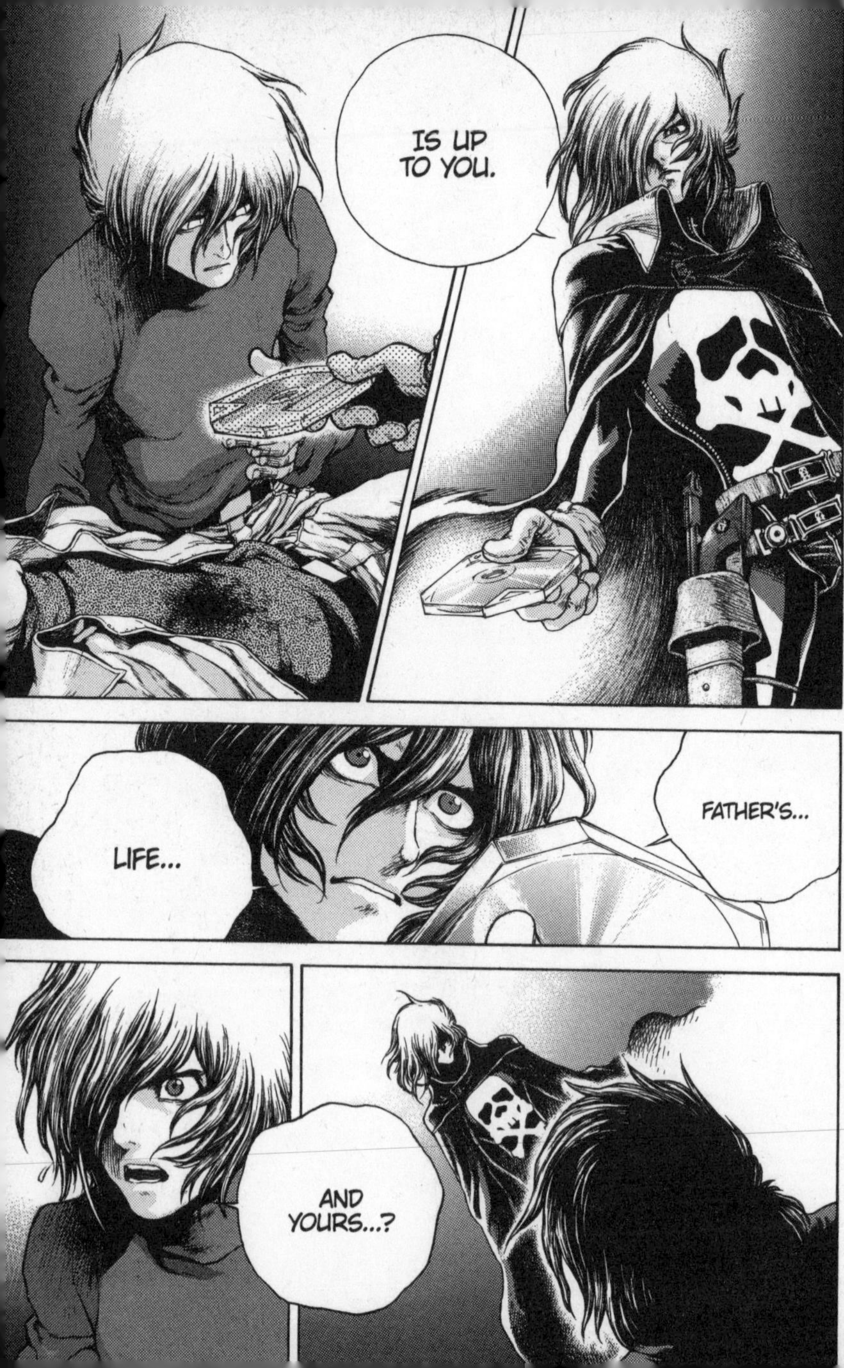
IS UP TO YOU.
FATHER'S...
LIFE...
AND YOURS...?

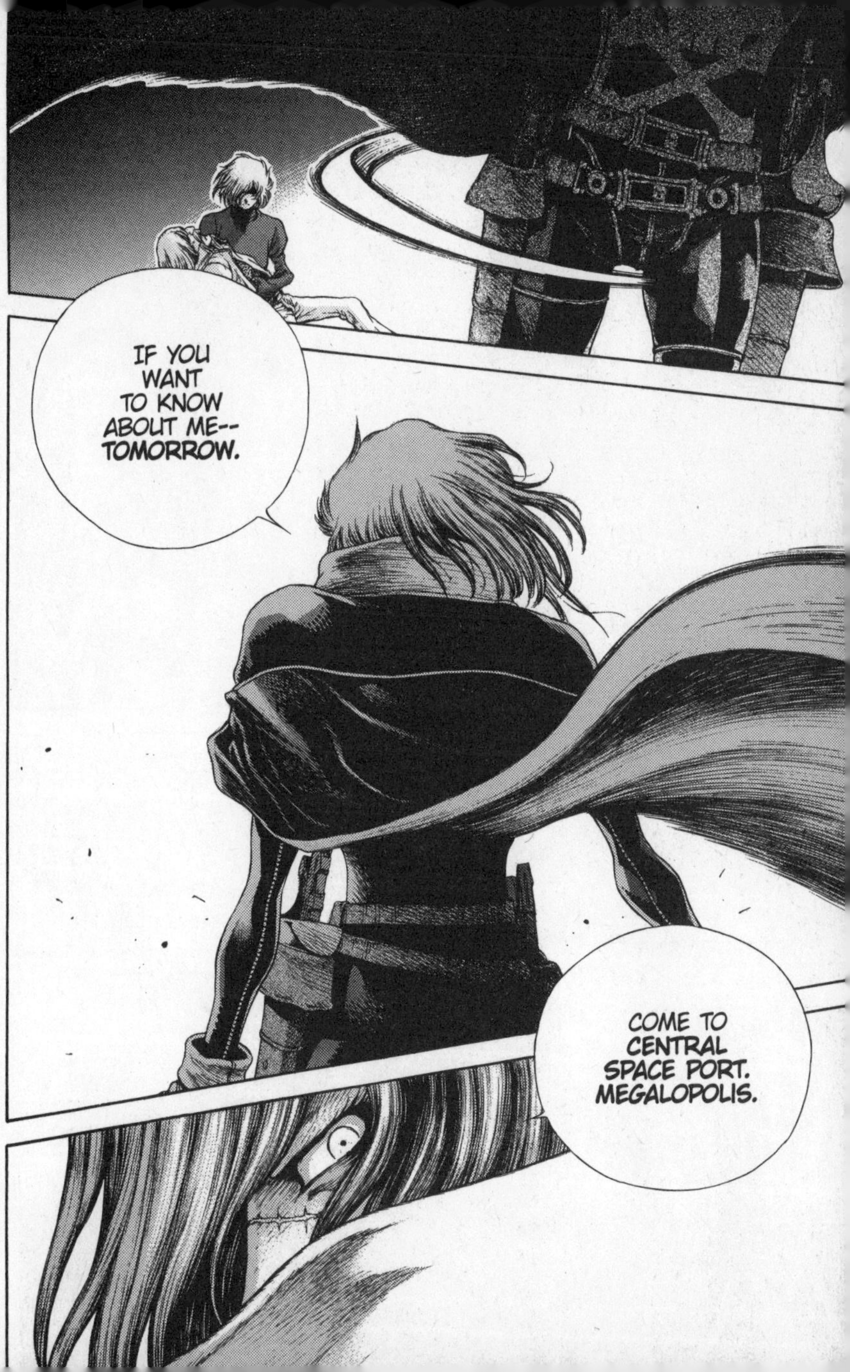
IF YOU WANT TO KNOW ABOUT ME-- TOMORROW.
COME TO CENTRAL SPACE PORT. MEGALOPOLIS.

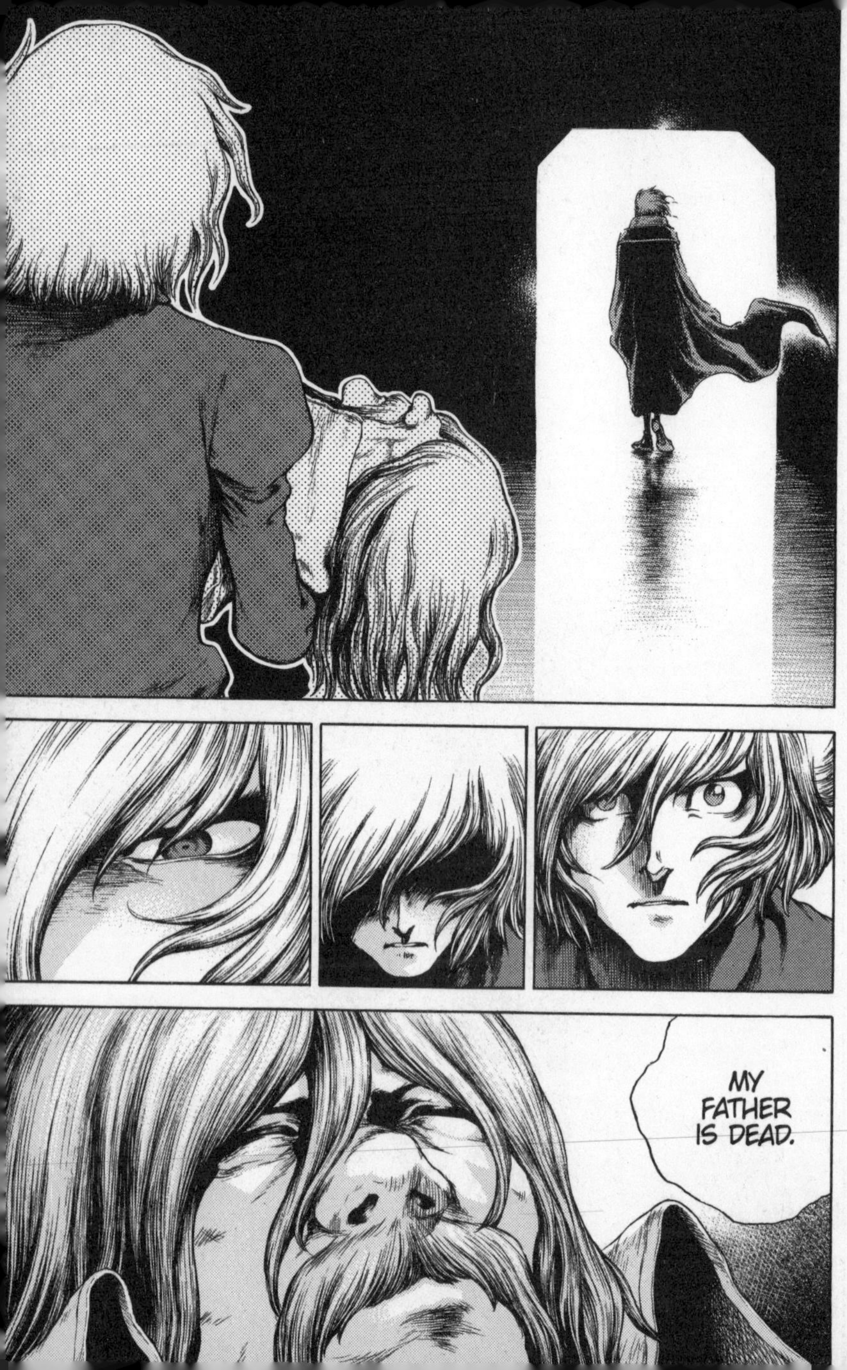
MY FATHER IS DEAD.

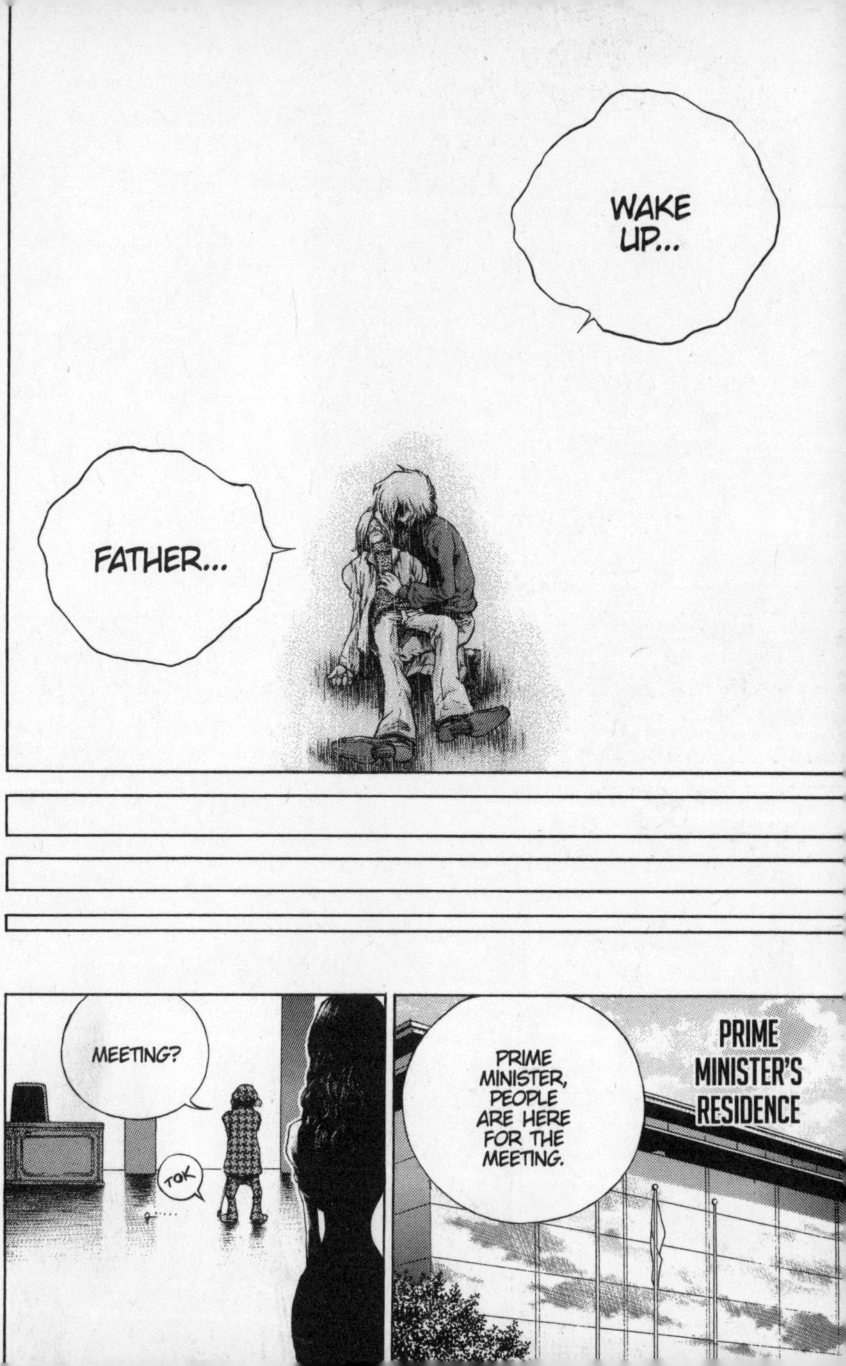
WAKE UP...
FATHER...
PRIME MINISTER'S RESIDENCE
PRIME MINISTER, PEOPLE ARE HERE FOR THE MEETING.
MEETING?
TOK

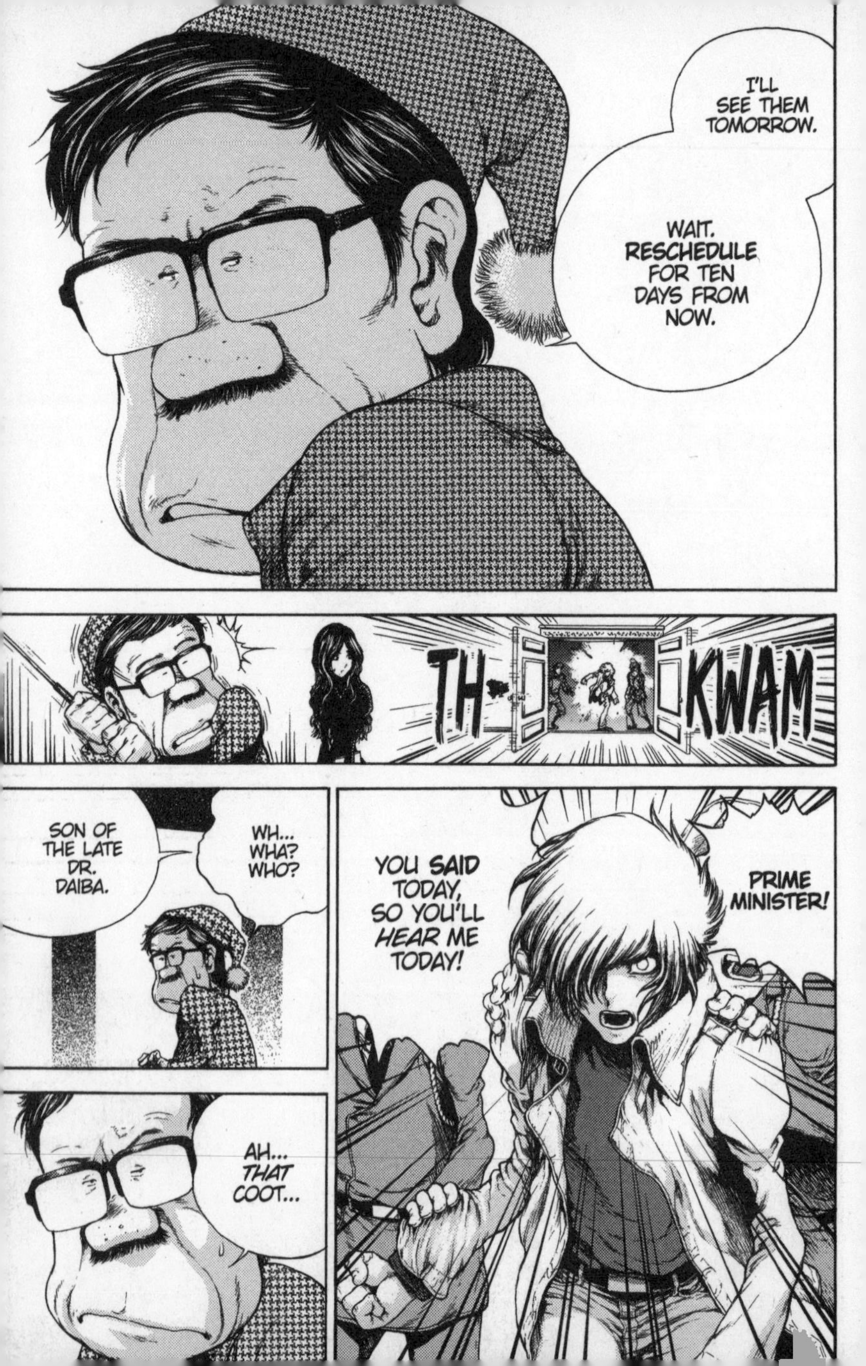
I'LL SEE THEM TOMORROW.
WAIT. RESCHEDULE FOR TEN DAYS FROM NOW.
TH
KWAM
PRIME MINISTER!
YOU SAID TODAY, SO YOU'LL HEAR ME TODAY!
WH... WHA? WHO?
SON OF THE LATE DR. DAIBA.
AH... THAT COOT...

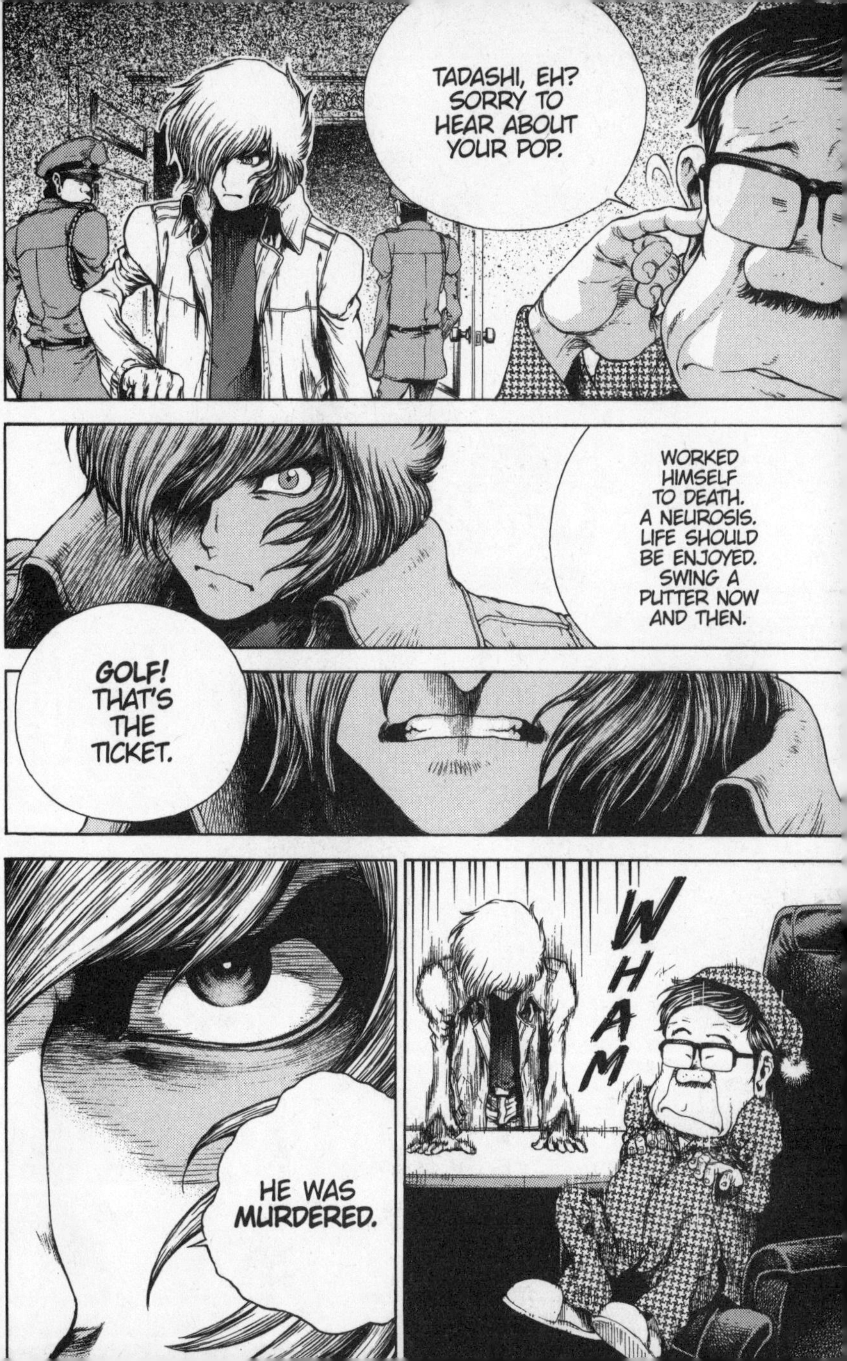
TADASHI, EH? SORRY TO HEAR ABOUT YOUR POP.
WORKED HIMSELF TO DEATH. A NEUROSIS. LIFE SHOULD BE ENJOYED. SWING A PUTTER NOW AND THEN.
GOLF! THAT'S THE TICKET.
WHAM
HE WAS MURDERED.

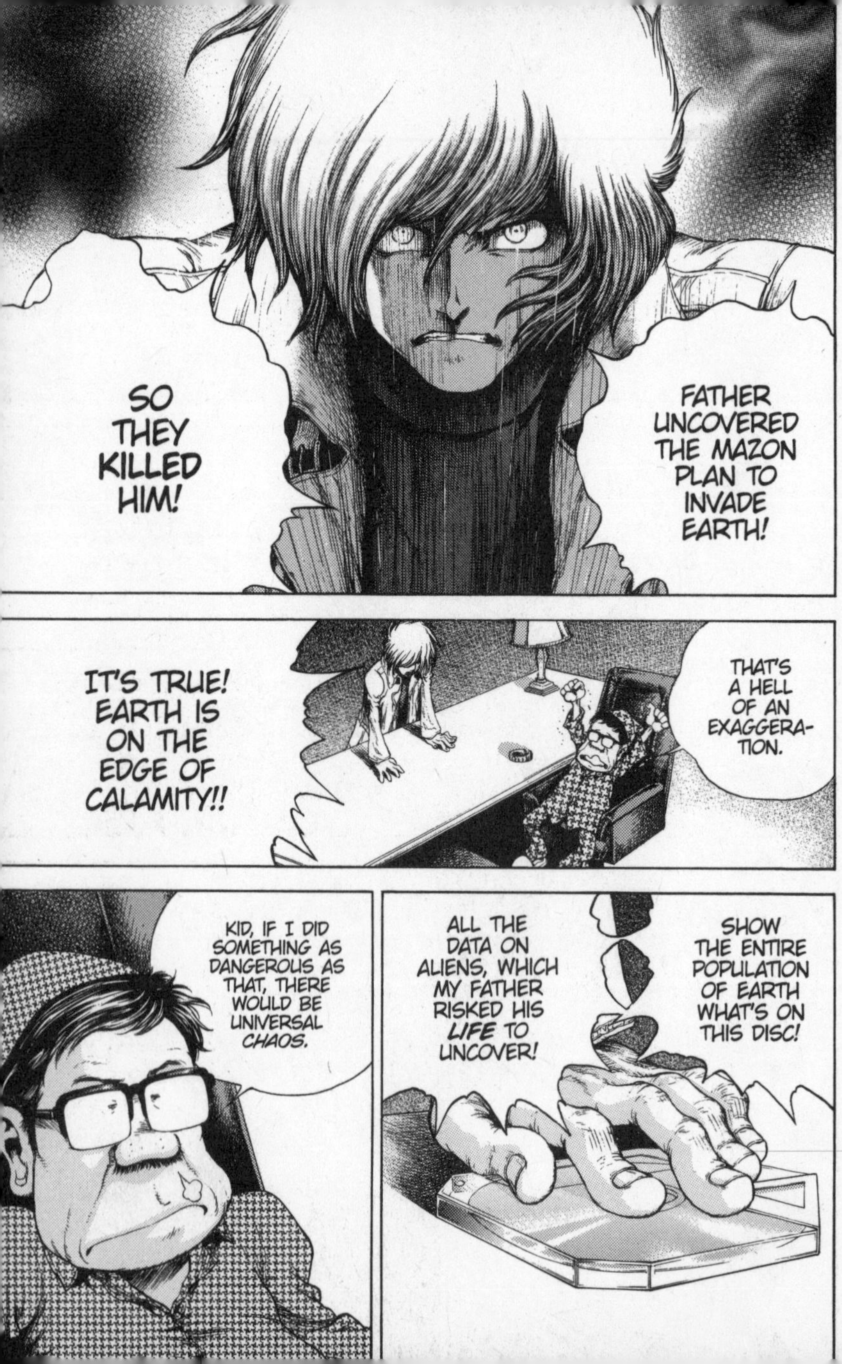
FATHER UNCOVERED THE MAZON PLAN TO INVADE EARTH!
SO THEY KILLED HIM!
THAT'S A HELL OF AN EXAGGERA-TION.
IT'S TRUE! EARTH IS ON THE EDGE OF CALAMITY!!
SHOW THE ENTIRE POPULATION OF EARTH WHAT'S ON THIS DISC!
ALL THE DATA ON ALIENS, WHICH MY FATHER RISKED HIS *LIFE* TO UNCOVER!
KID, IF I DID SOMETHING AS DANGEROUS AS THAT, THERE WOULD BE UNIVERSAL *CHAOS.*

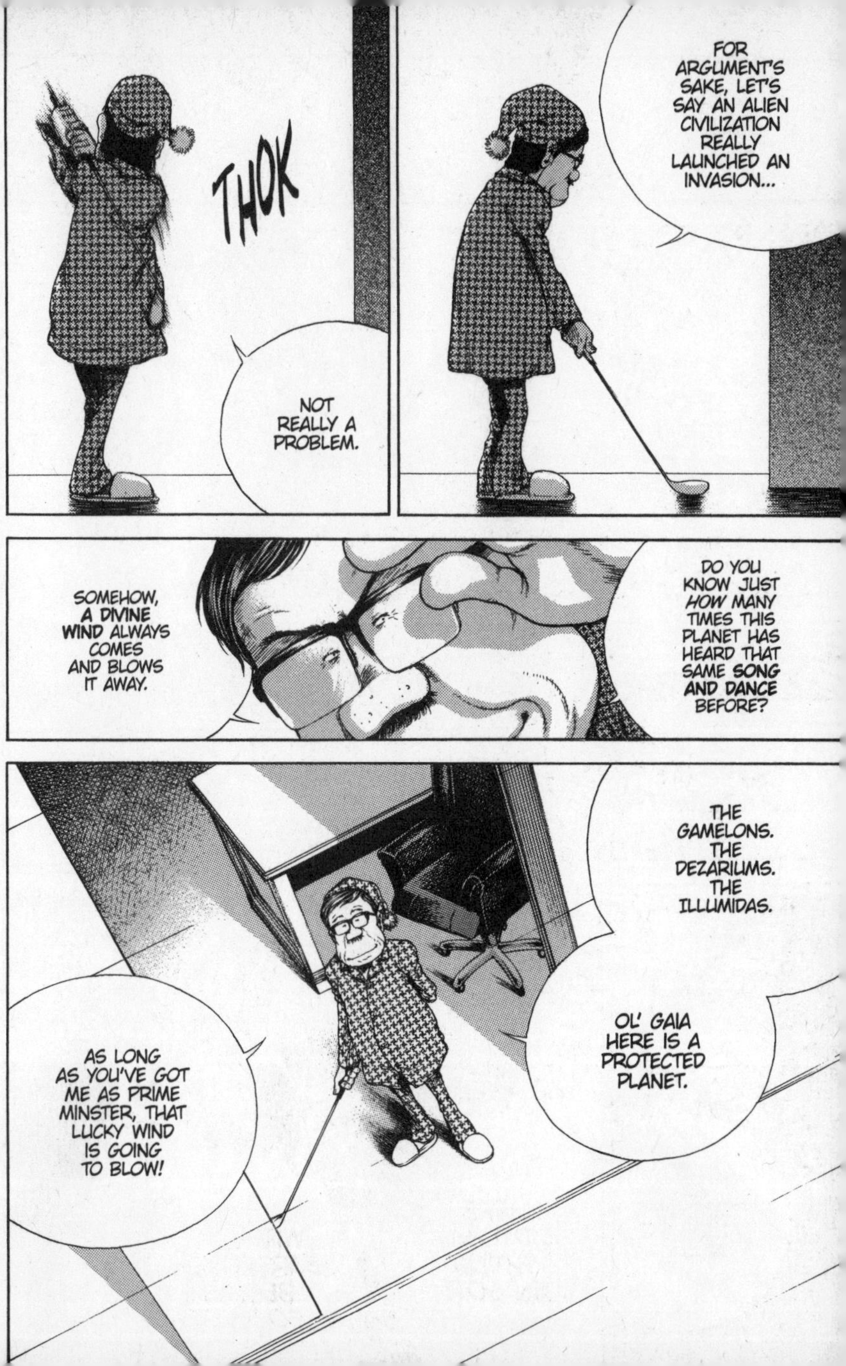
FOR ARGUMENT'S SAKE, LET'S SAY AN ALIEN CIVILIZATION REALLY LAUNCHED AN INVASION...
THOK
NOT REALLY A PROBLEM.
DO YOU KNOW JUST *HOW* MANY TIMES THIS PLANET HAS HEARD THAT SAME **SONG AND DANCE** BEFORE?
SOMEHOW, **A DIVINE WIND** ALWAYS COMES AND BLOWS IT AWAY.
THE GAMELONS. THE DEZARIUMS. THE ILLUMIDAS.
OL' GAIA HERE IS A PROTECTED PLANET.
AS LONG AS YOU'VE GOT ME AS PRIME MINSTER, THAT LUCKY WIND IS GOING TO BLOW!

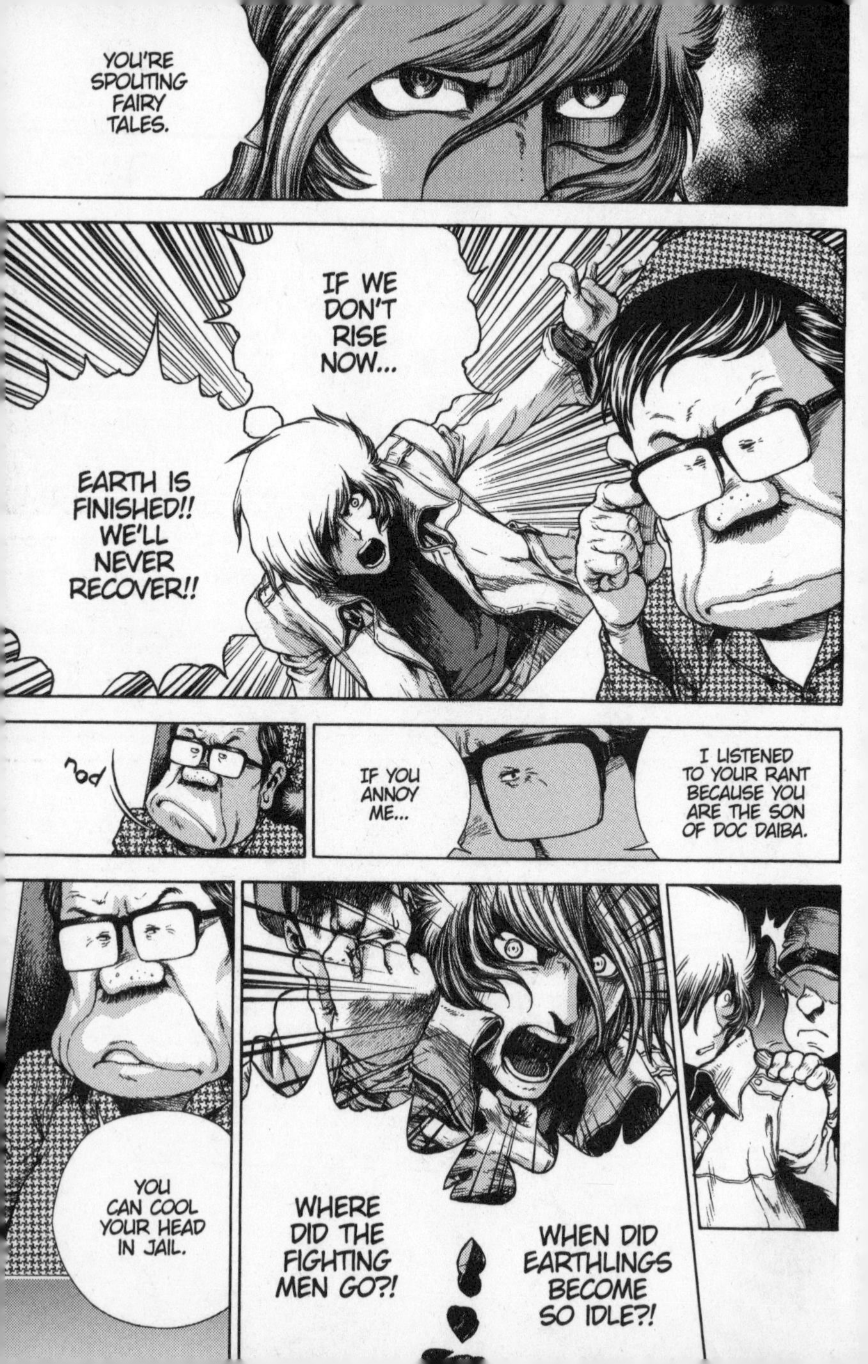
YOU'RE SPOUTING FAIRY TALES.
IF WE DON'T RISE NOW...
EARTH IS FINISHED!! WE'LL NEVER RECOVER!!
I LISTENED TO YOUR RANT BECAUSE YOU ARE THE SON OF DOC DAIBA.
IF YOU ANNOY ME...
poy
WHERE DID THE FIGHTING MEN GO?!
WHEN DID EARTHLINGS BECOME SO IDLE?!
YOU CAN COOL YOUR HEAD IN JAIL.

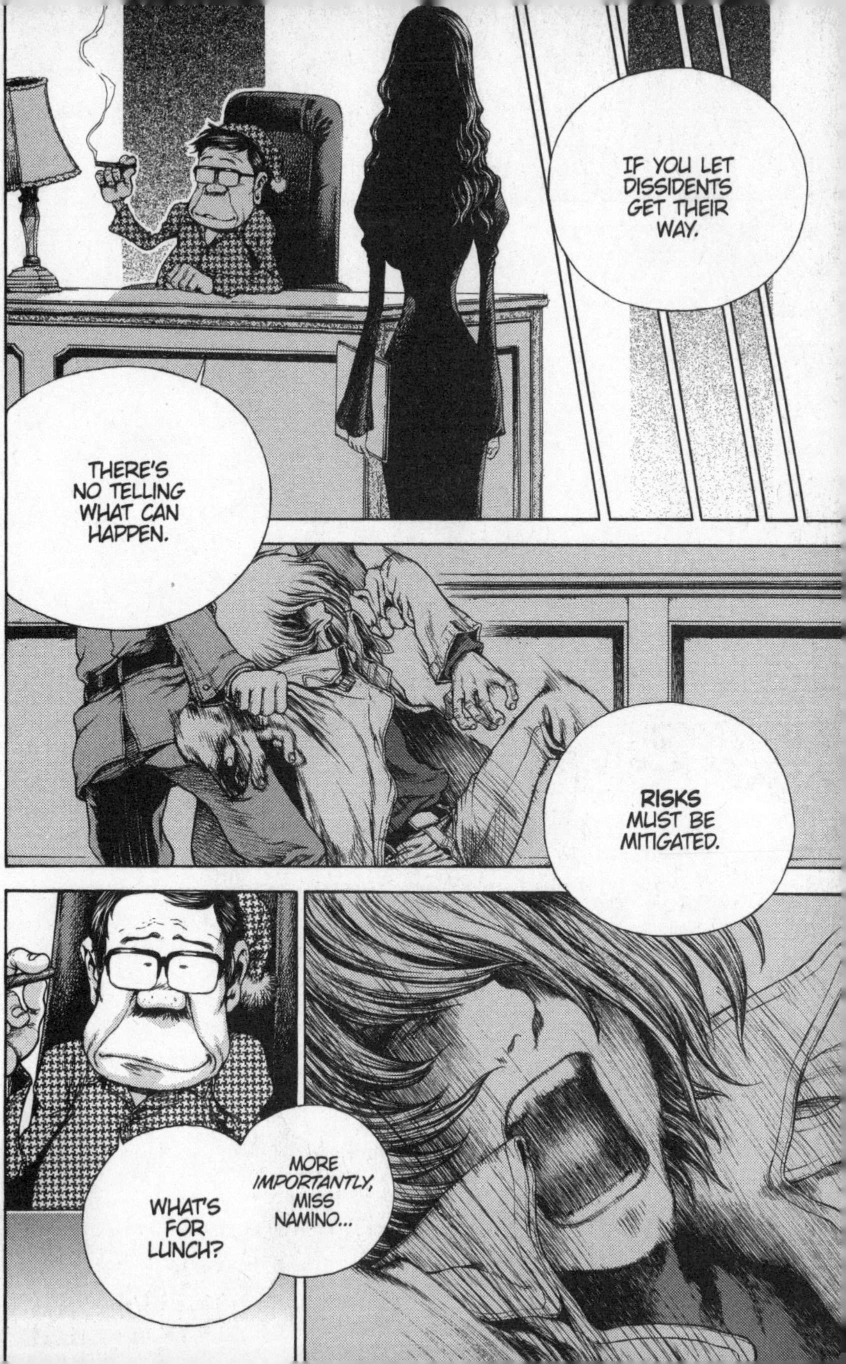
IF YOU LET DISSIDENTS GET THEIR WAY.
THERE'S NO TELLING WHAT CAN HAPPEN.
RISKS MUST BE MITIGATED.
MORE IMPORTANTLY, MISS NAMINO...
WHAT'S FOR LUNCH?

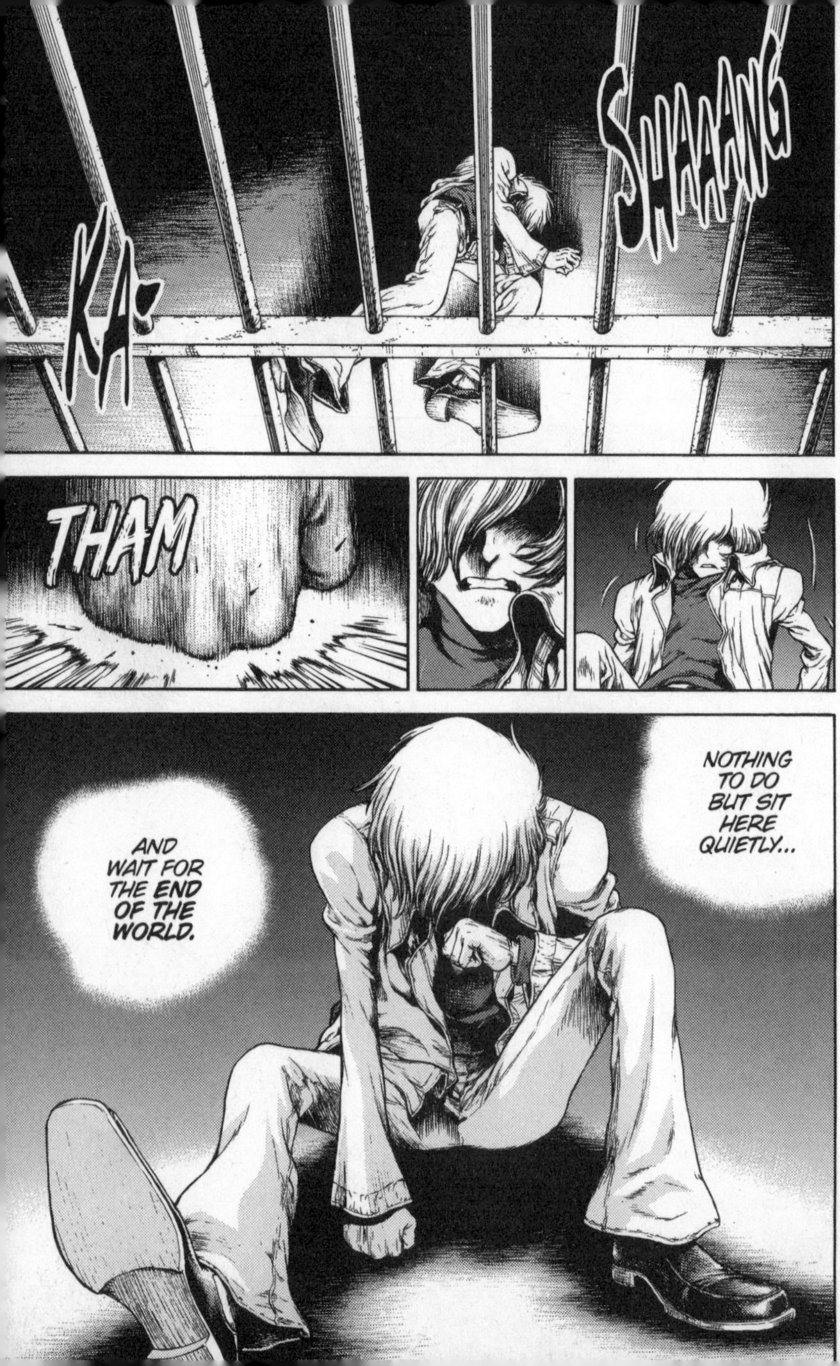
SHAANG
KA!
THAM!
NOTHING TO DO BUT SIT HERE QUIETLY...
AND WAIT FOR THE END OF THE WORLD.

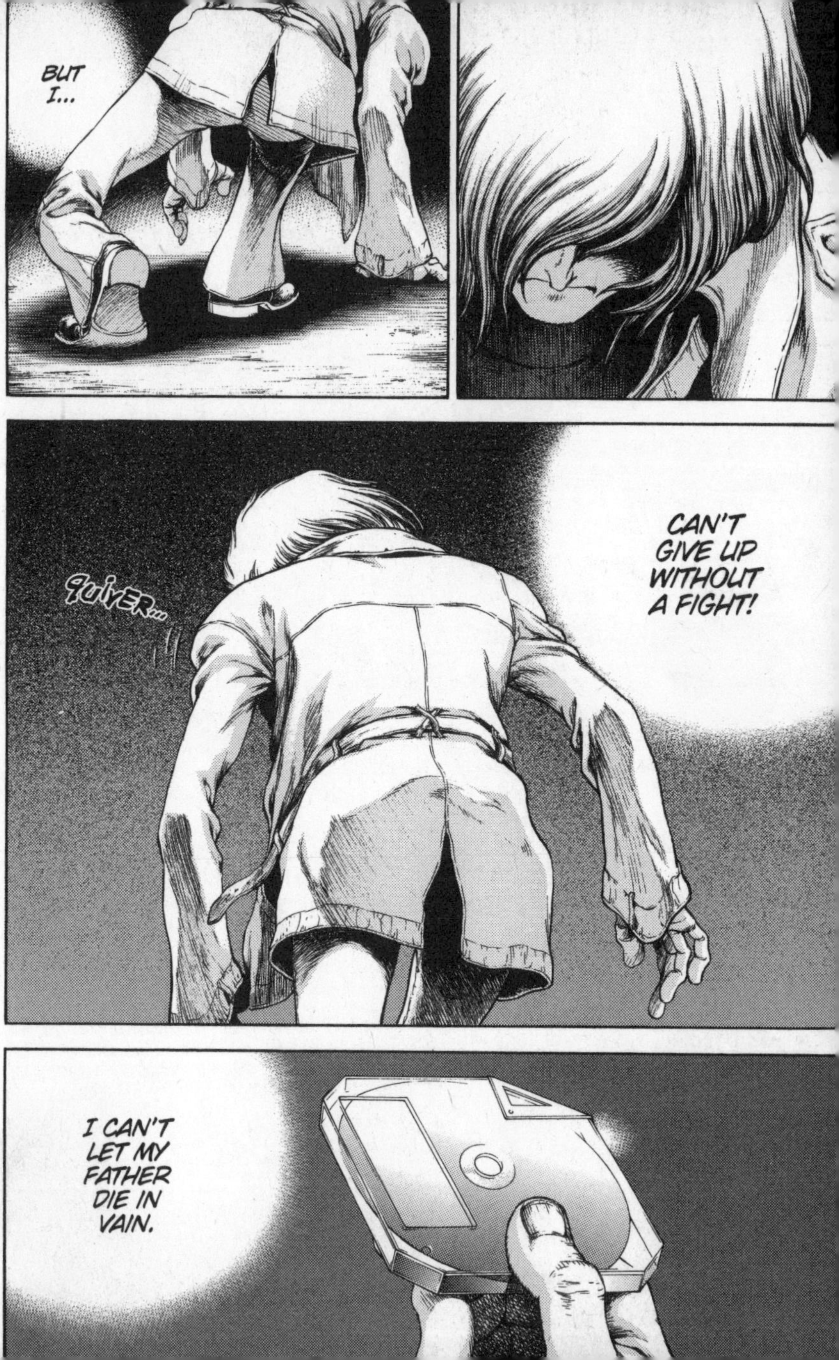
BUT I...
CAN'T GIVE UP WITHOUT A FIGHT!
QUIVER...
I CAN'T LET MY FATHER DIE IN VAIN.

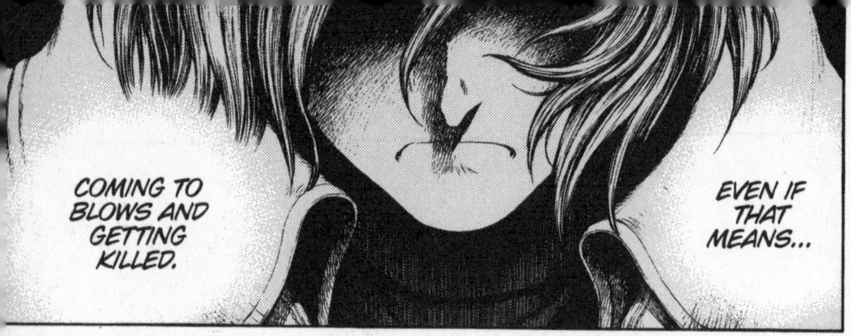
EVEN IF THAT MEANS...
COMING TO BLOWS AND GETTING KILLED.
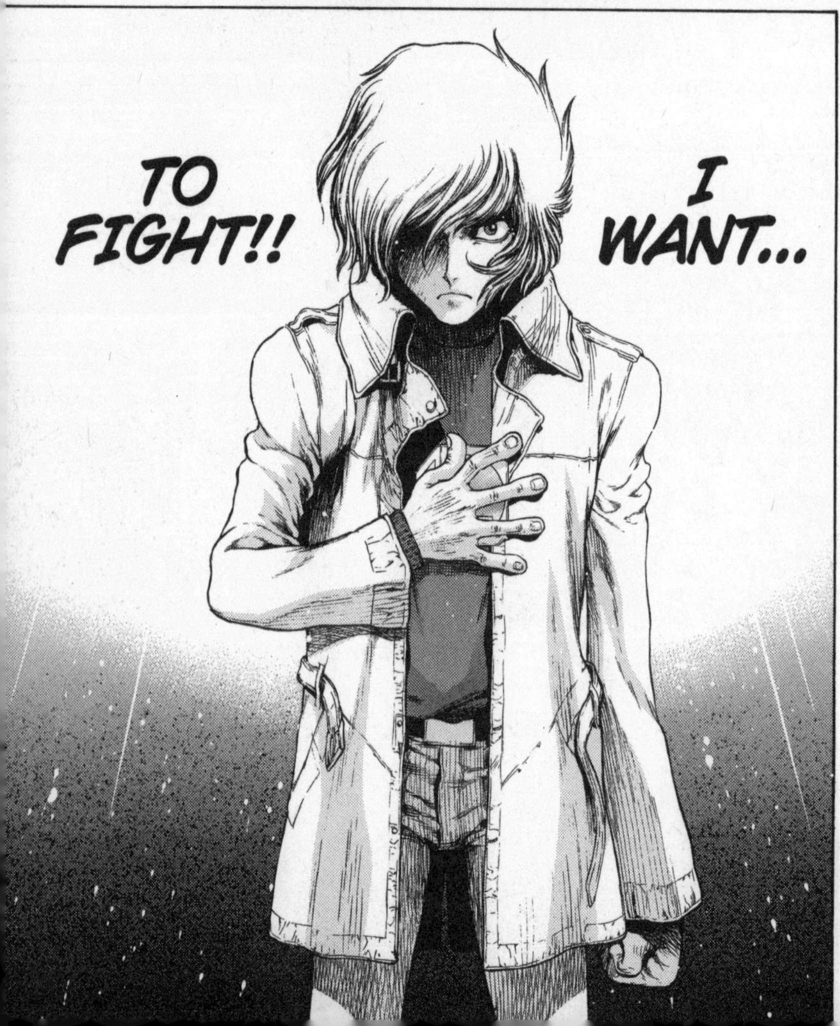
I WANT...
TO FIGHT!!

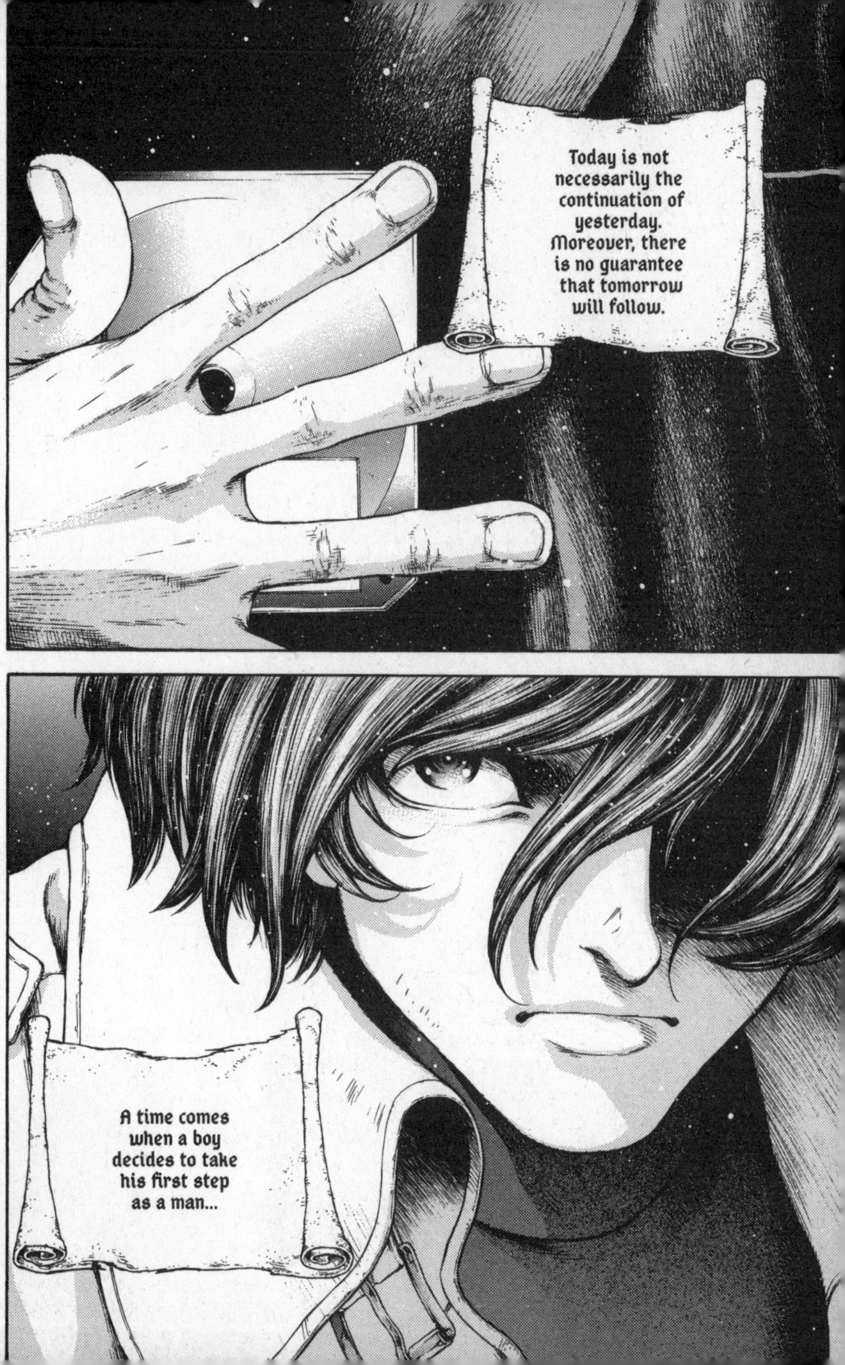
Today is not necessarily the continuation of yesterday. Moreover, there is no guarantee that tomorrow will follow.
A time comes when a boy decides to take his first step as a man...

CAPTAIN HARLOCK 1
SPACE PIRATE DIMENSIONAL VOYAGE

CAPTAIN HARLOCK 1
SPACE PIRATE DIMENSIONAL VOYAGE

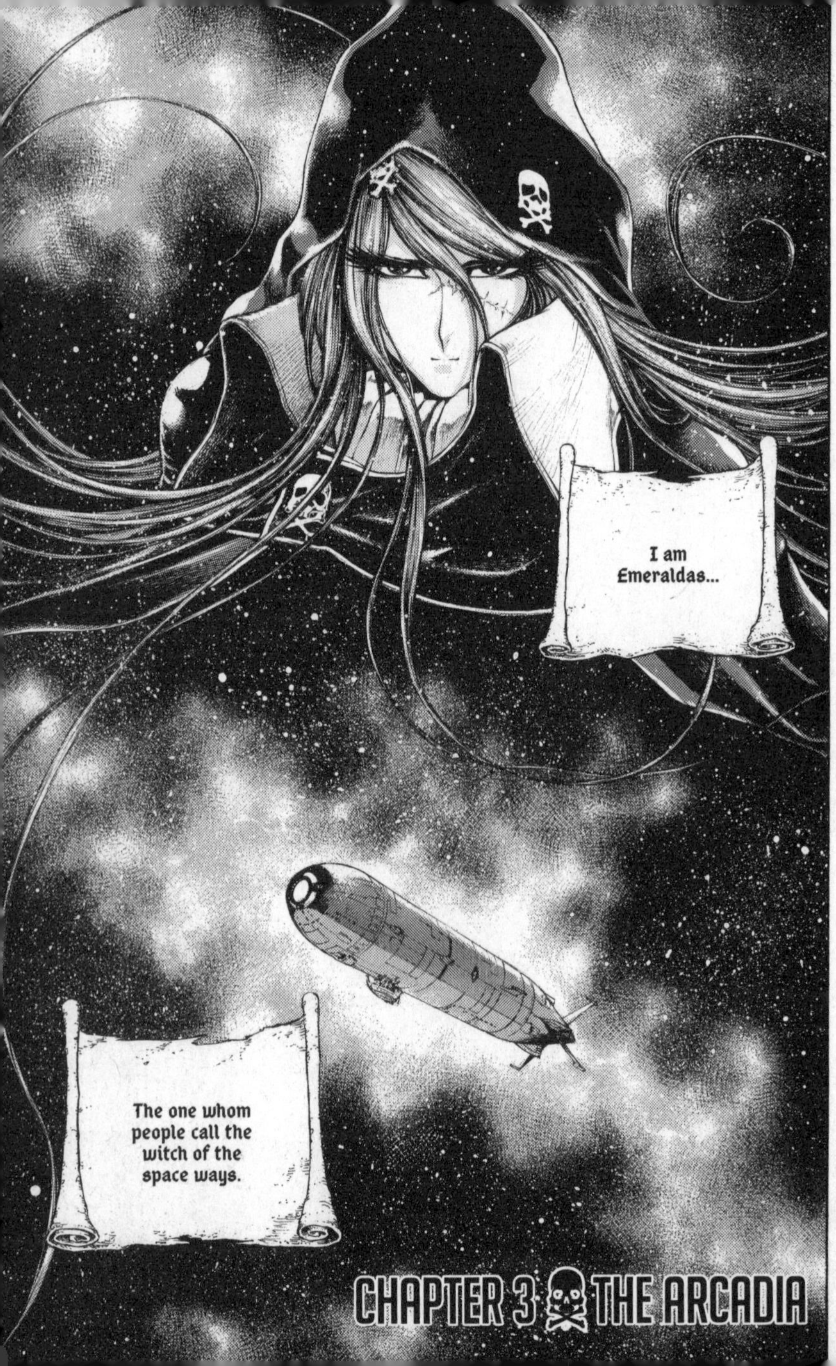
I am Emeraldas...
The one whom people call the witch of the space ways.
CHAPTER 3 THE ARCADIA

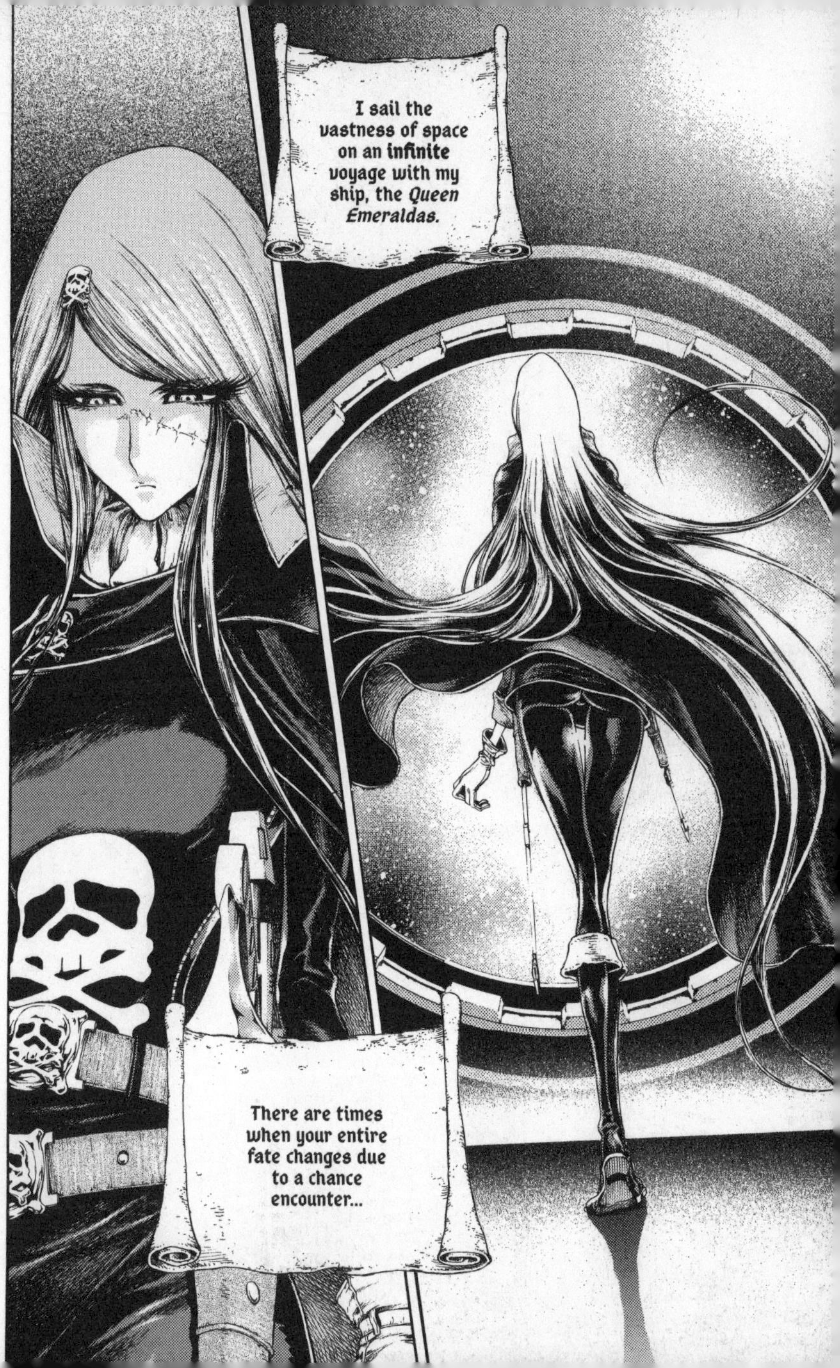
I sail the vastness of space on an infinite voyage with my ship, the Queen Emeraldas.
There are times when your entire fate changes due to a chance encounter...

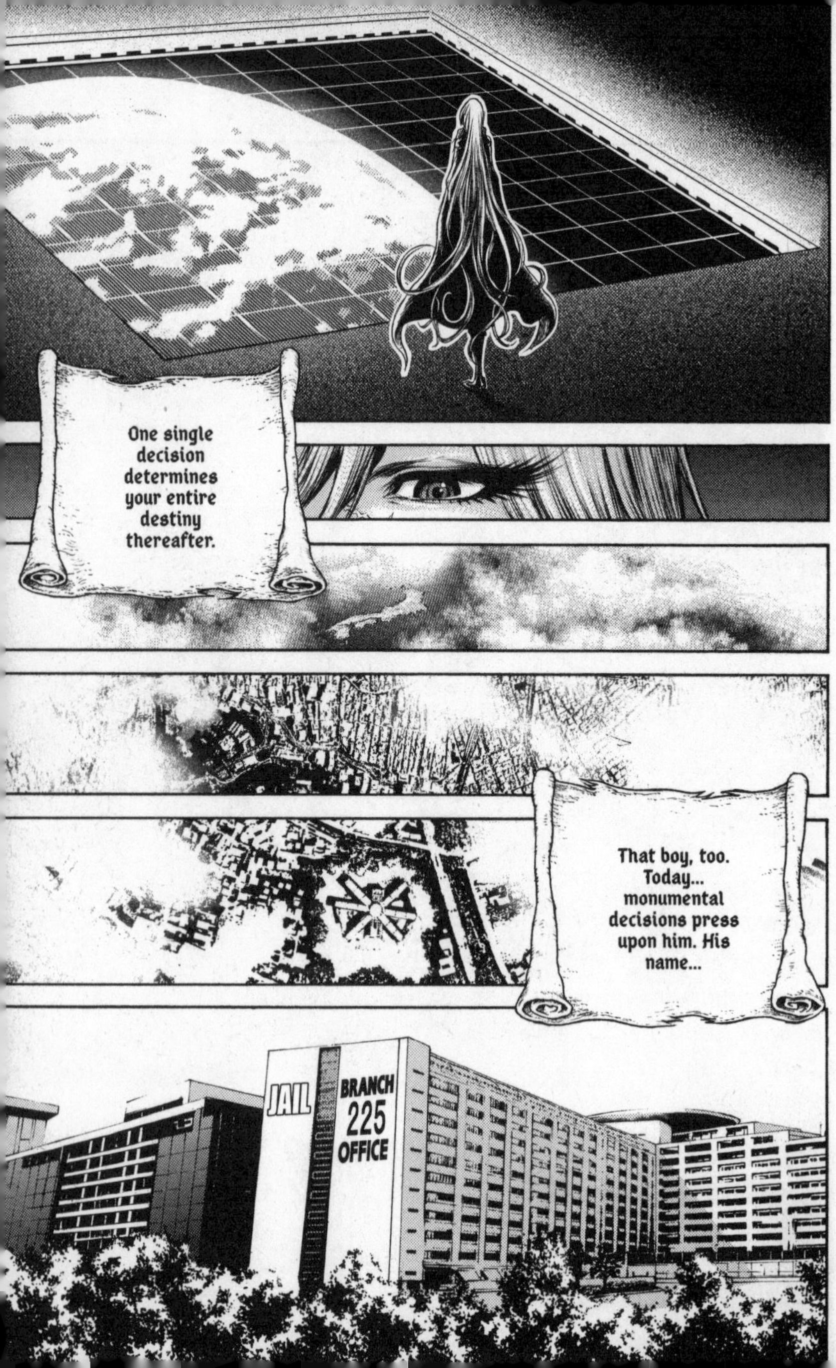
One single decision determines your entire destiny thereafter.
That boy, too. Today... monumental decisions press upon him. His name...
BRANCH 225 OFFICE
JAIL

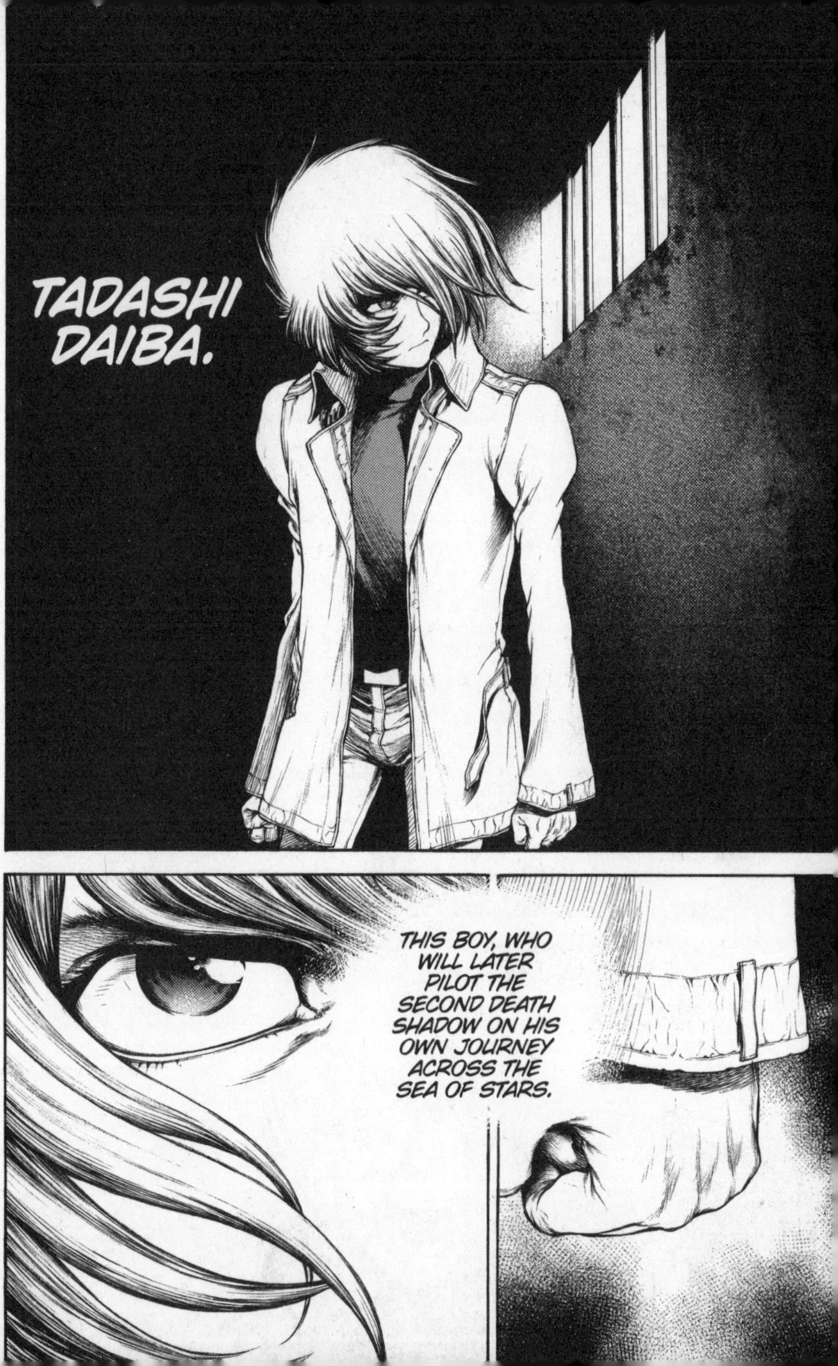
TADASHI DAIBA.
THIS BOY, WHO WILL LATER PILOT THE SECOND DEATH SHADOW ON HIS OWN JOURNEY ACROSS THE SEA OF STARS.

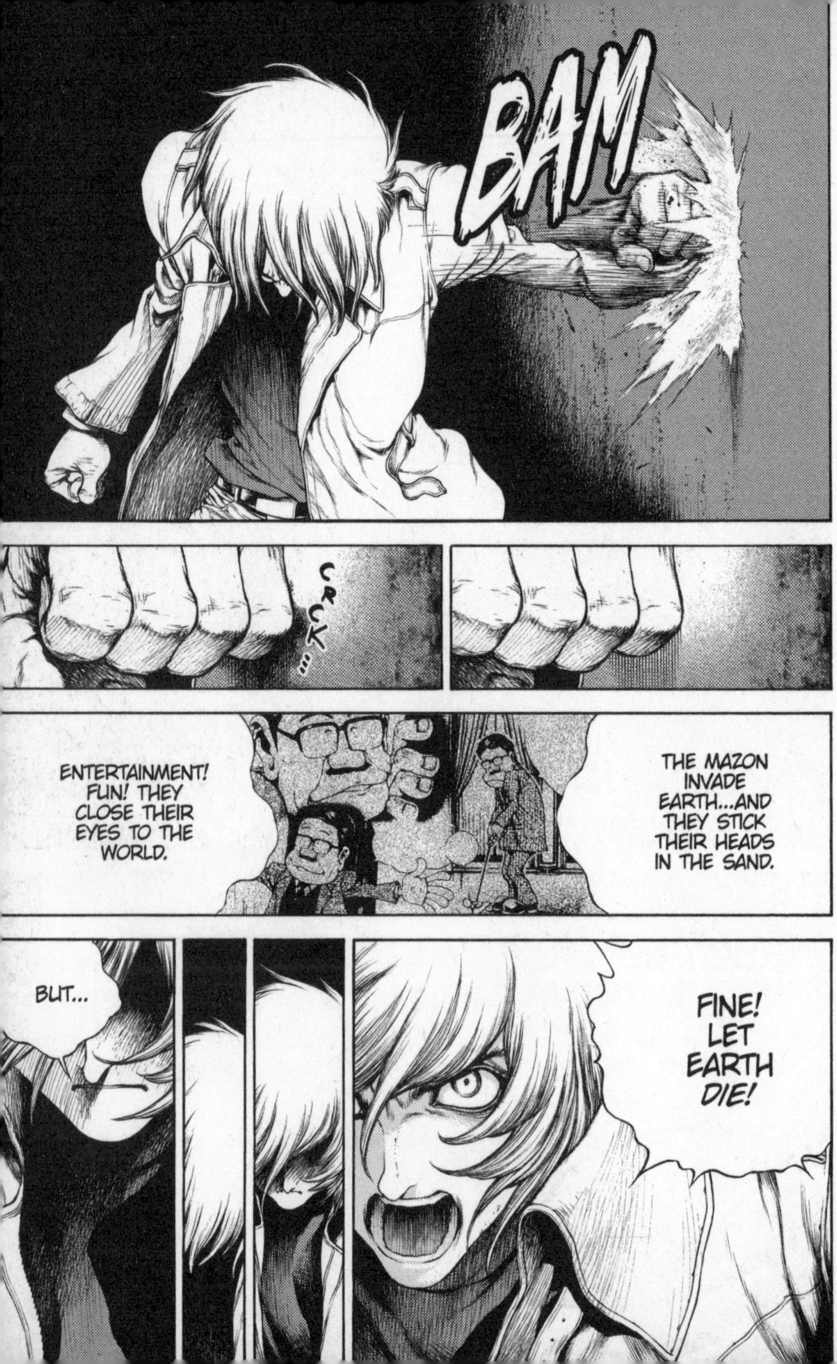
BAM
CRCK...
THE MAZON INVADE EARTH...AND THEY STICK THEIR HEADS IN THE SAND.
ENTERTAINMENT! FUN! THEY CLOSE THEIR EYES TO THE WORLD.
FINE! LET EARTH DIE!
BUT...

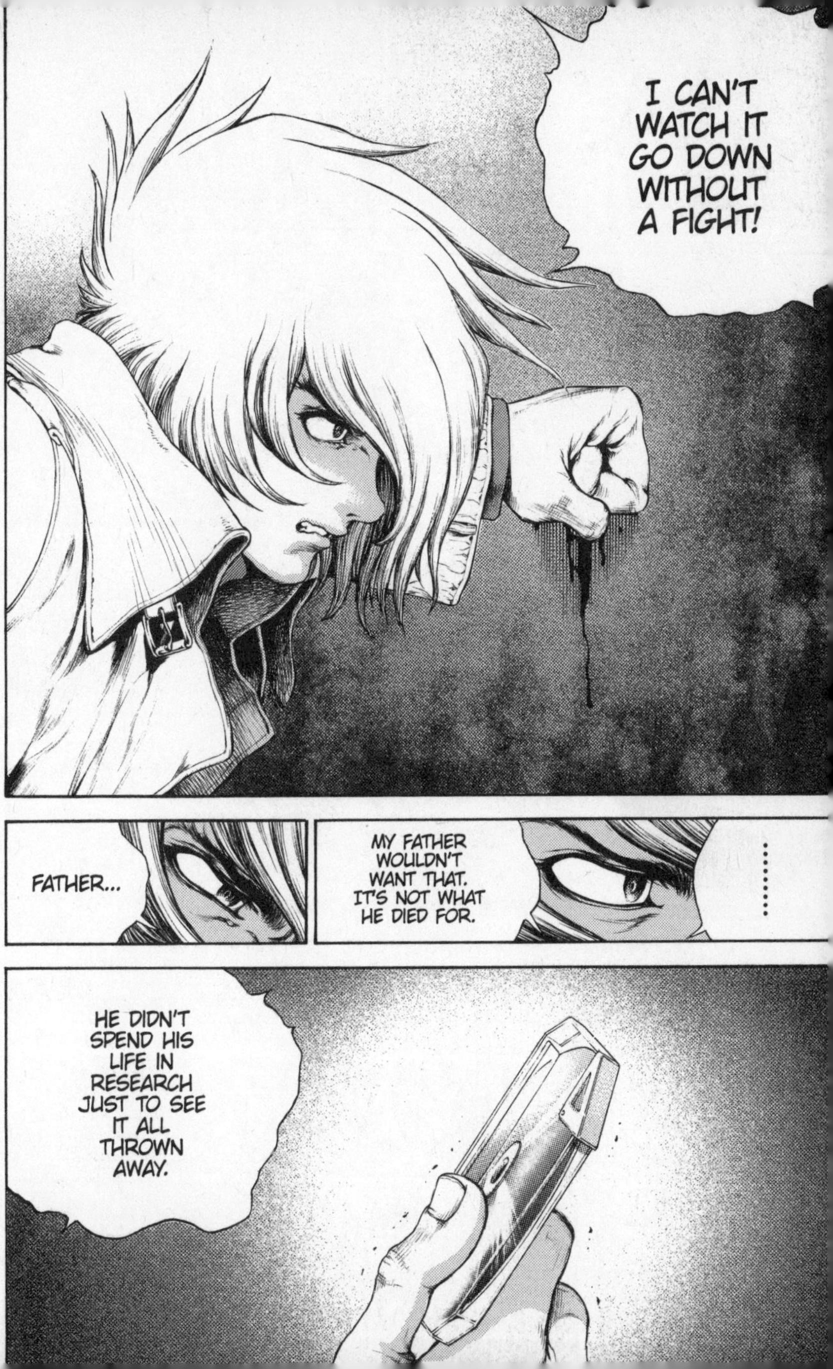
I CAN'T WATCH IT GO DOWN WITHOUT A FIGHT!
....
MY FATHER WOULDN'T WANT THAT. IT'S NOT WHAT HE DIED FOR.
FATHER...
HE DIDN'T SPEND HIS LIFE IN RESEARCH JUST TO SEE IT ALL THROWN AWAY.

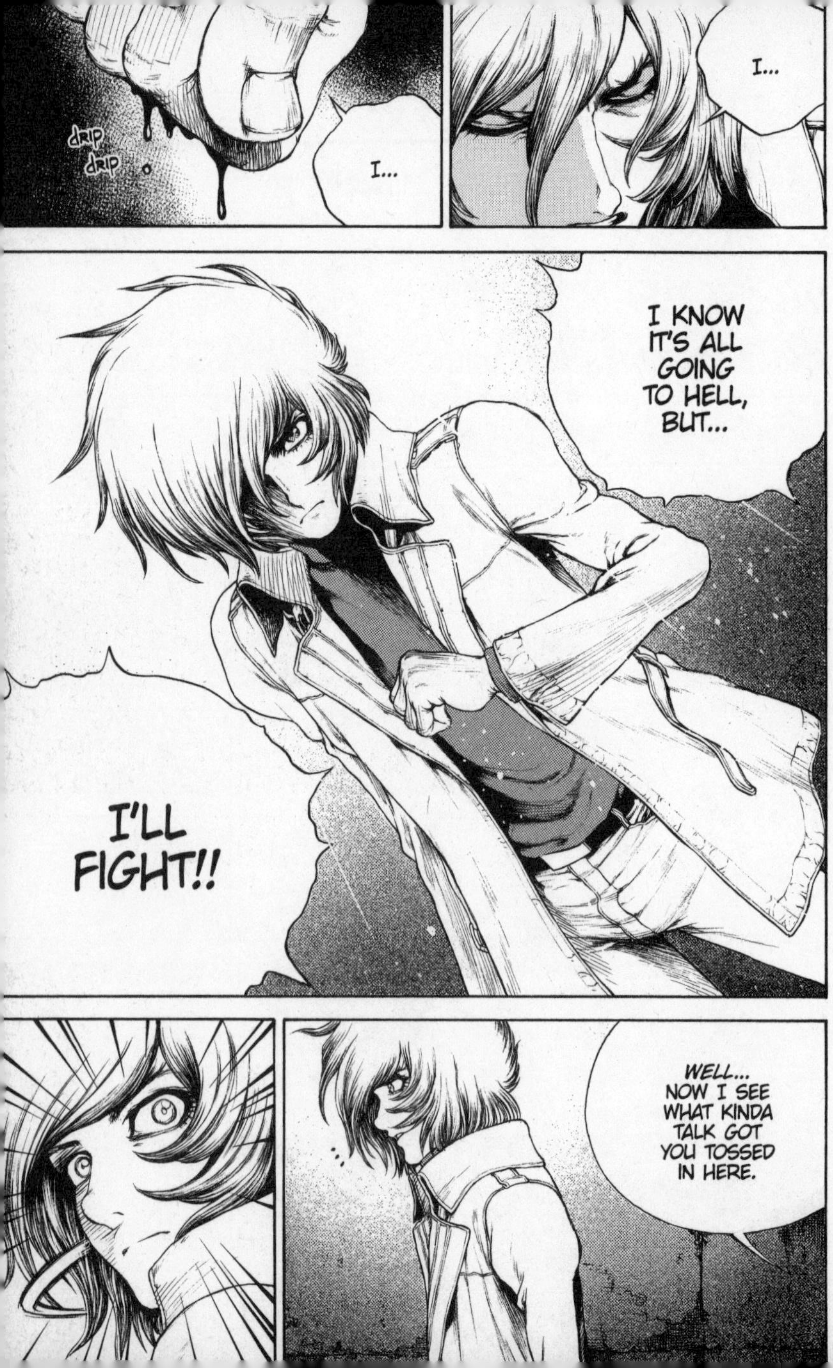
I...
drip
drip
I...
I KNOW IT'S ALL GOING TO HELL, BUT...
I'LL FIGHT!!
WELL... NOW I SEE WHAT KINDA TALK GOT YOU TOSSED IN HERE.
...

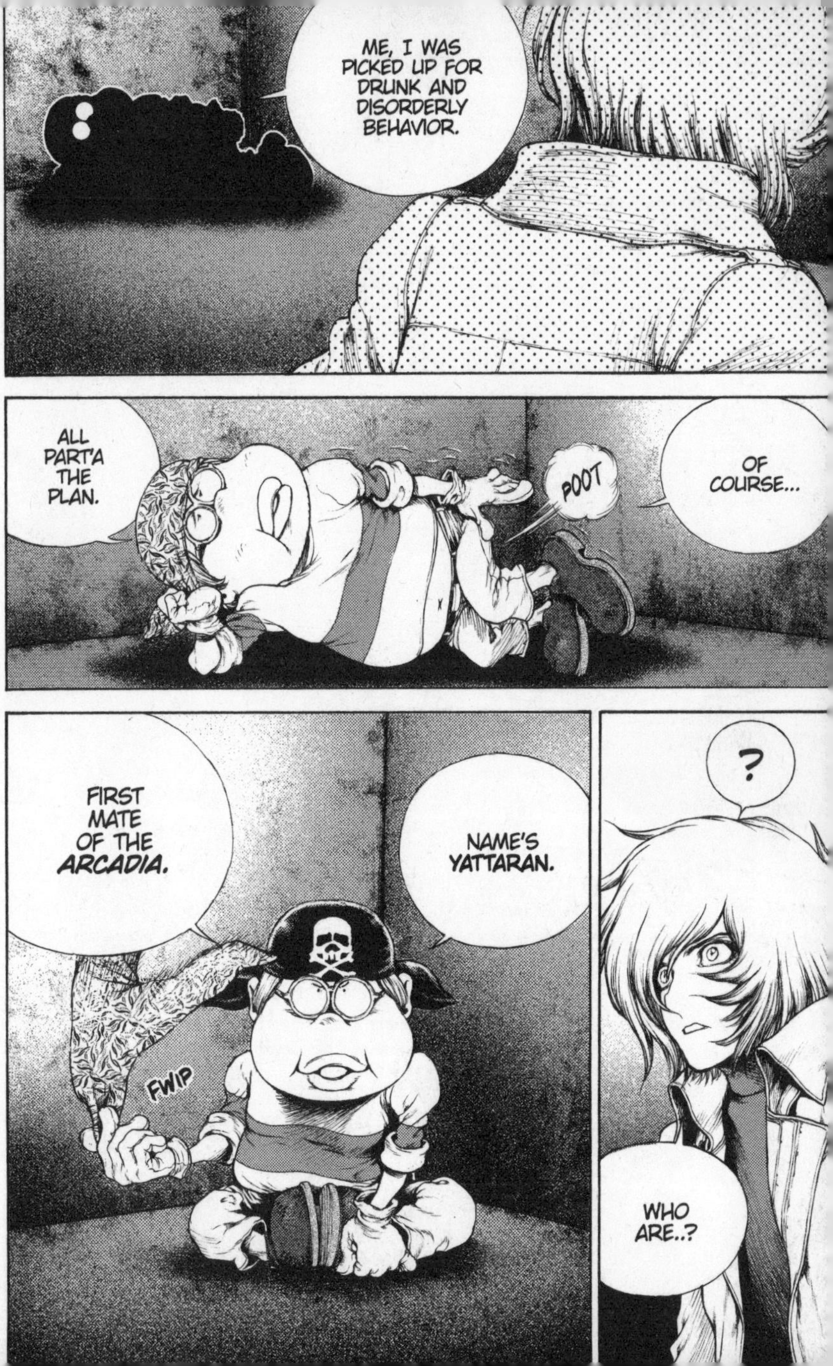
ME, I WAS PICKED UP FOR DRUNK AND DISORDERLY BEHAVIOR.
OF COURSE...
POOT
ALL PART'A THE PLAN.
?
WHO ARE..?
NAME'S YATTARAN.
FIRST MATE OF THE *ARCADIA.*
FWIP

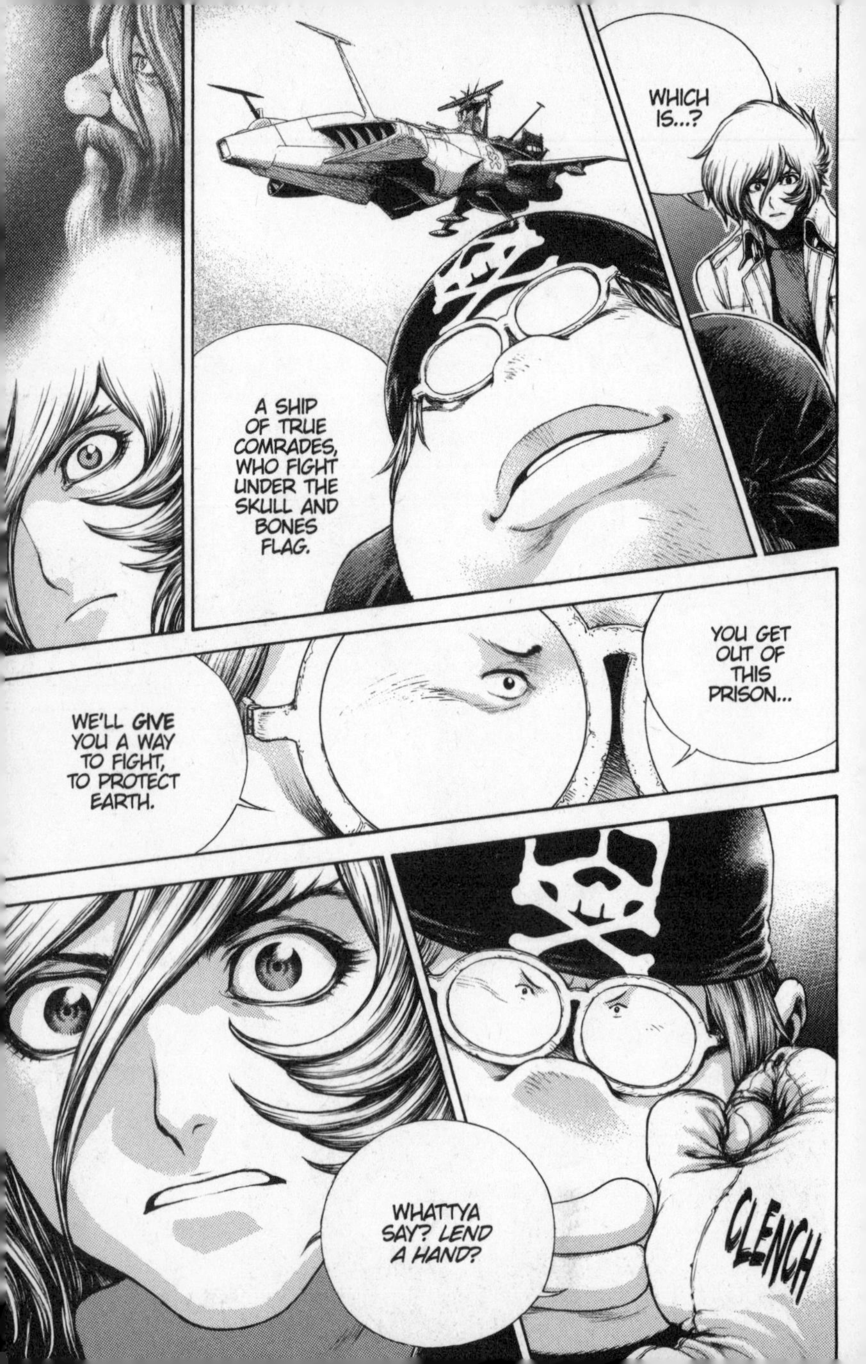
WHICH IS...?
A SHIP OF TRUE COMRADES, WHO FIGHT UNDER THE SKULL AND BONES FLAG.
YOU GET OUT OF THIS PRISON...
WE'LL GIVE YOU A WAY TO FIGHT, TO PROTECT EARTH.
WHATTYA SAY? LEND A HAND?
CLENCH

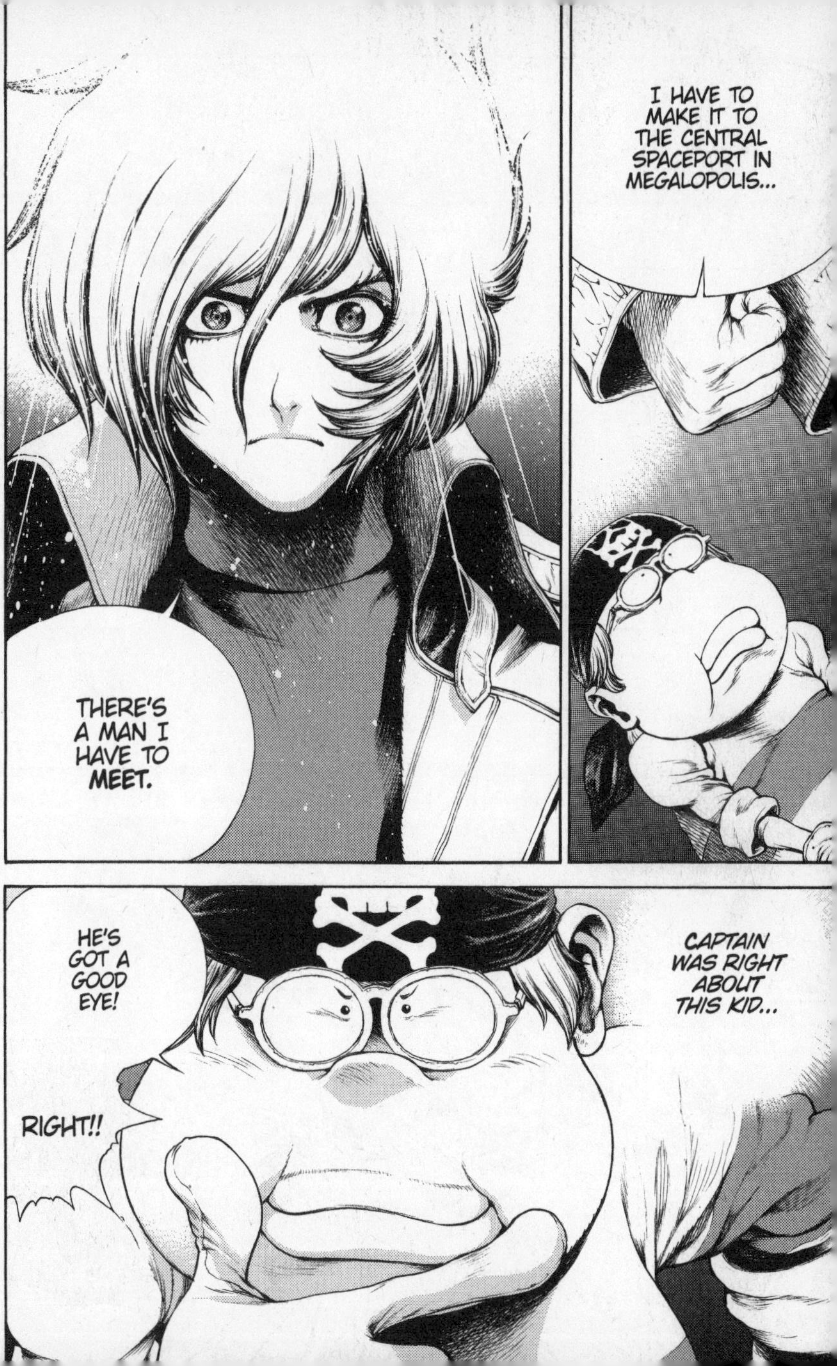
I HAVE TO MAKE IT TO THE CENTRAL SPACEPORT IN MEGALOPOLIS...
THERE'S A MAN I HAVE TO MEET.
CAPTAIN WAS RIGHT ABOUT THIS KID...
HE'S GOT A GOOD EYE!
RIGHT!!

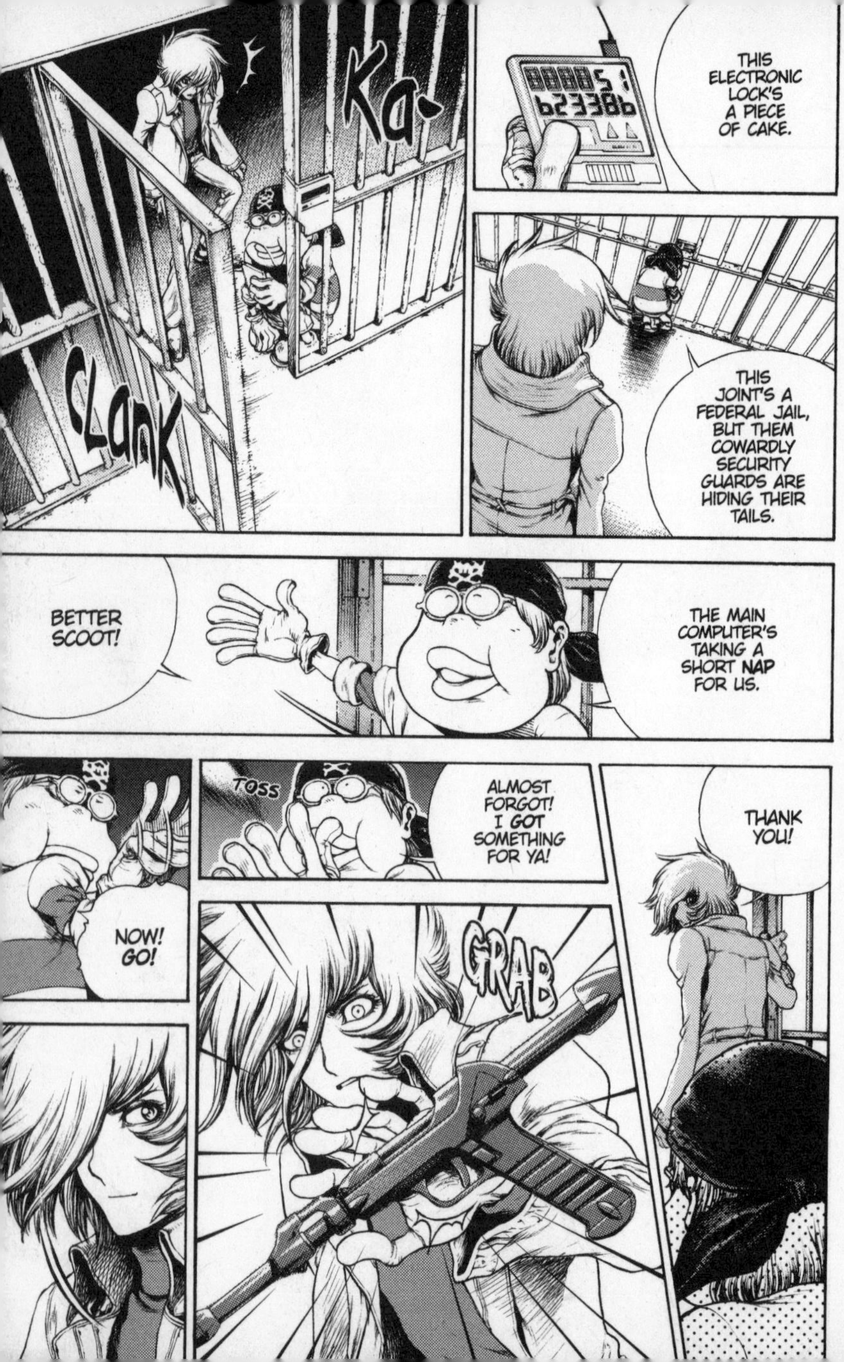

THIS ELECTRONIC LOCK'S A PIECE OF CAKE.
THIS JOINT'S A FEDERAL JAIL, BUT THEM COWARDLY SECURITY GUARDS ARE HIDING THEIR TAILS.
Ka
CLANK
THE MAIN COMPUTER'S TAKING A SHORT NAP FOR US.
BETTER SCOOT!
THANK YOU!
TOSS
ALMOST FORGOT! I GOT SOMETHING FOR YA!
NOW! GO!
GRAB

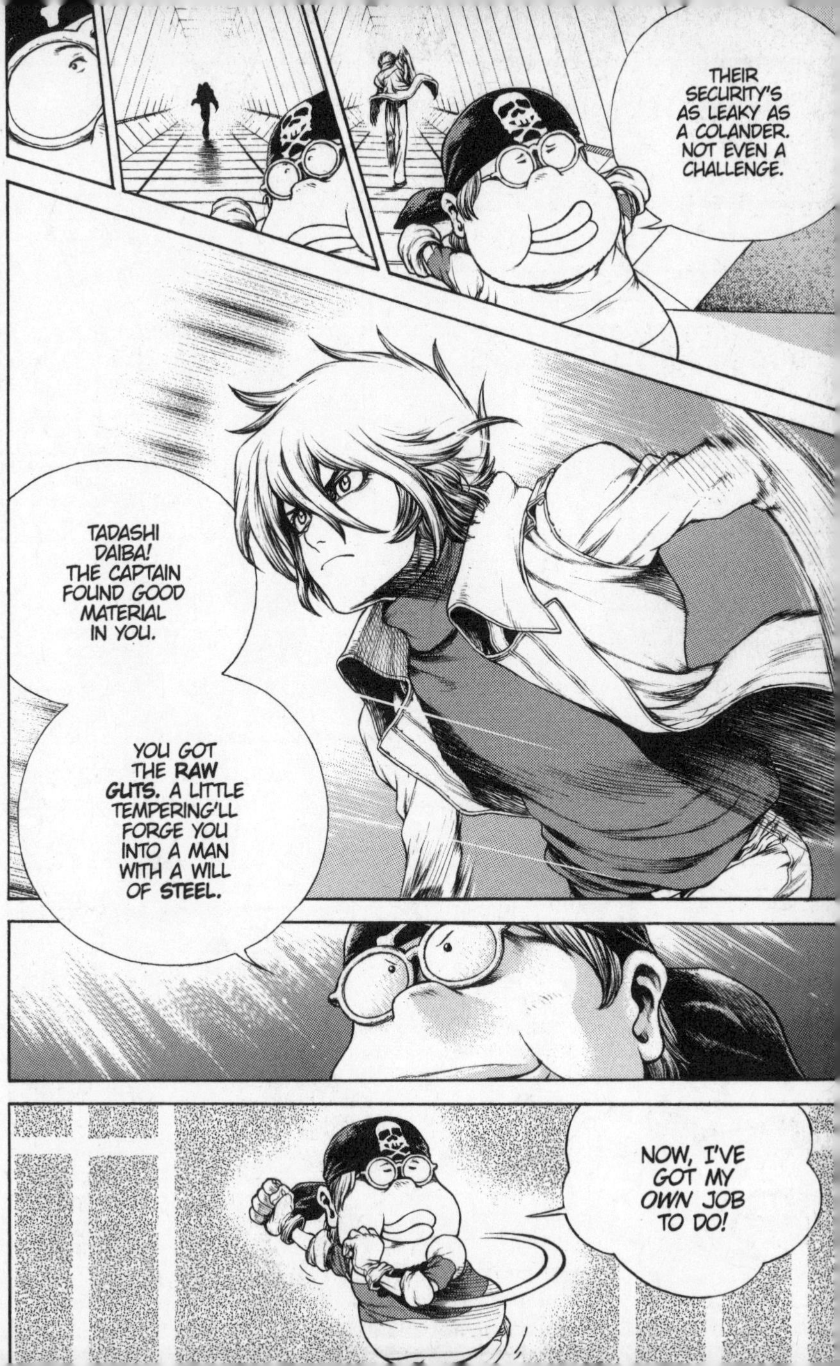
THEIR SECURITY'S AS LEAKY AS A COLANDER. NOT EVEN A CHALLENGE.
TADASHI DAIBA! THE CAPTAIN FOUND GOOD MATERIAL IN YOU.
YOU GOT THE **RAW GUTS**. A LITTLE TEMPERING'LL FORGE YOU INTO A MAN WITH A WILL OF **STEEL**.
NOW, I'VE GOT MY *OWN* JOB TO DO!

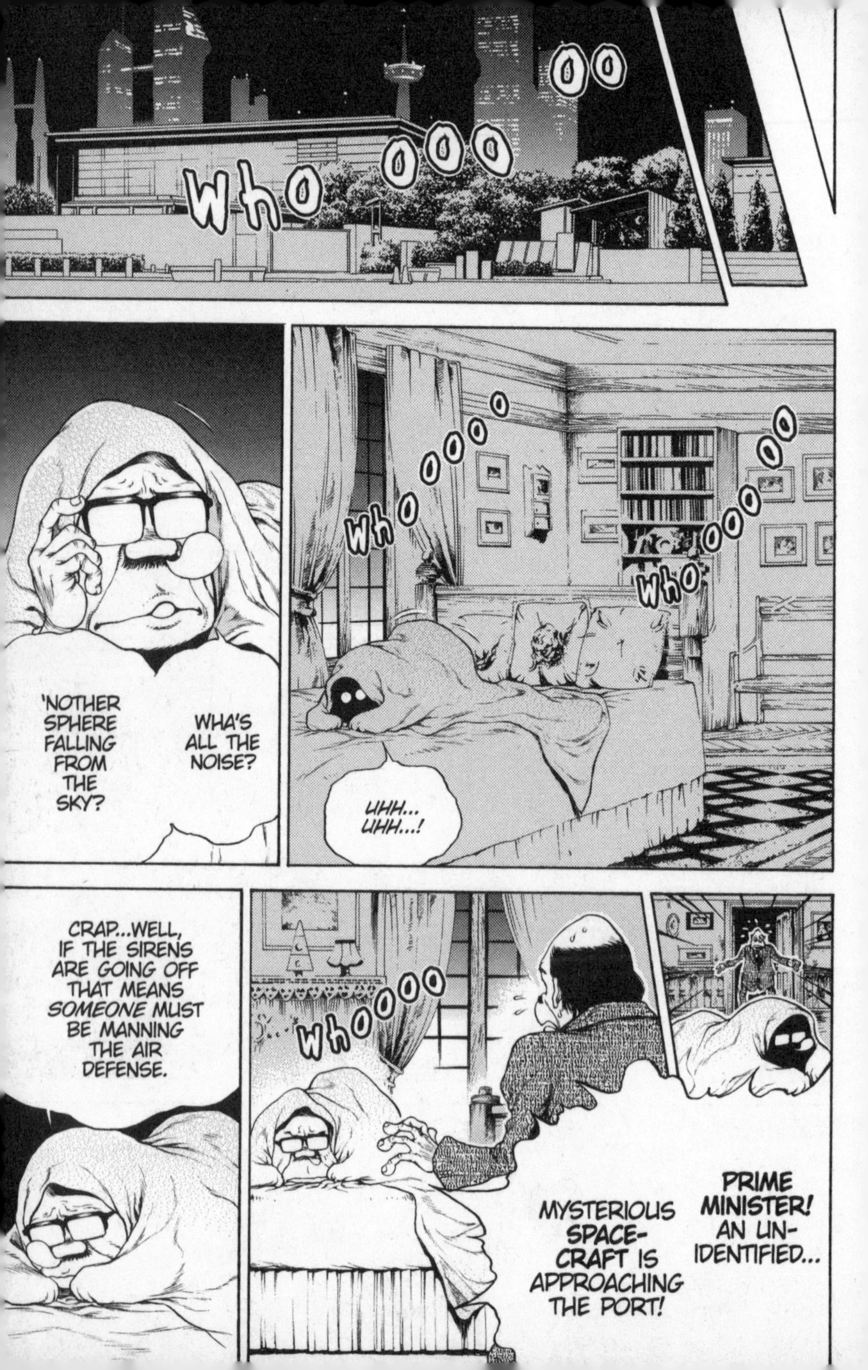
Whoooooo
Whoooooo
Whoooooooo
UHH... UHH...!
WHA'S ALL THE NOISE?
'NOTHER SPHERE FALLING FROM THE SKY?
PRIME MINISTER! AN UN-IDENTIFIED...
MYSTERIOUS SPACE-CRAFT IS APPROACHING THE PORT!
Whoooo
CRAP...WELL, IF THE SIRENS ARE GOING OFF THAT MEANS *SOMEONE* MUST BE MANNING THE AIR DEFENSE.

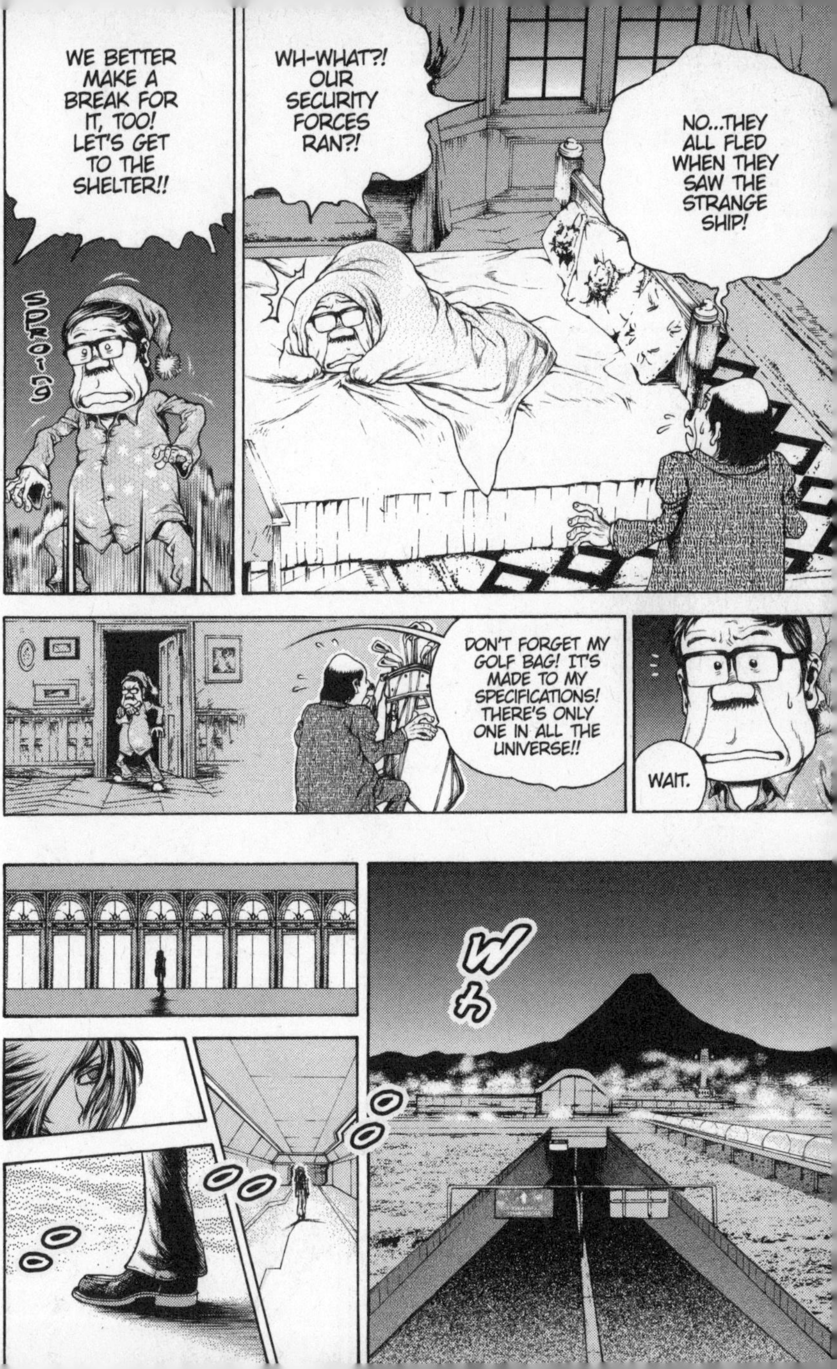
WH-WHAT?! OUR SECURITY FORCES RAN?!
NO...THEY ALL FLED WHEN THEY SAW THE STRANGE SHIP!
WE BETTER MAKE A BREAK FOR IT, TOO! LET'S GET TO THE SHELTER!!
SPROING
WAIT.
DON'T FORGET MY GOLF BAG! IT'S MADE TO MY SPECIFICATIONS! THERE'S ONLY ONE IN ALL THE UNIVERSE!!
Wh

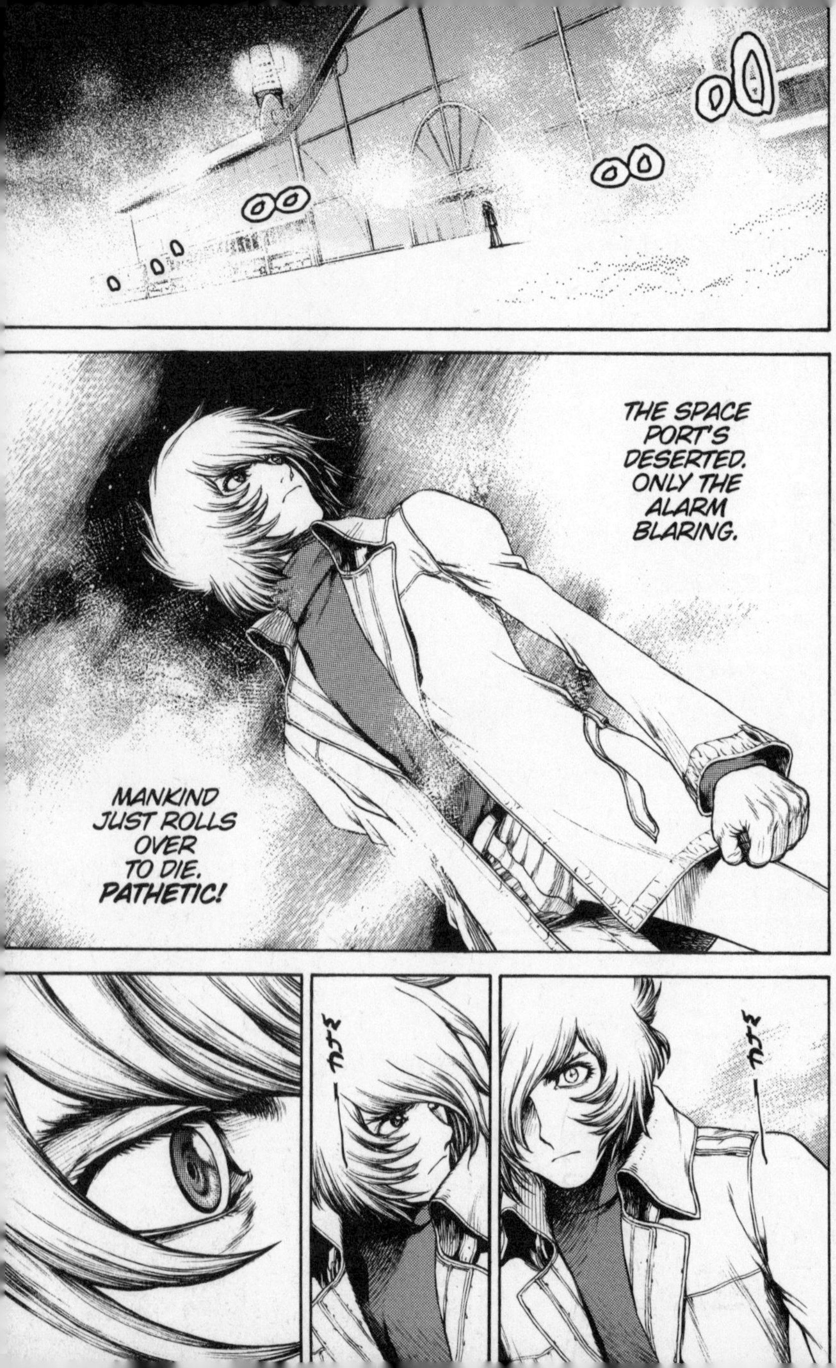
THE SPACE PORT'S DESERTED. ONLY THE ALARM BLARING.
MANKIND JUST ROLLS OVER TO DIE. PATHETIC!

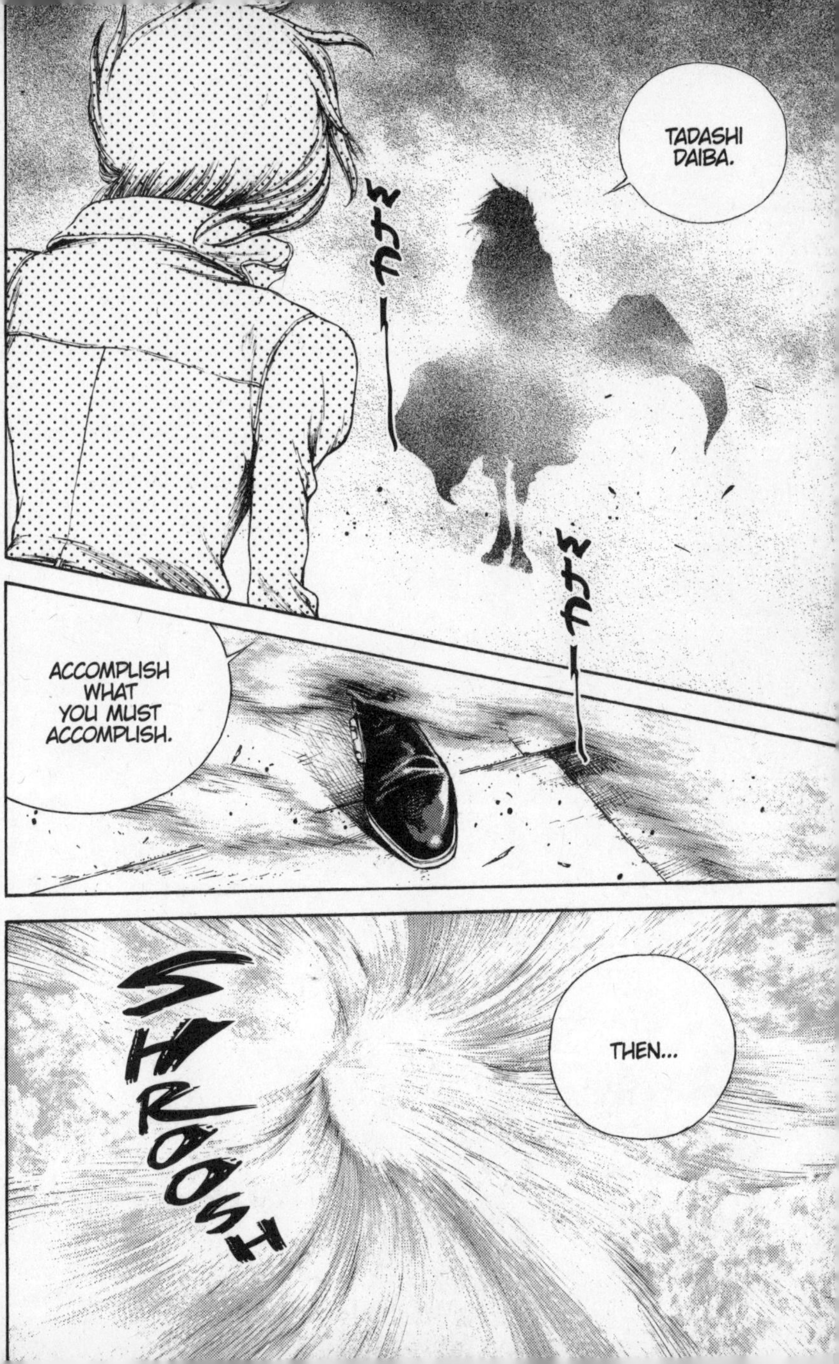
TADASHI DAIBA.
ACCOMPLISH WHAT YOU MUST ACCOMPLISH.
THEN...
SHROOSH

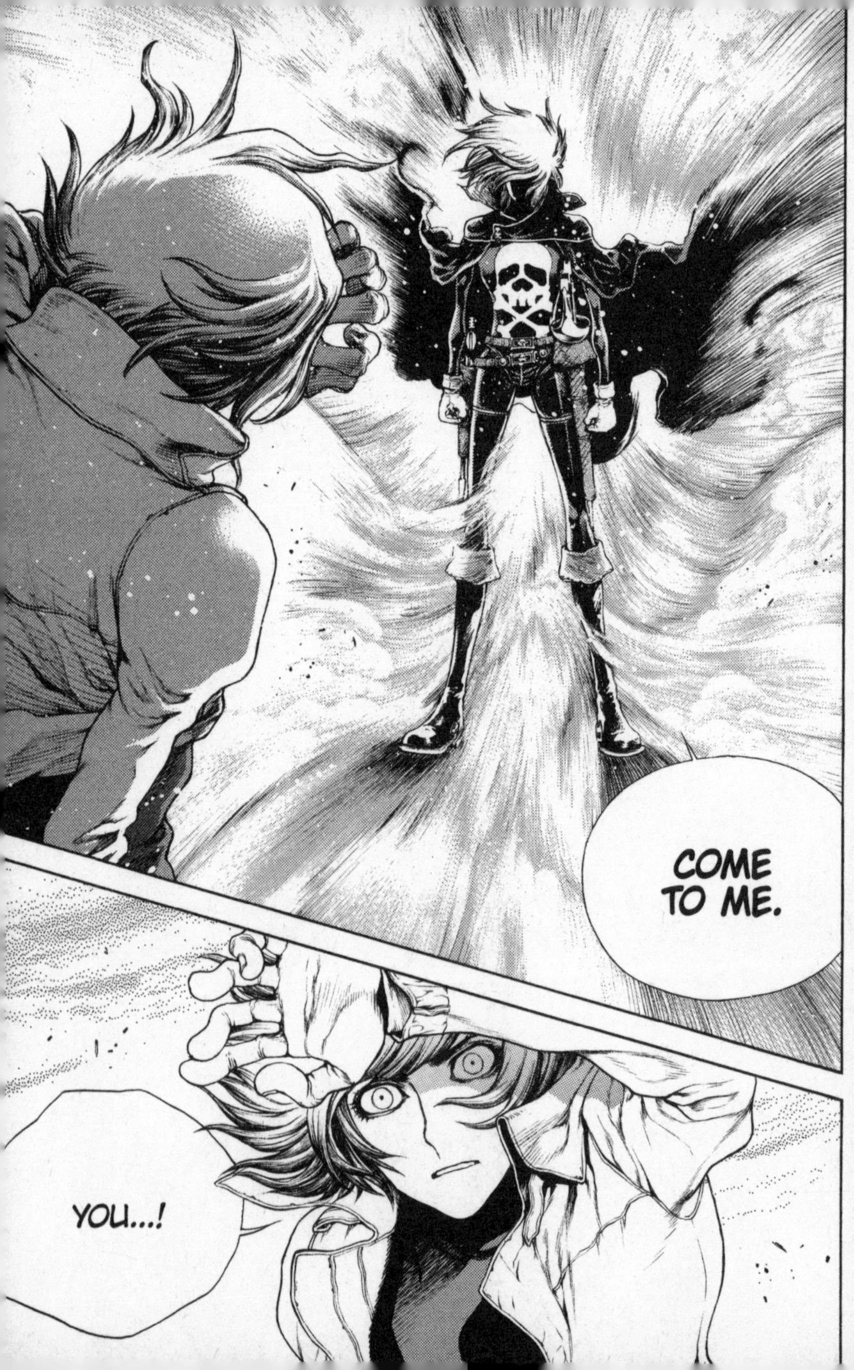
COME TO ME.
YOU...!

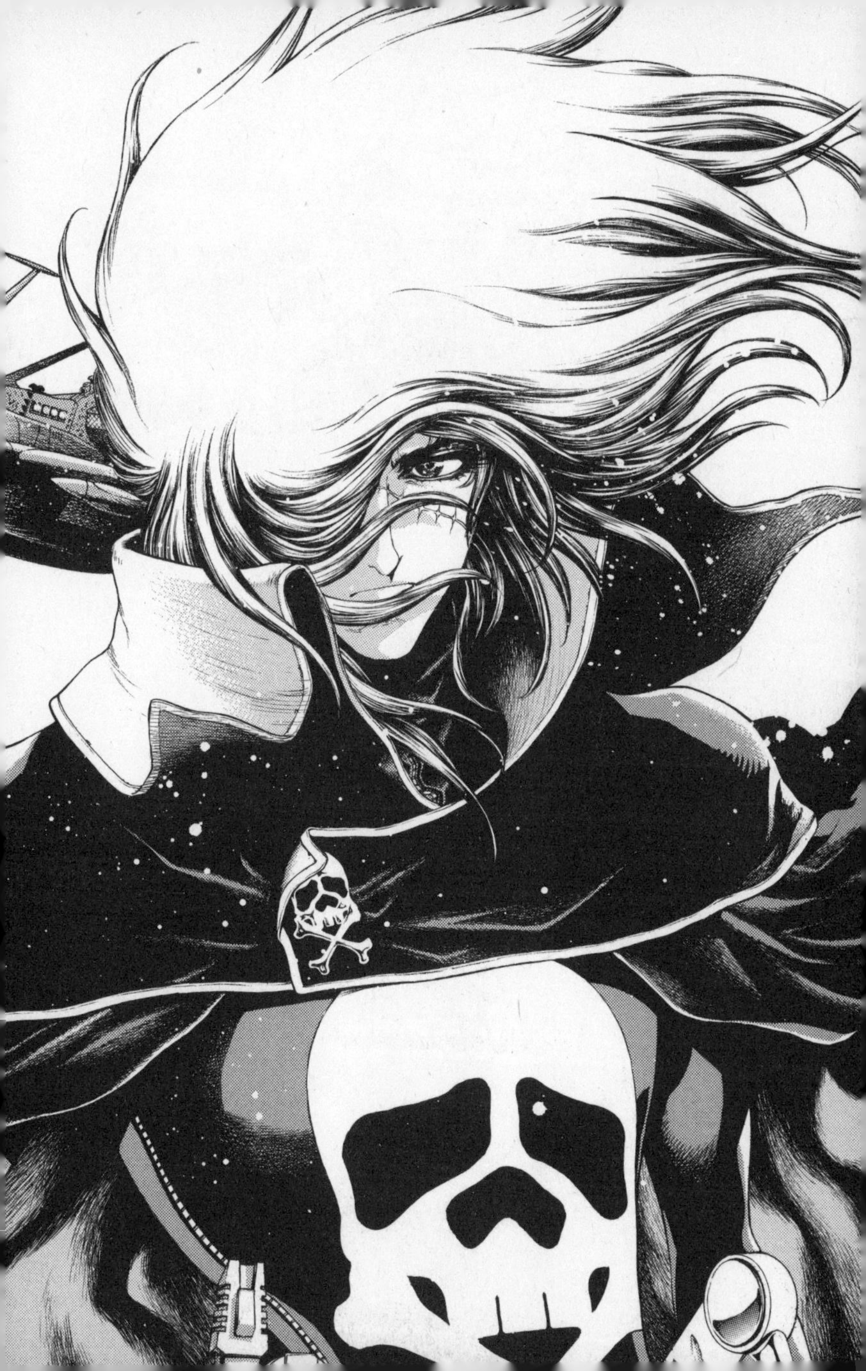

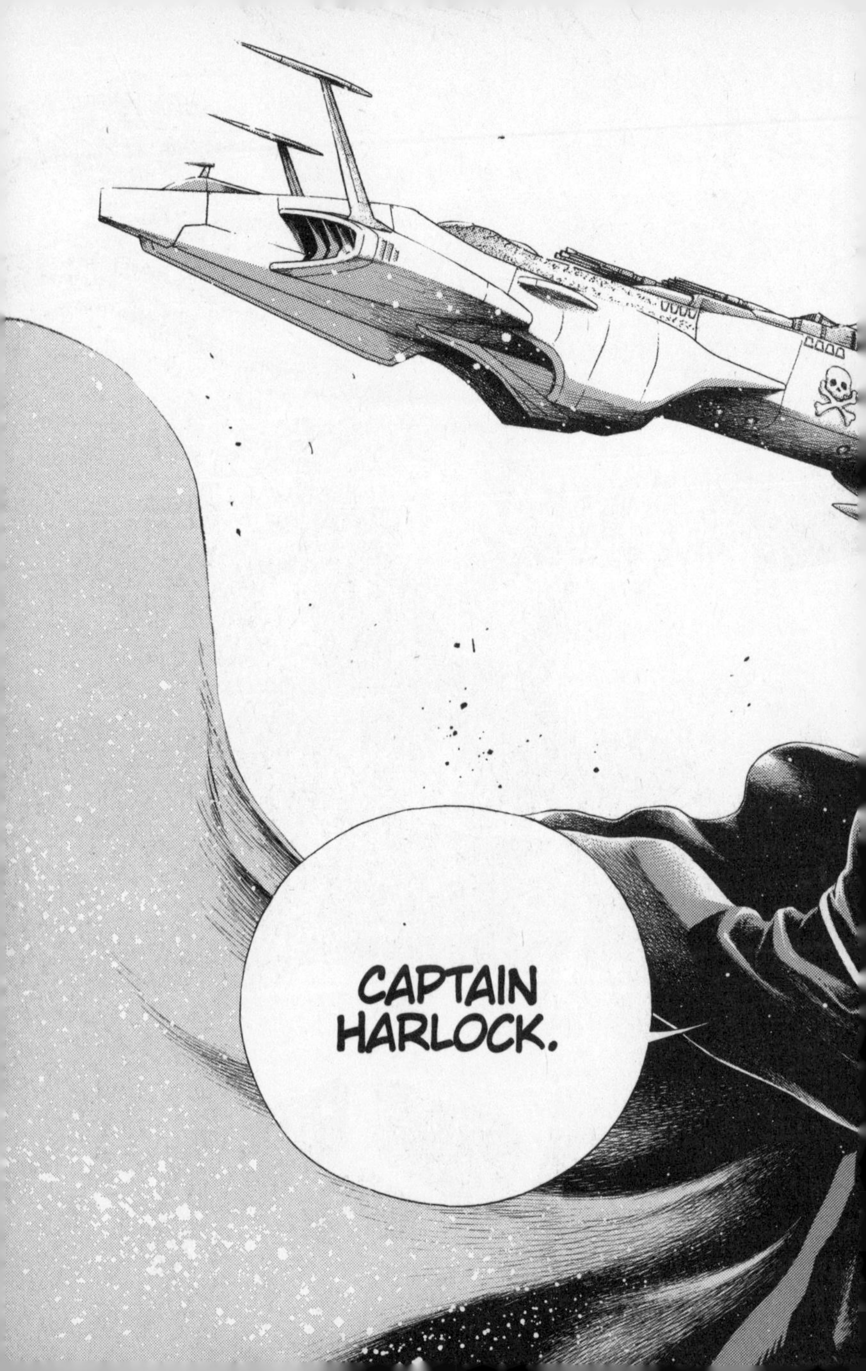
CAPTAIN HARLOCK.

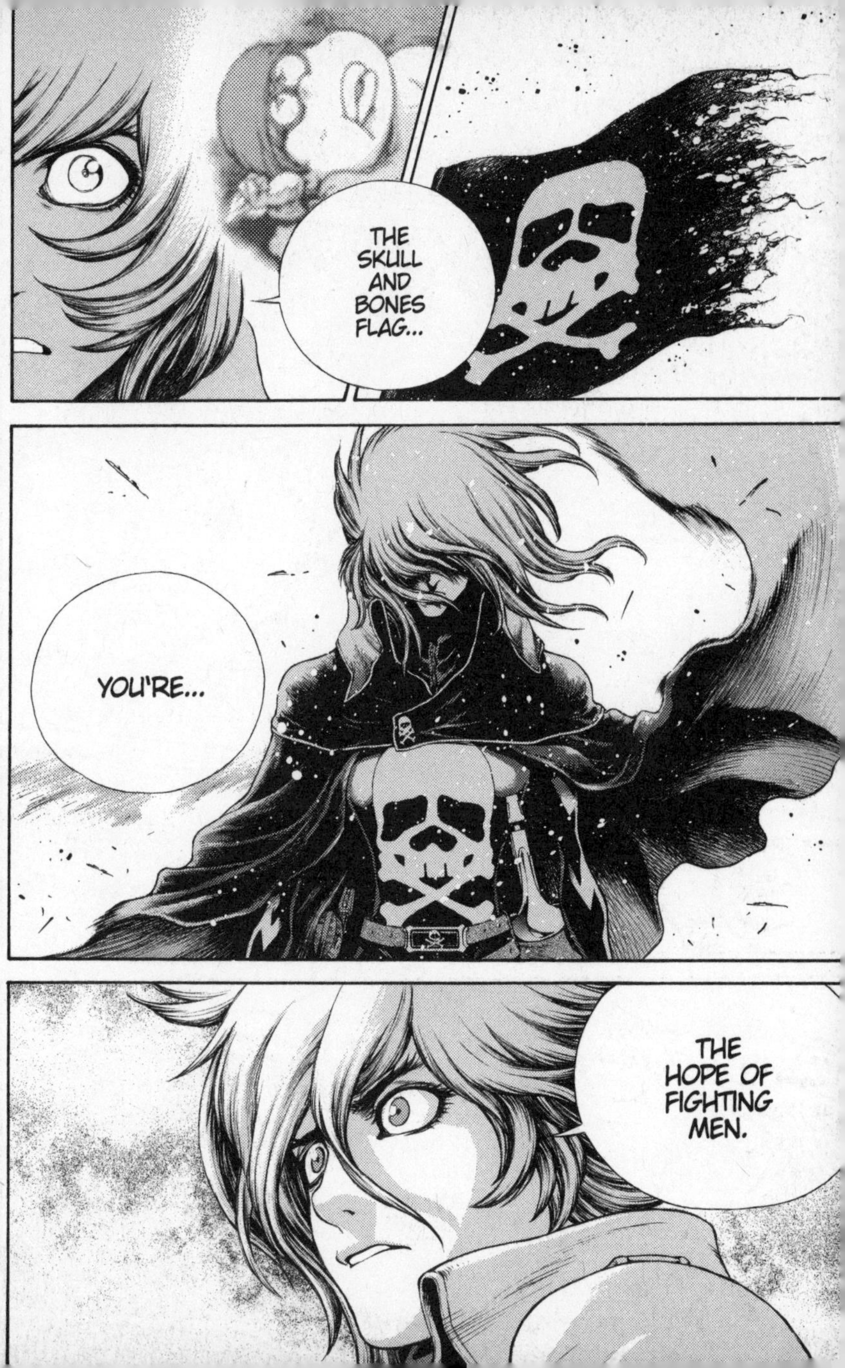
THE SKULL AND BONES FLAG...
YOU'RE...
THE HOPE OF FIGHTING MEN.

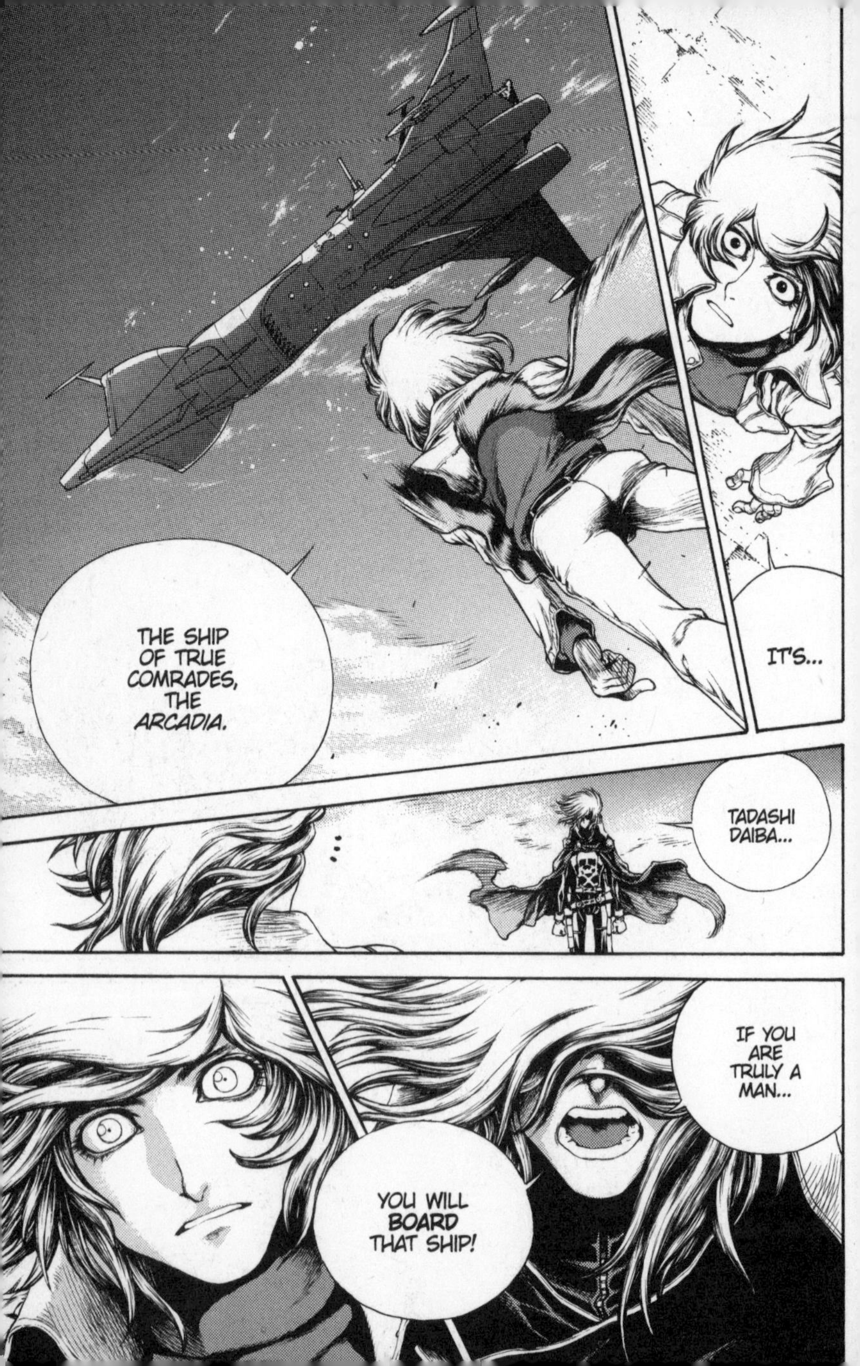
IT'S...
THE SHIP OF TRUE COMRADES, THE ARCADIA.
TADASHI DAIBA...
...
IF YOU ARE TRULY A MAN...
YOU WILL BOARD THAT SHIP!

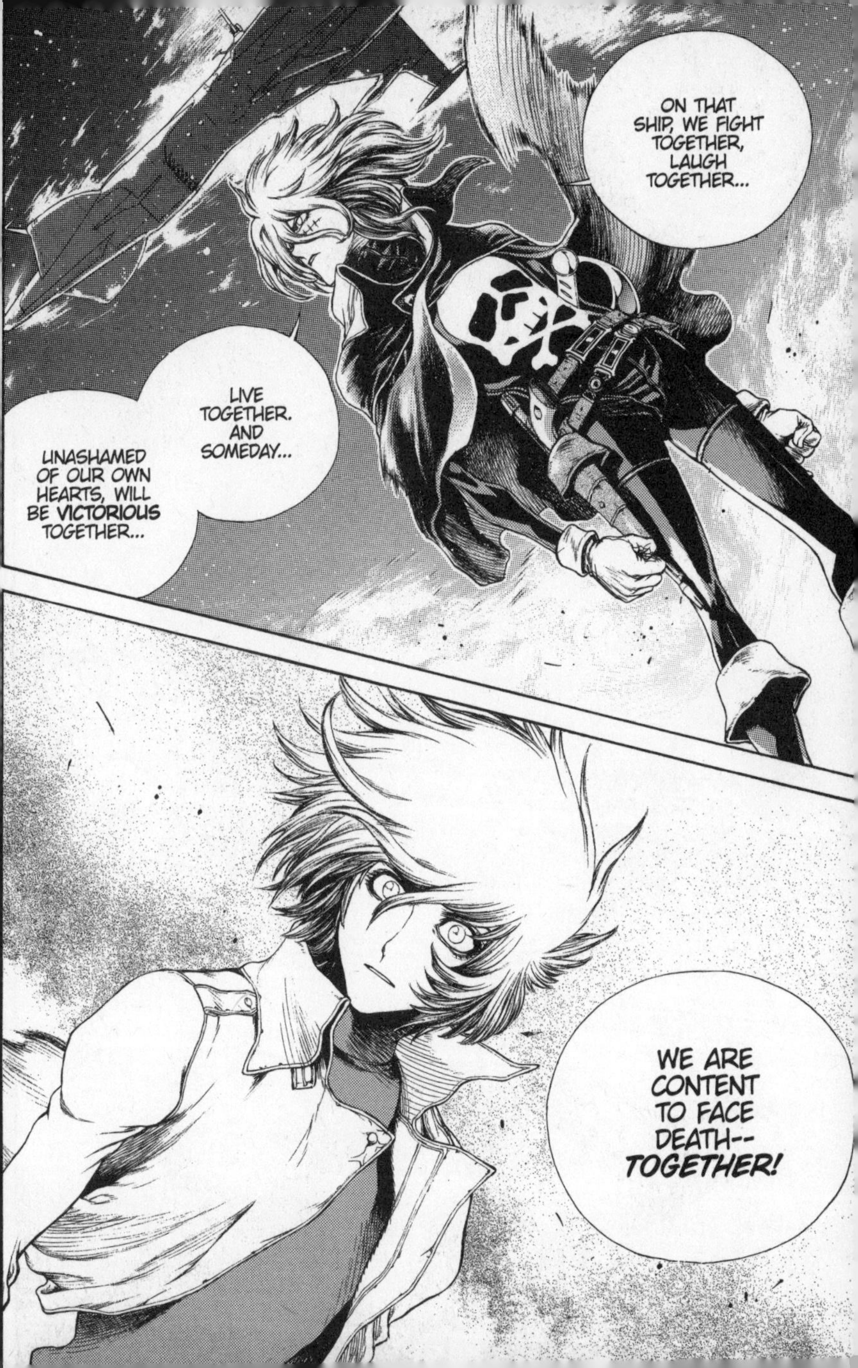
ON THAT SHIP, WE FIGHT TOGETHER, LAUGH TOGETHER...
LIVE TOGETHER. AND SOMEDAY...
UNASHAMED OF OUR OWN HEARTS, WILL BE VICTORIOUS TOGETHER...
WE ARE CONTENT TO FACE DEATH-- TOGETHER!

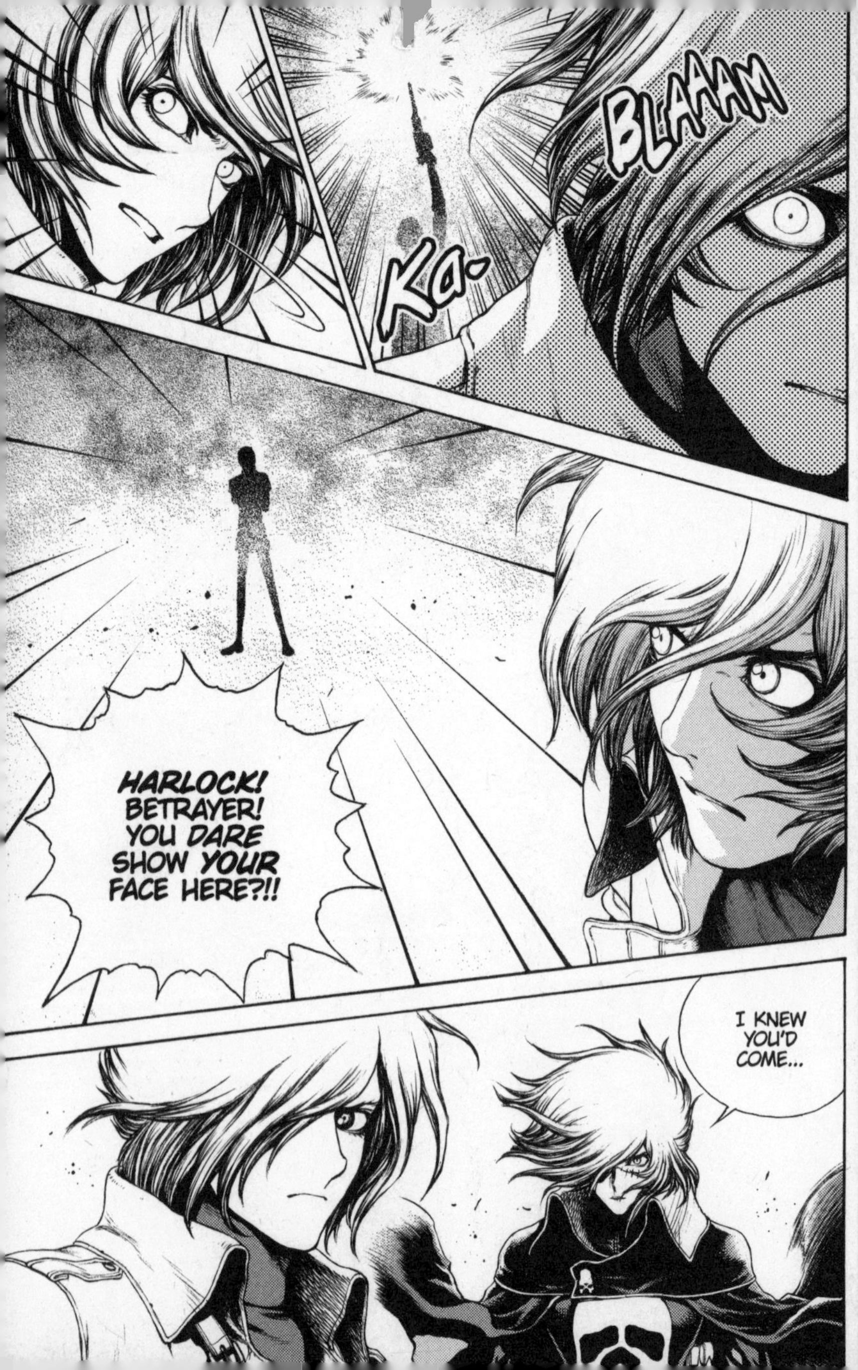
BLAAAM
KA-
HARLOCK! BETRAYER! YOU DARE SHOW YOUR FACE HERE?!!
I KNEW YOU'D COME...

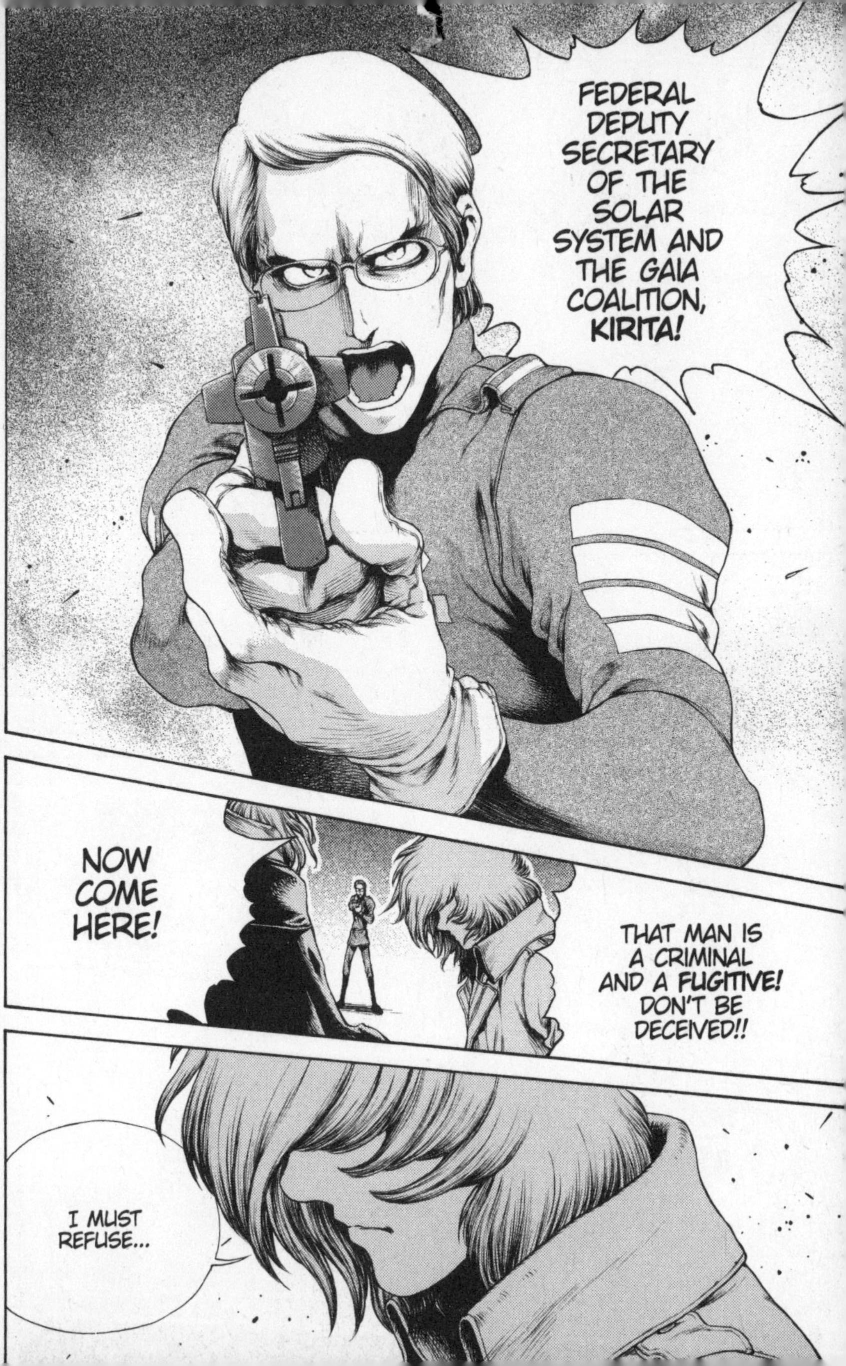
FEDERAL DEPUTY SECRETARY OF THE SOLAR SYSTEM AND THE GAIA COALITION, KIRITA!
THAT MAN IS A CRIMINAL AND A FUGITIVE! DON'T BE DECEIVED!!
NOW COME HERE!
I MUST REFUSE...

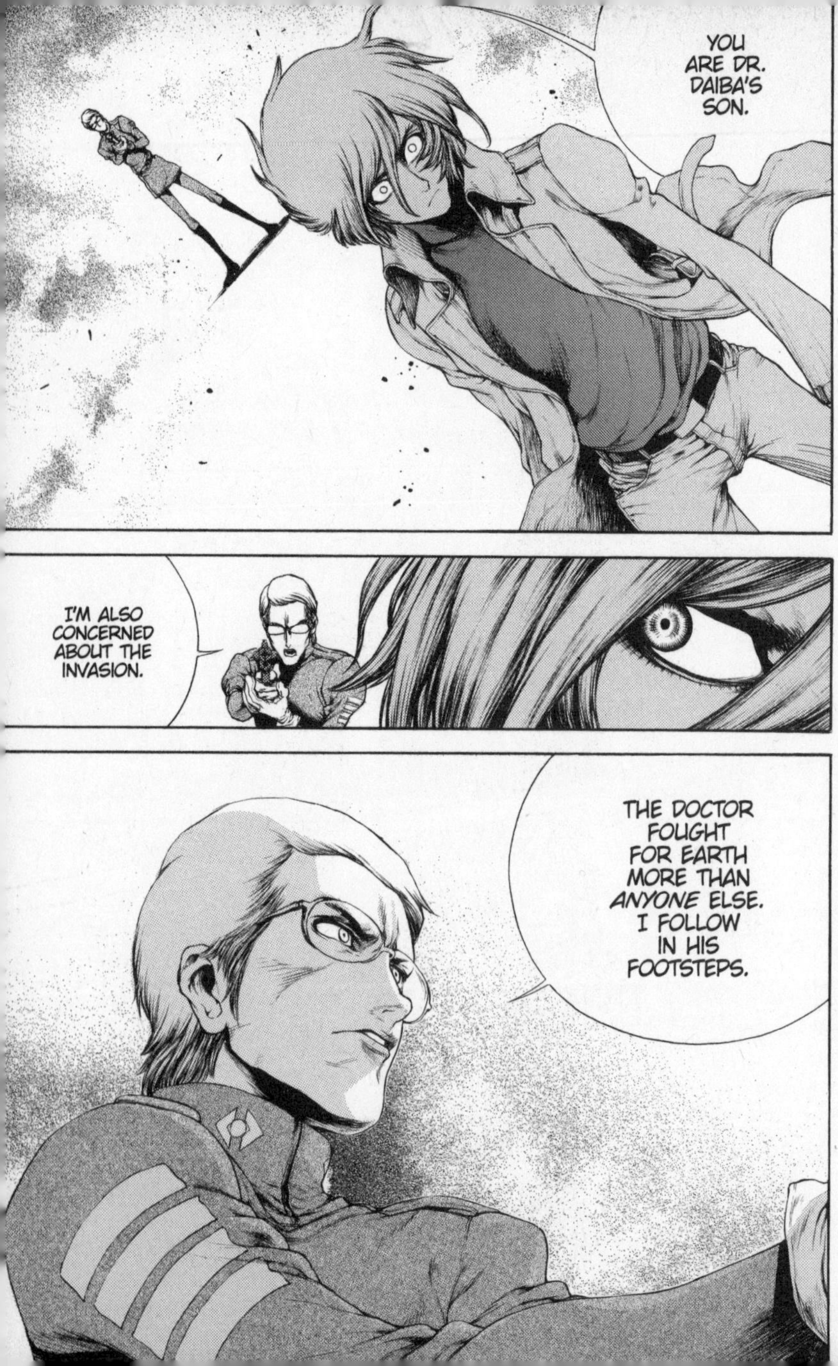
YOU ARE DR. DAIBA'S SON.
I'M ALSO CONCERNED ABOUT THE INVASION.
THE DOCTOR FOUGHT FOR EARTH MORE THAN *ANYONE* ELSE. I FOLLOW IN HIS FOOTSTEPS.

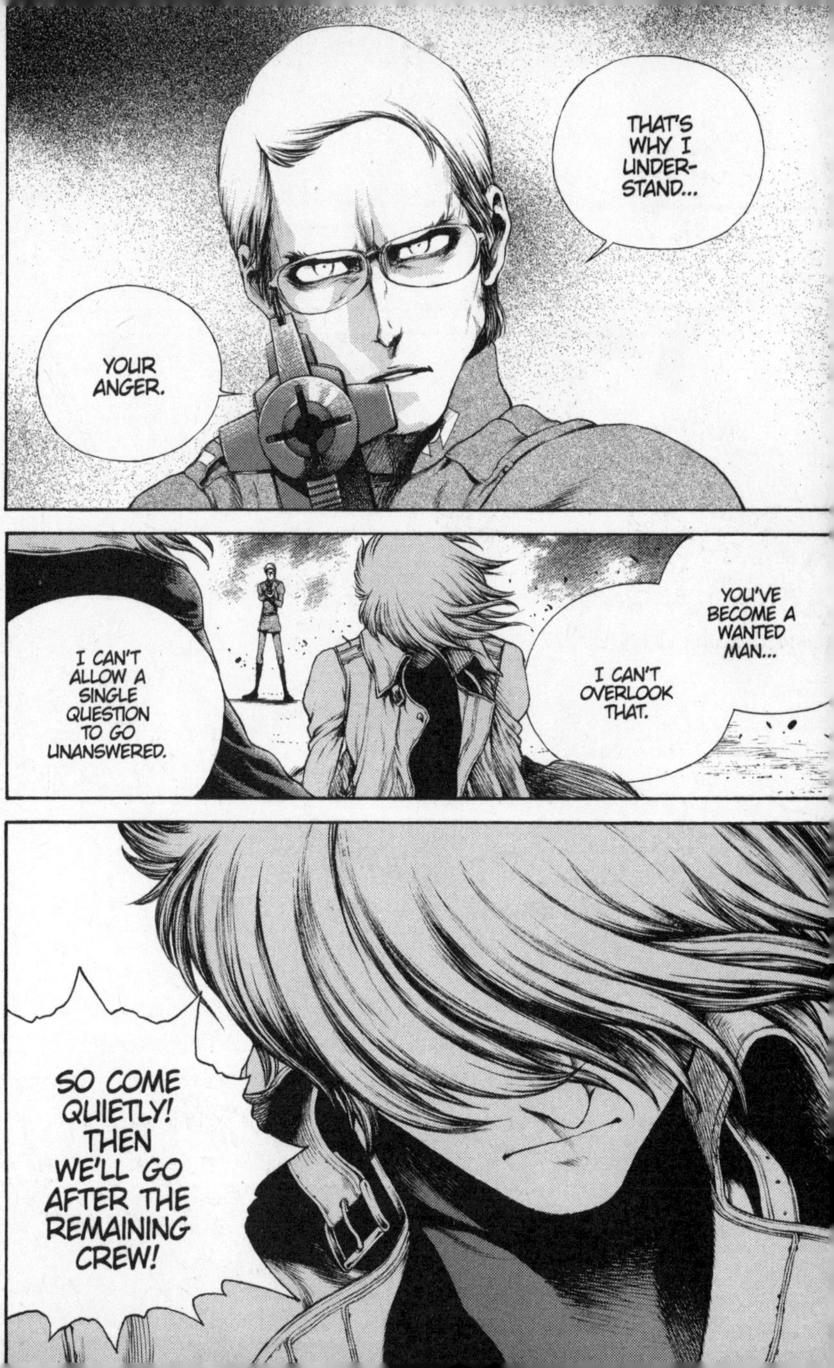
THAT'S WHY I UNDER-STAND...
YOUR ANGER.
YOU'VE BECOME A WANTED MAN...
I CAN'T OVERLOOK THAT.
I CAN'T ALLOW A SINGLE QUESTION TO GO UNANSWERED.
SO COME QUIETLY! THEN WE'LL GO AFTER THE REMAINING CREW!

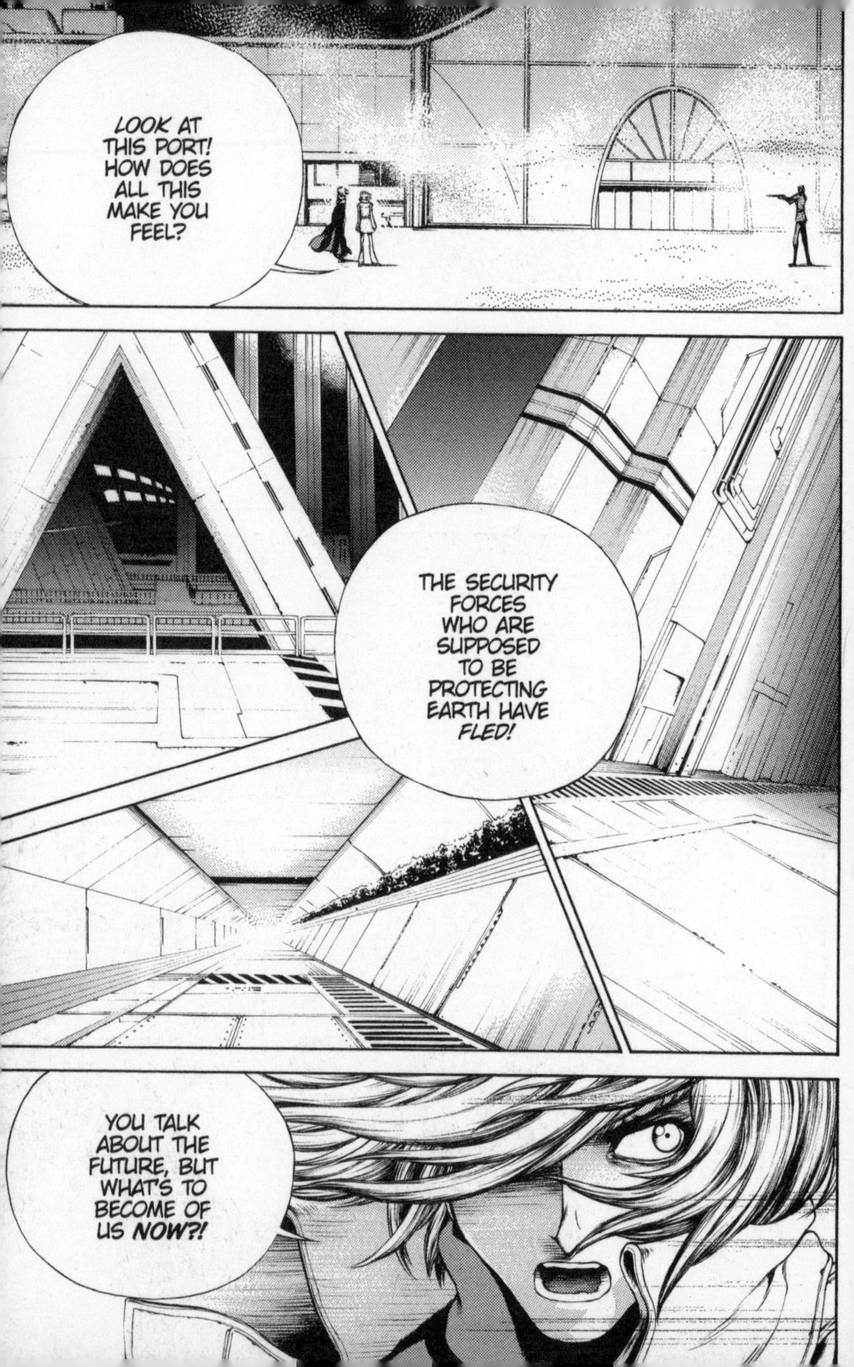
LOOK AT THIS PORT! HOW DOES ALL THIS MAKE YOU FEEL?
THE SECURITY FORCES WHO ARE SUPPOSED TO BE PROTECTING EARTH HAVE FLED!
YOU TALK ABOUT THE FUTURE, BUT WHAT'S TO BECOME OF US NOW?!

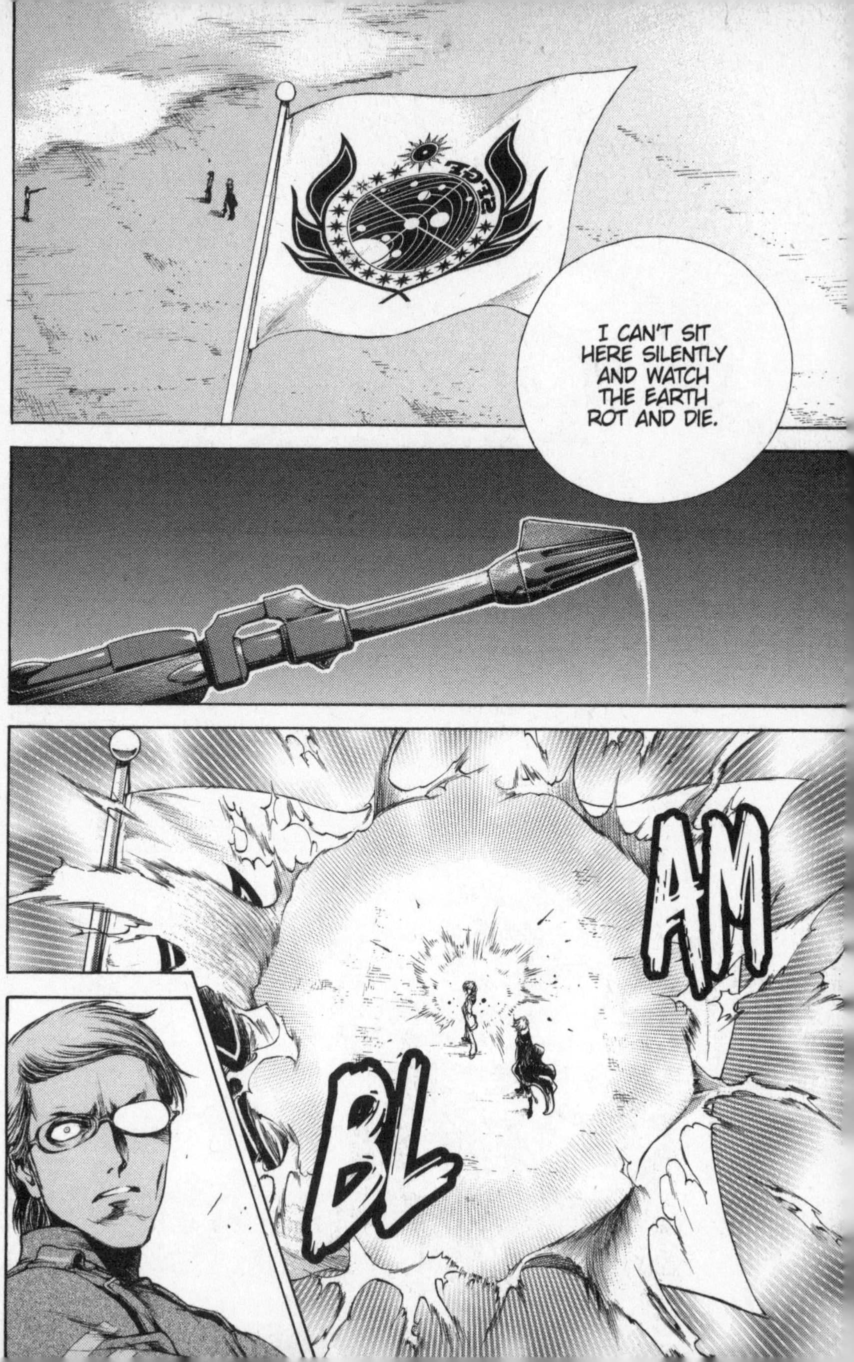
I CAN'T SIT HERE SILENTLY AND WATCH THE EARTH ROT AND DIE.
BL
AM

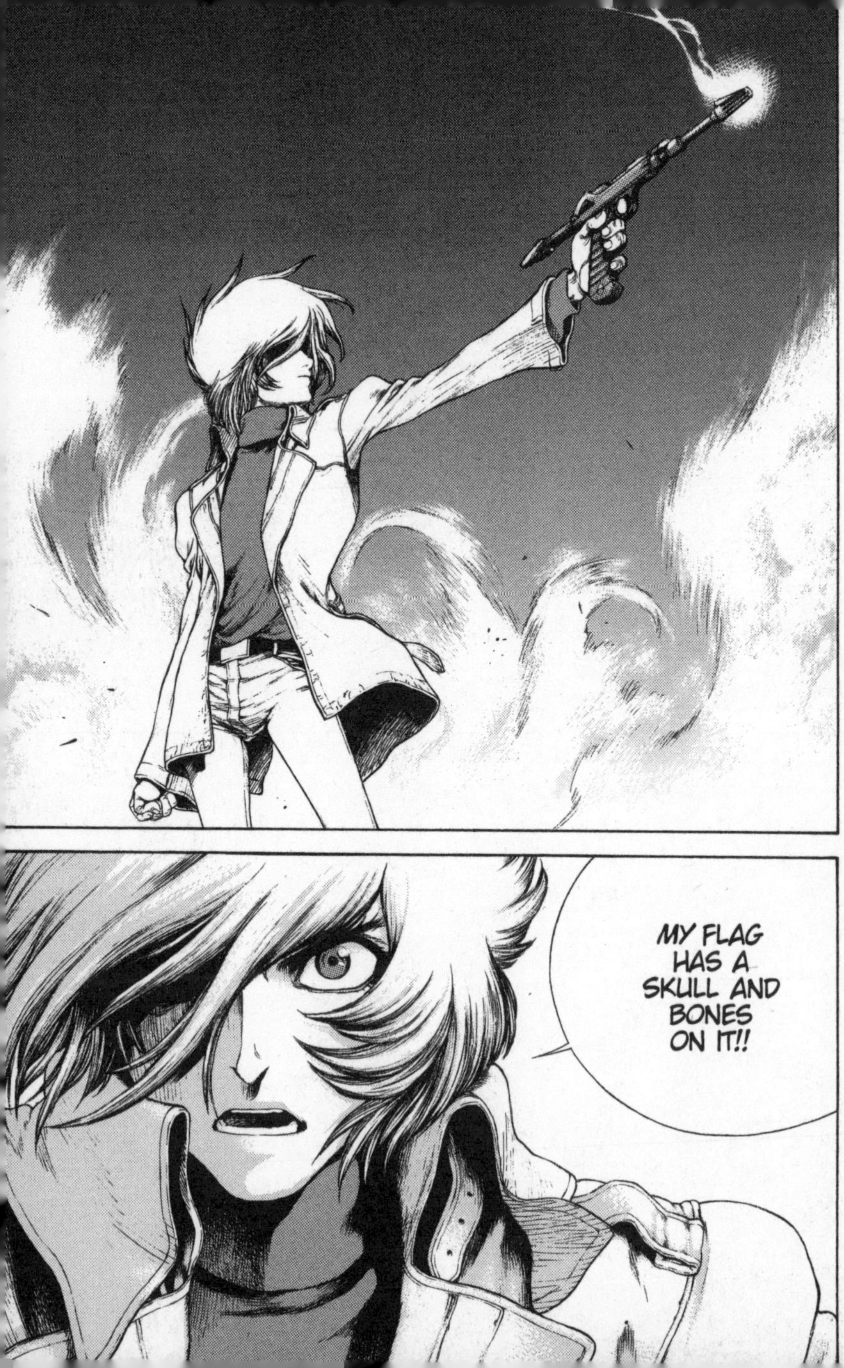
MY FLAG HAS A SKULL AND BONES ON IT!!

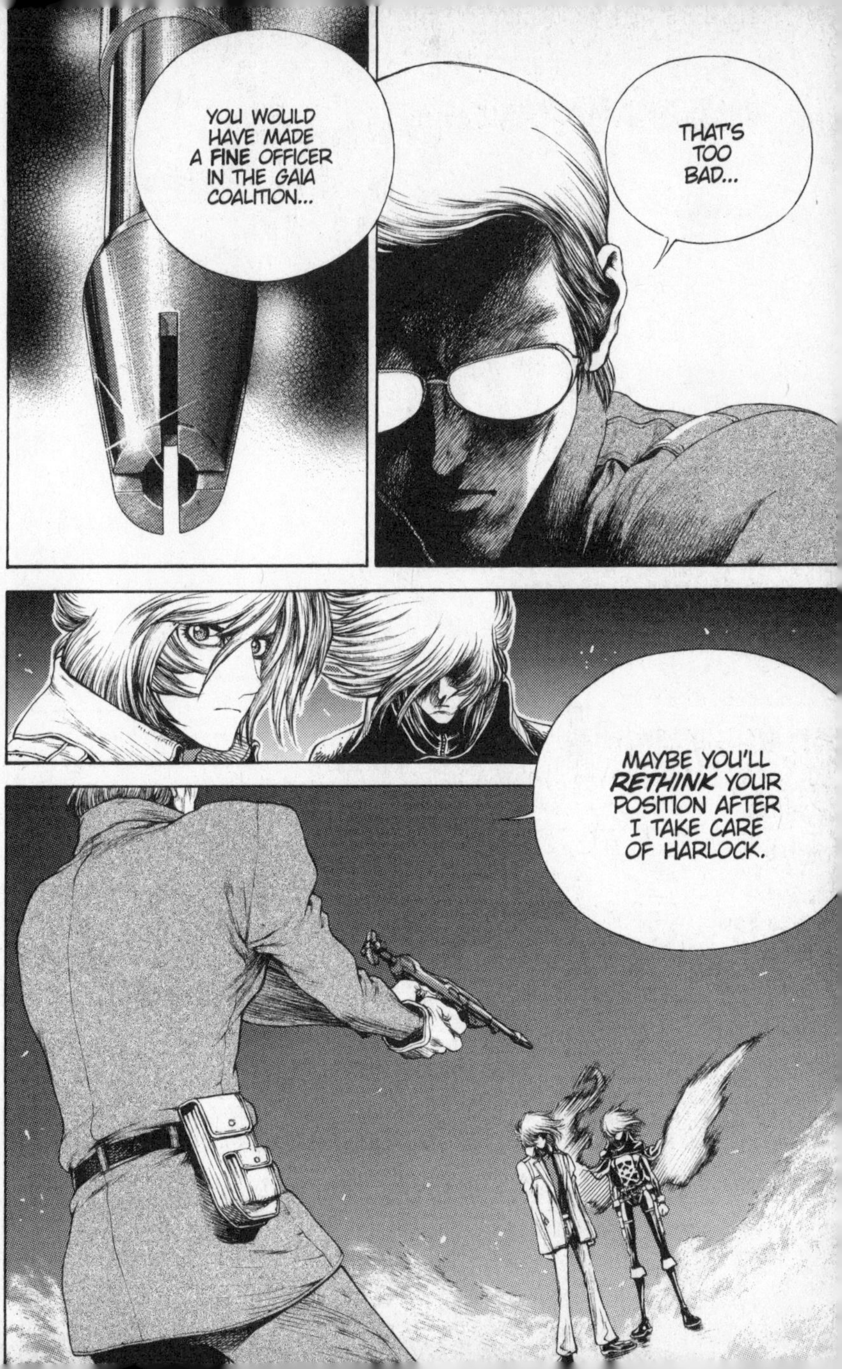
THAT'S TOO BAD...
YOU WOULD HAVE MADE A FINE OFFICER IN THE GAIA COALITION...
MAYBE YOU'LL RETHINK YOUR POSITION AFTER I TAKE CARE OF HARLOCK.

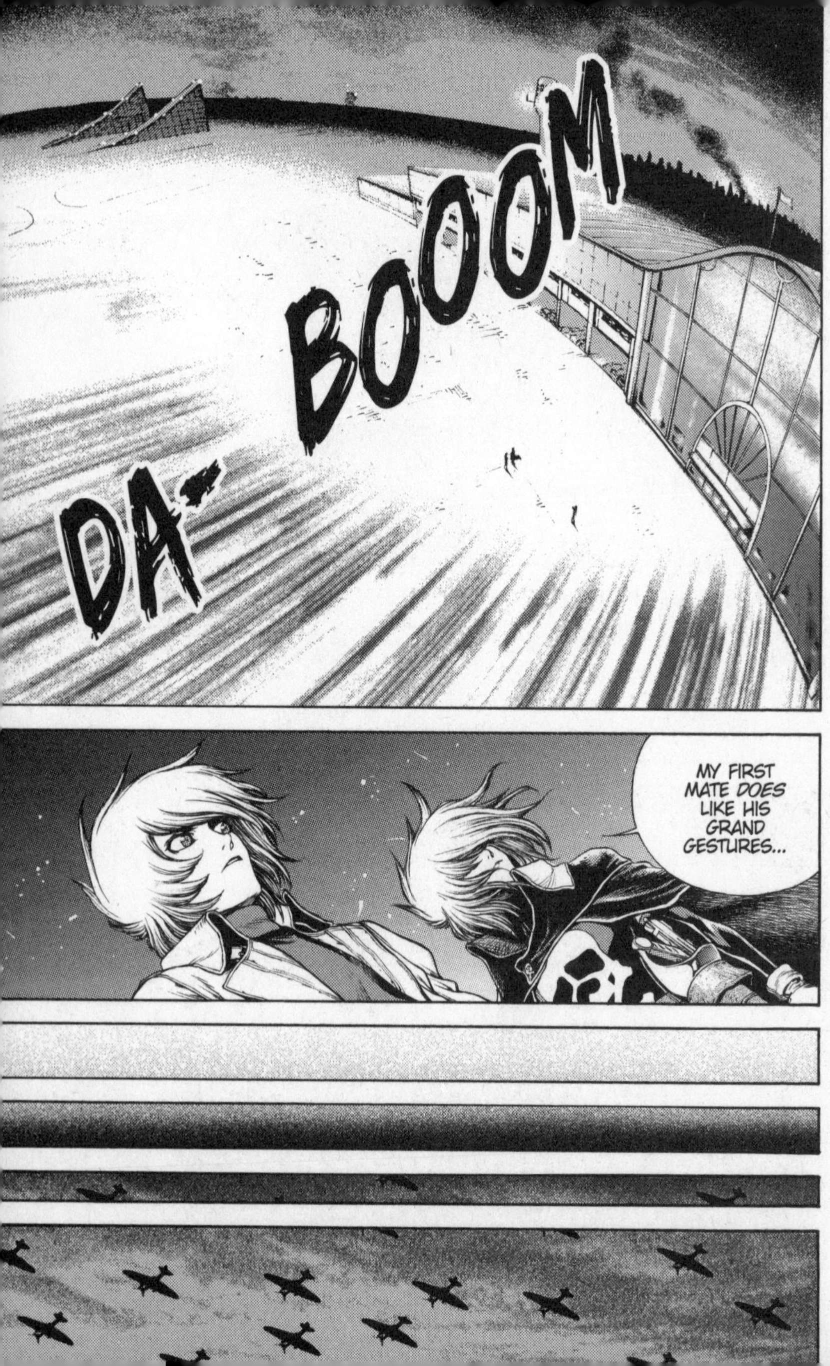
DA- BOOOM
MY FIRST MATE *DOES* LIKE HIS GRAND GESTURES...

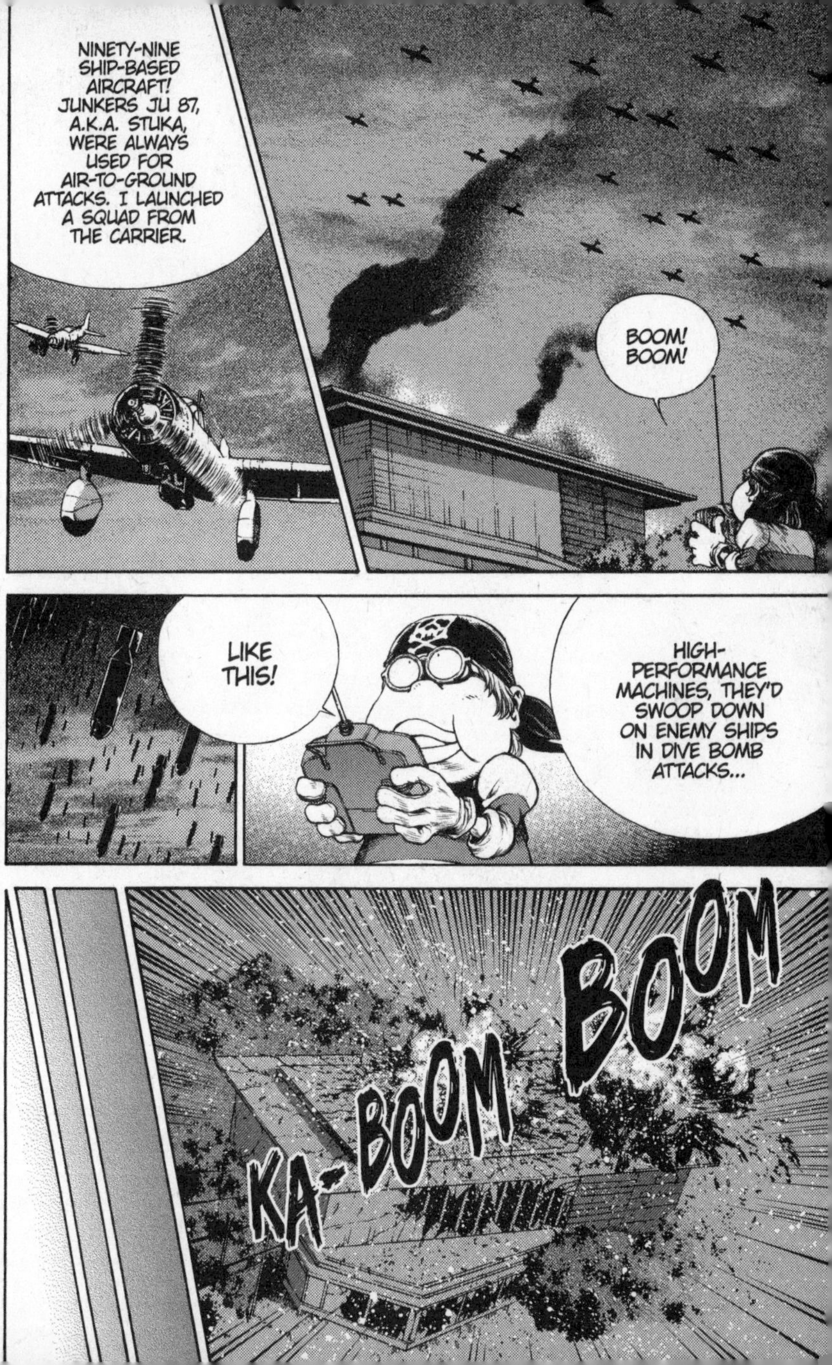
BOOM! BOOM!
NINETY-NINE SHIP-BASED AIRCRAFT! JUNKERS JU 87, A.K.A. STUKA, WERE ALWAYS USED FOR AIR-TO-GROUND ATTACKS. I LAUNCHED A SQUAD FROM THE CARRIER.
HIGH-PERFORMANCE MACHINES, THEY'D SWOOP DOWN ON ENEMY SHIPS IN DIVE BOMB ATTACKS...
LIKE THIS!
KA-BOOM
BOOM
BOOM

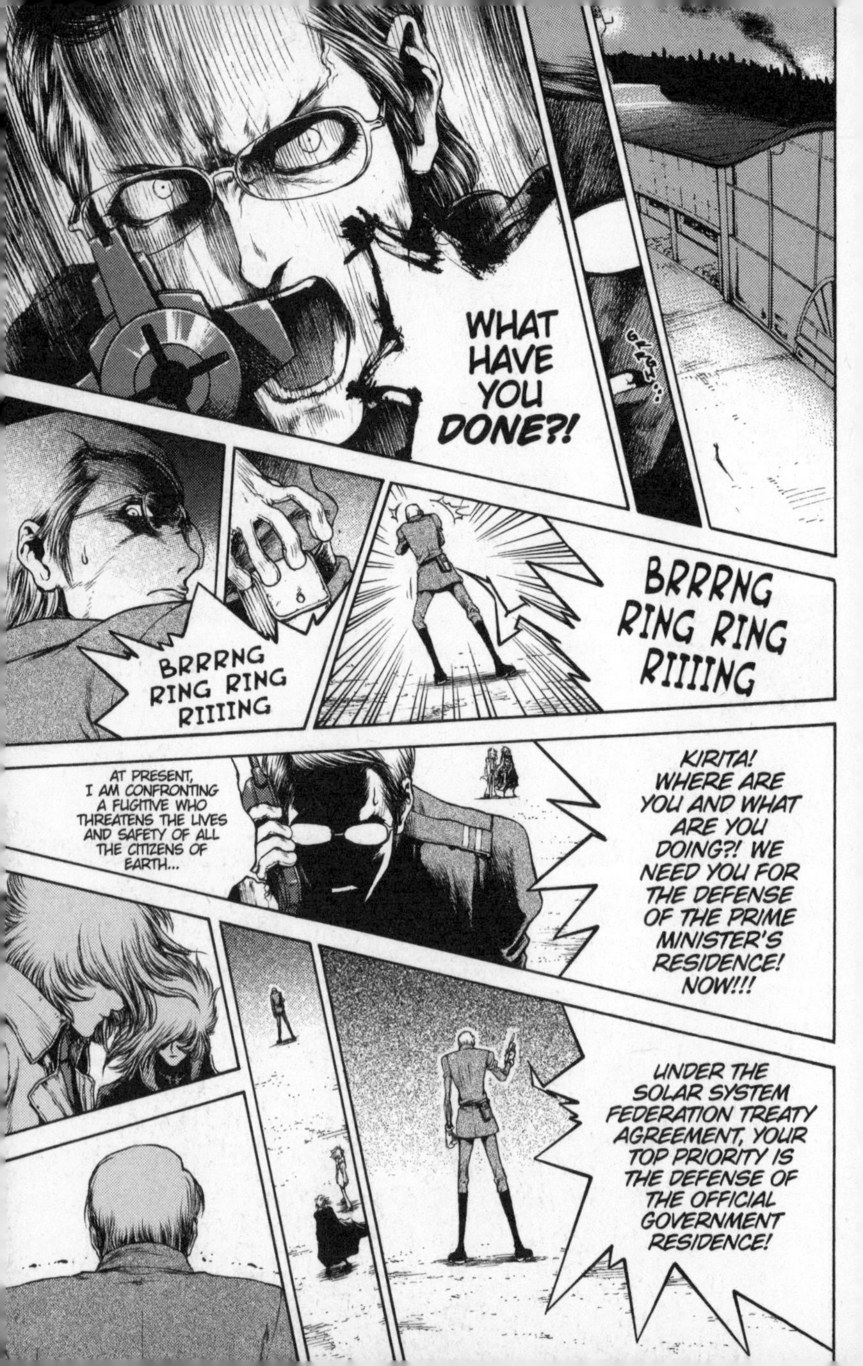
GRRGH..
WHAT HAVE YOU DONE?!
BRRRNG RING RING RIIIING
BRRRNG RING RING RIIIING
KIRITA! WHERE ARE YOU AND WHAT ARE YOU DOING?! WE NEED YOU FOR THE DEFENSE OF THE PRIME MINISTER'S RESIDENCE! NOW!!!
AT PRESENT, I AM CONFRONTING A FUGITIVE WHO THREATENS THE LIVES AND SAFETY OF ALL THE CITIZENS OF EARTH...
UNDER THE SOLAR SYSTEM FEDERATION TREATY AGREEMENT, YOUR TOP PRIORITY IS THE DEFENSE OF THE OFFICIAL GOVERNMENT RESIDENCE!

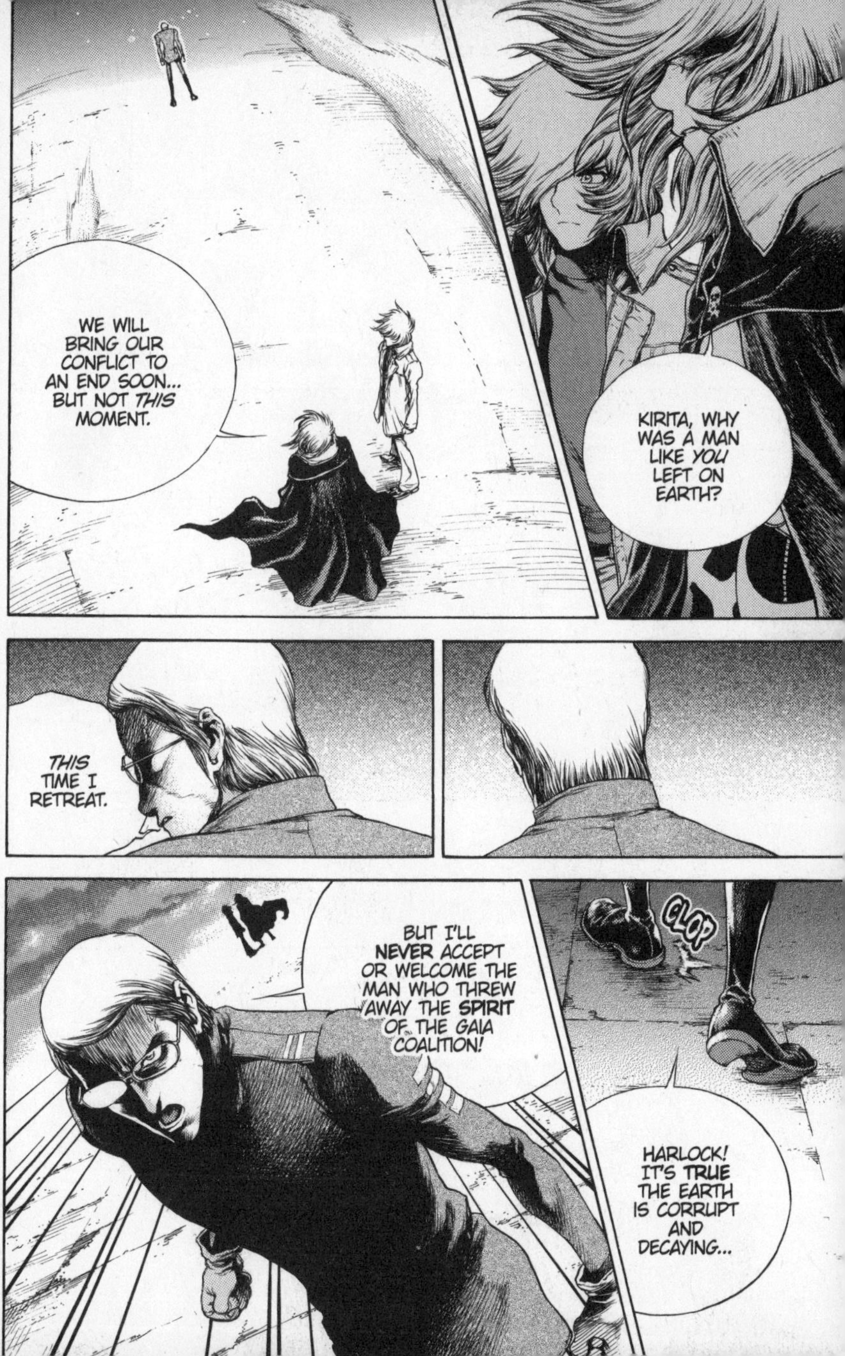
KIRITA, WHY WAS A MAN LIKE *YOU* LEFT ON EARTH?
WE WILL BRING OUR CONFLICT TO AN END SOON... BUT NOT *THIS* MOMENT.
THIS TIME I RETREAT.
CLOP
HARLOCK! IT'S **TRUE** THE EARTH IS CORRUPT AND DECAYING...
BUT I'LL **NEVER** ACCEPT OR WELCOME THE MAN WHO THREW AWAY THE **SPIRIT** OF THE GAIA COALITION!

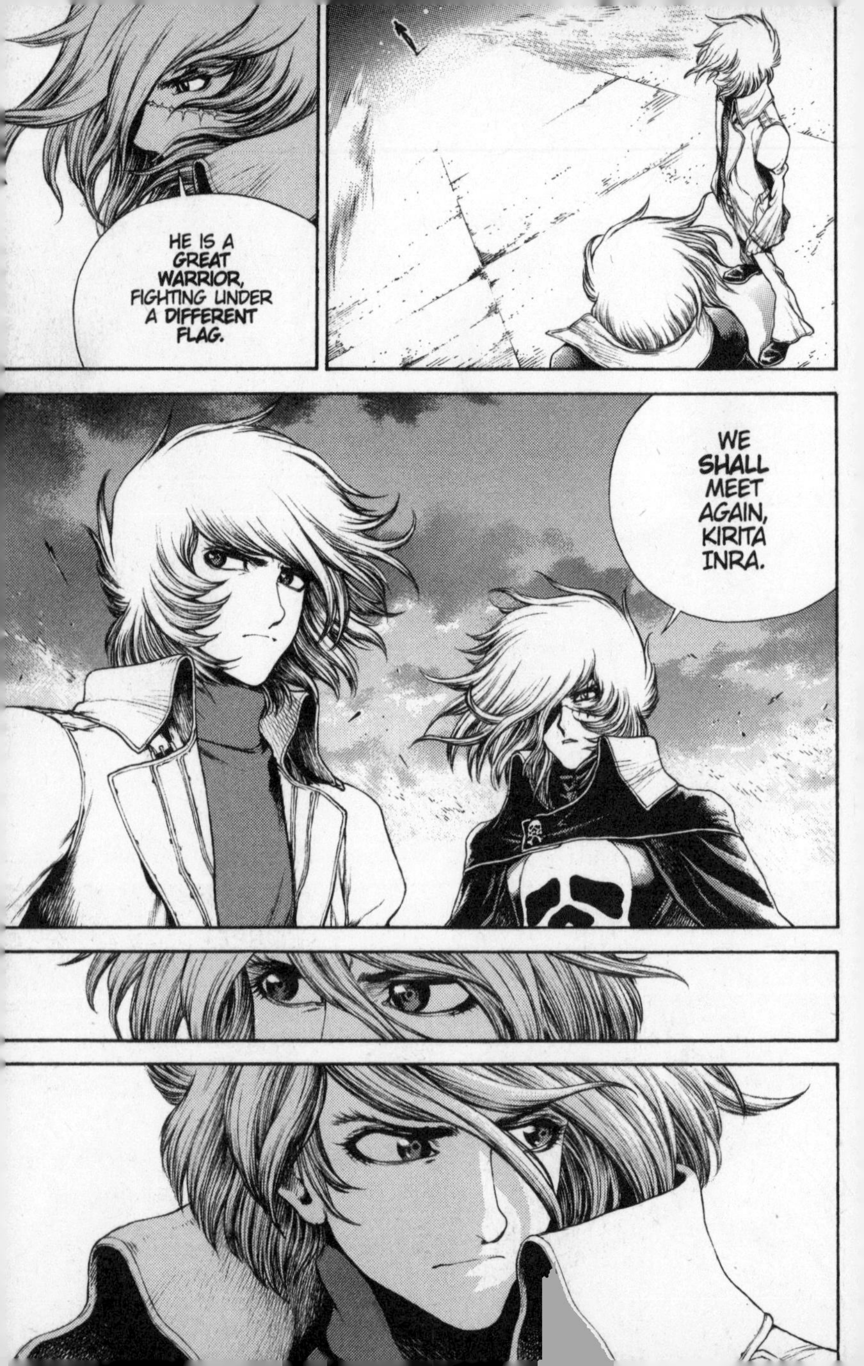
HE IS A GREAT WARRIOR, FIGHTING UNDER A DIFFERENT FLAG.
WE SHALL MEET AGAIN, KIRITA INRA.

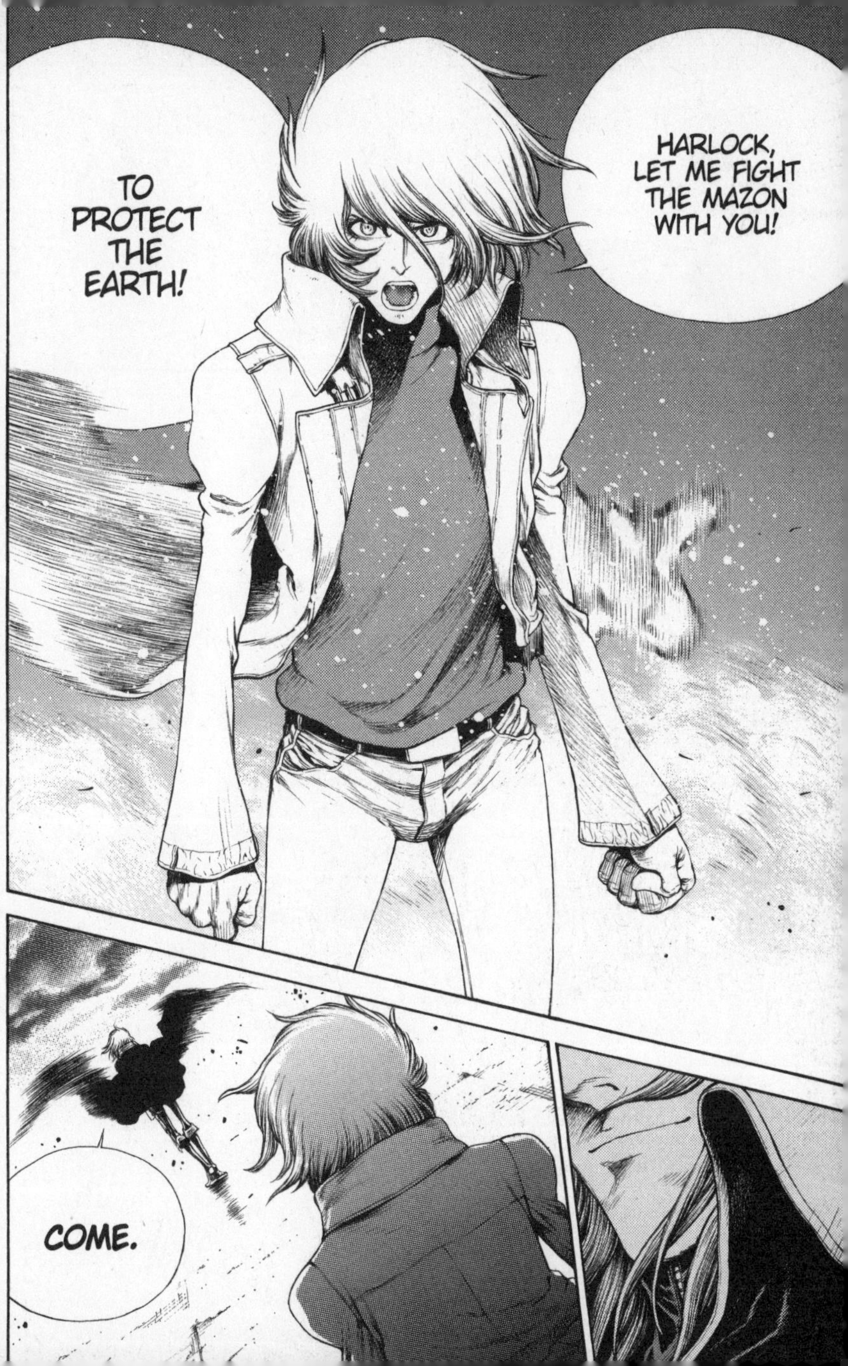
HARLOCK, LET ME FIGHT THE MAZON WITH YOU!
TO PROTECT THE EARTH!
COME.

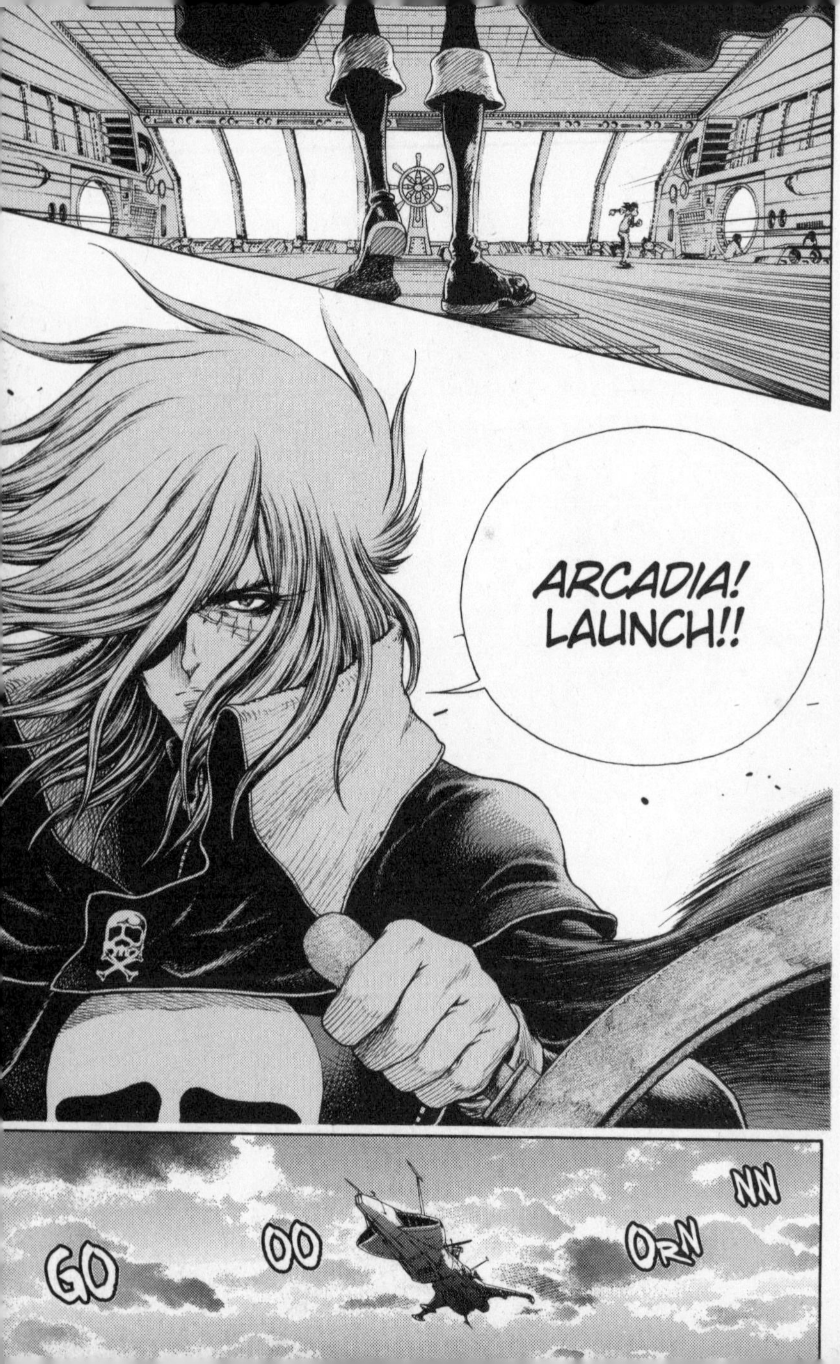
ARCADIA! LAUNCH!!
GO OO ORN NN

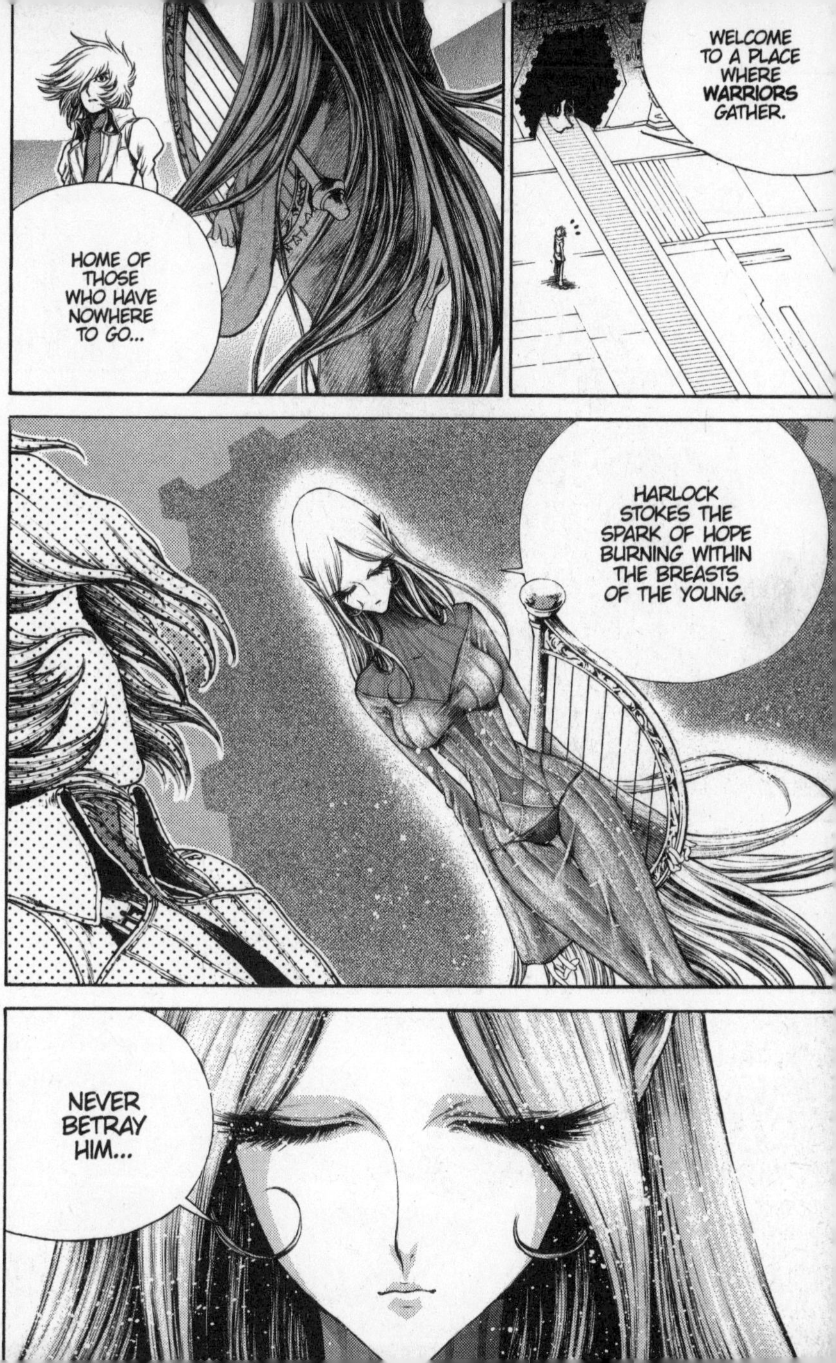
WELCOME TO A PLACE WHERE WARRIORS GATHER.
HOME OF THOSE WHO HAVE NOWHERE TO GO...
HARLOCK STOKES THE SPARK OF HOPE BURNING WITHIN THE BREASTS OF THE YOUNG.
NEVER BETRAY HIM...

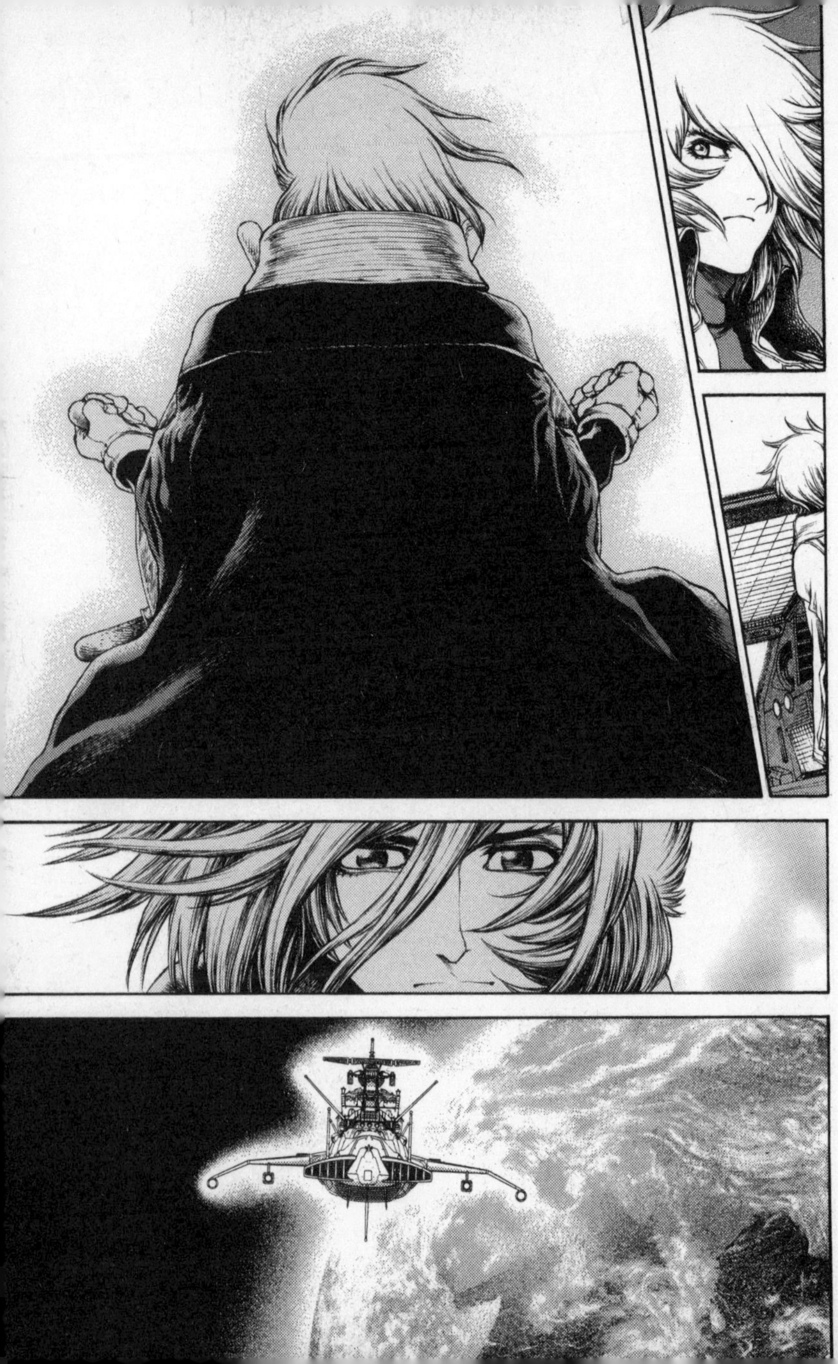

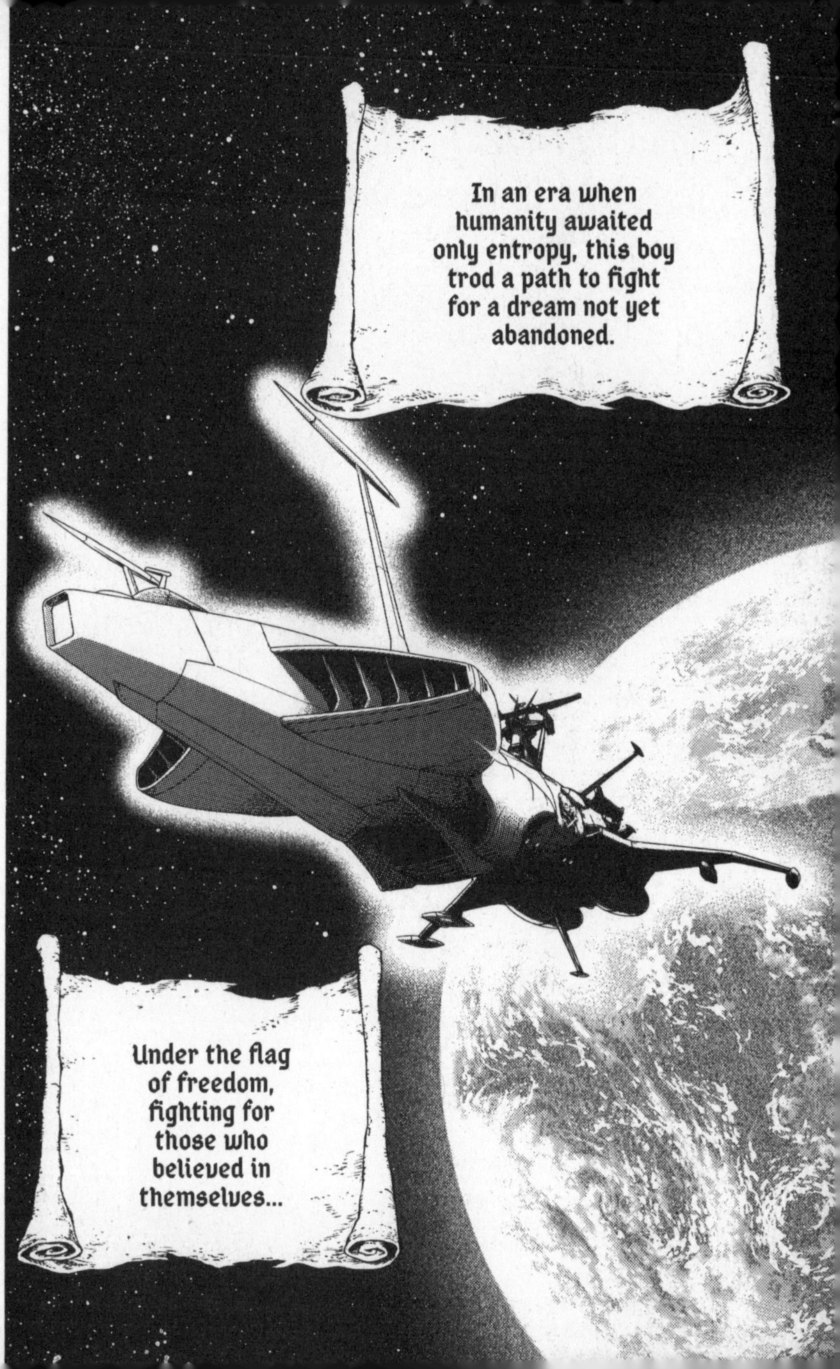
In an era when humanity awaited only entropy, this boy trod a path to fight for a dream not yet abandoned.
Under the flag of freedom, fighting for those who believed in themselves...

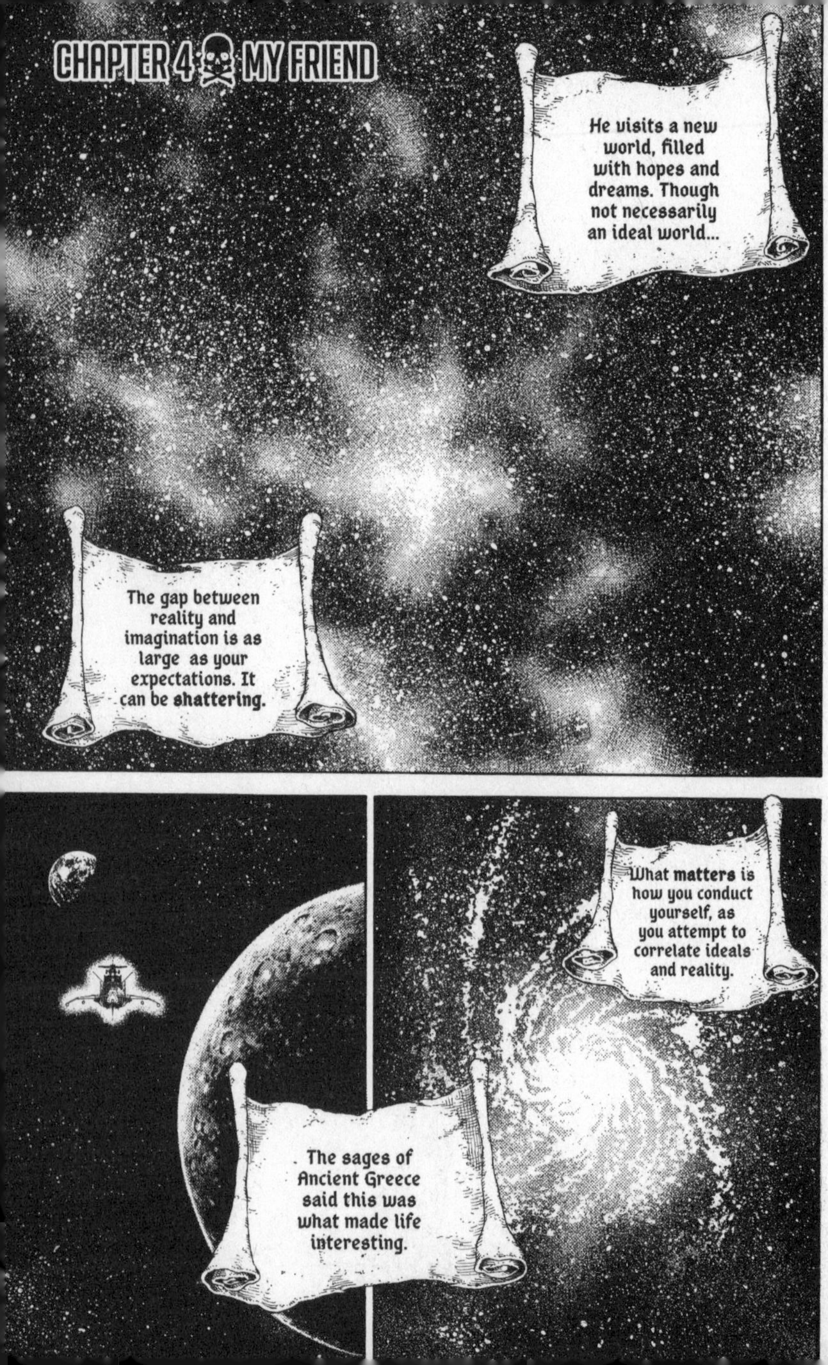
CHAPTER 4 MY FRIEND
He visits a new world, filled with hopes and dreams. Though not necessarily an ideal world...
The gap between reality and imagination is as large as your expectations. It can be shattering.
What matters is how you conduct yourself, as you attempt to correlate ideals and reality.
The sages of Ancient Greece said this was what made life interesting.

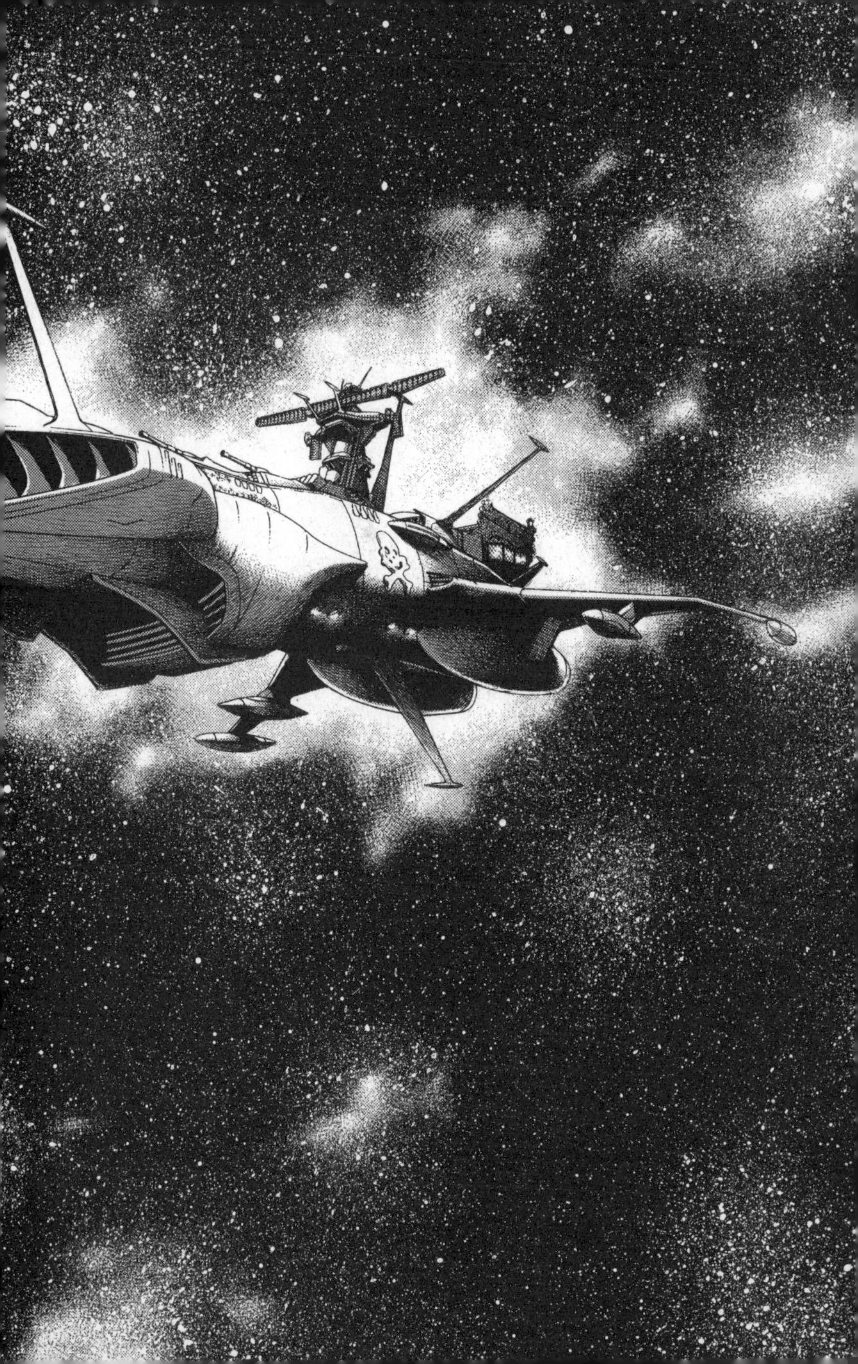

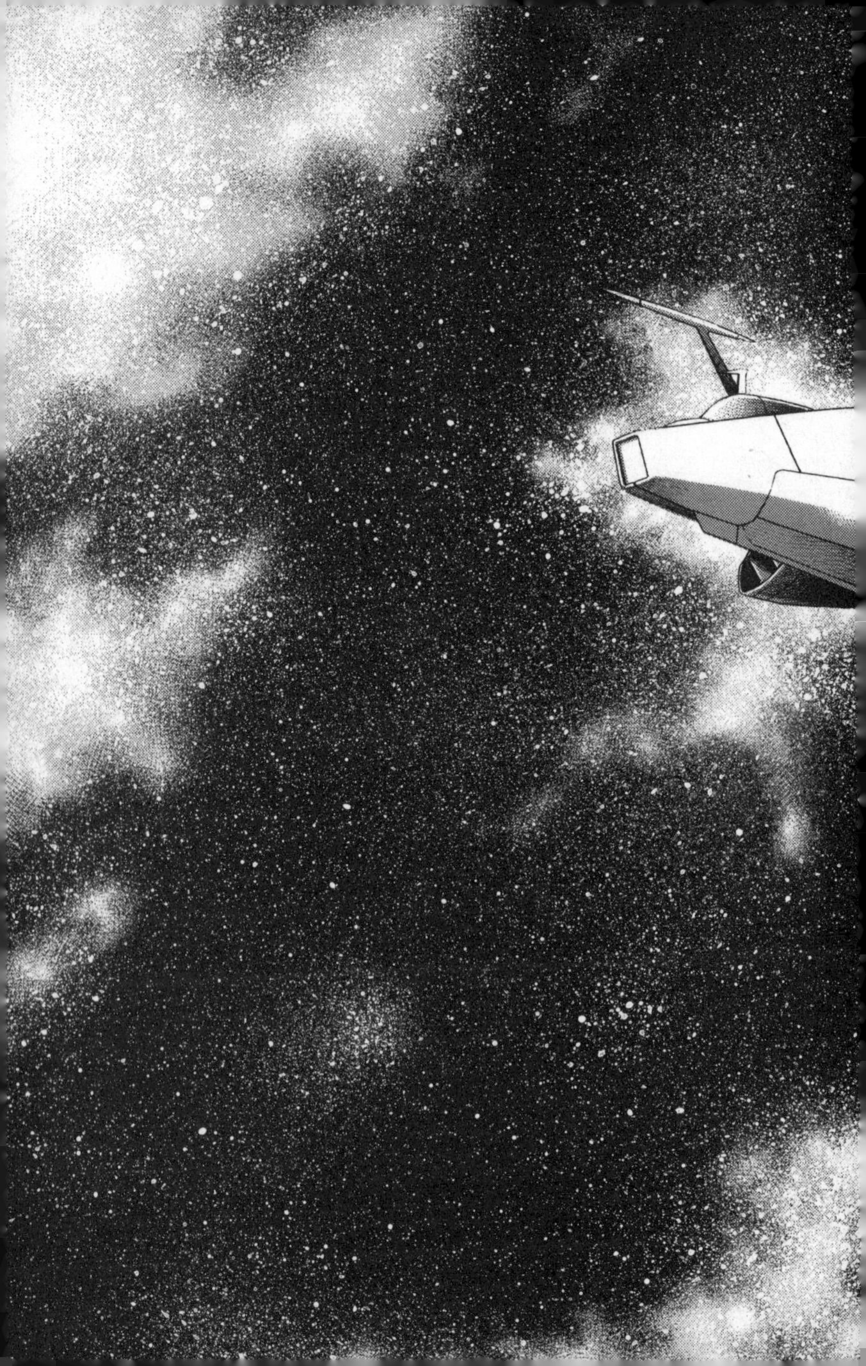

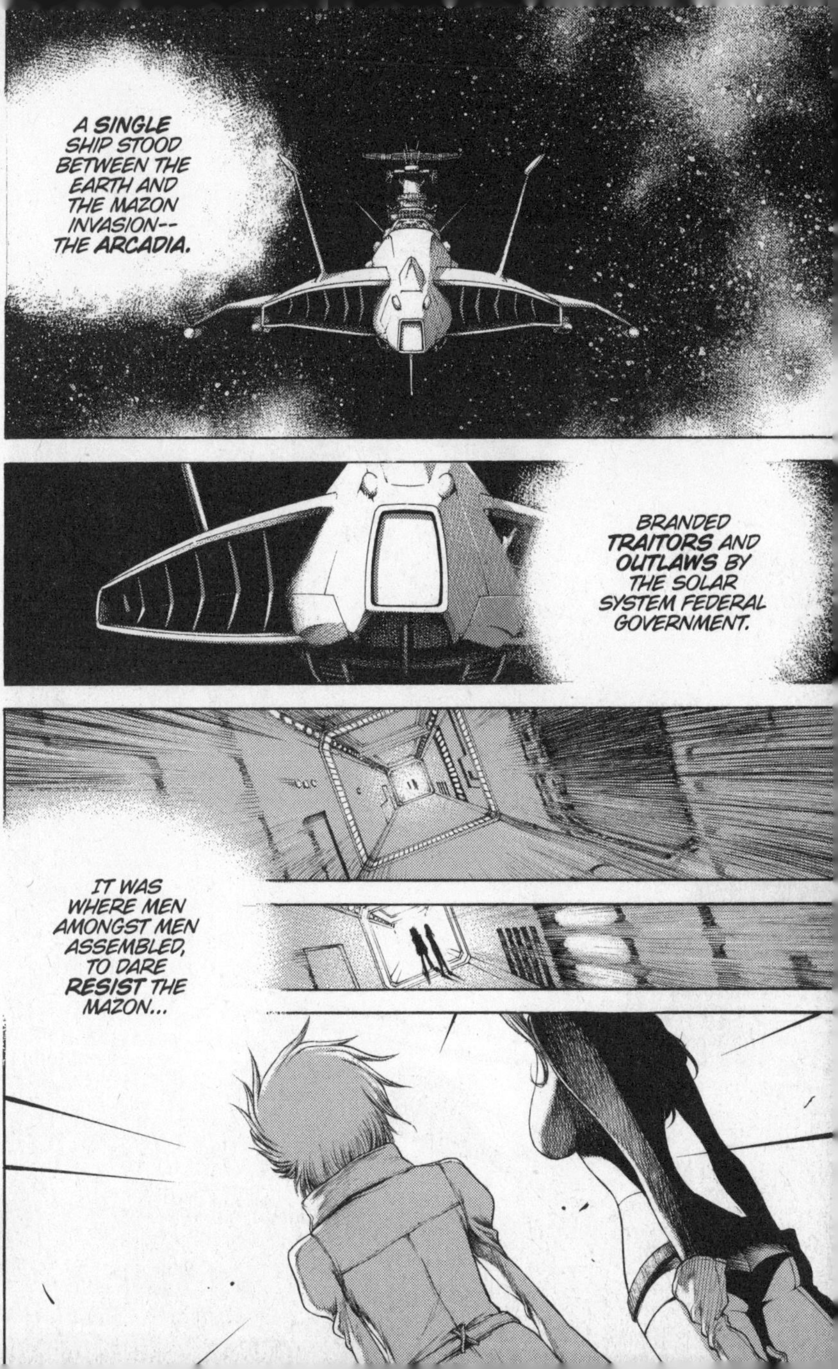
A SINGLE SHIP STOOD BETWEEN THE EARTH AND THE MAZON INVASION-- THE ARCADIA.
BRANDED TRAITORS AND OUTLAWS BY THE SOLAR SYSTEM FEDERAL GOVERNMENT.
IT WAS WHERE MEN AMONGST MEN ASSEMBLED, TO DARE RESIST THE MAZON...

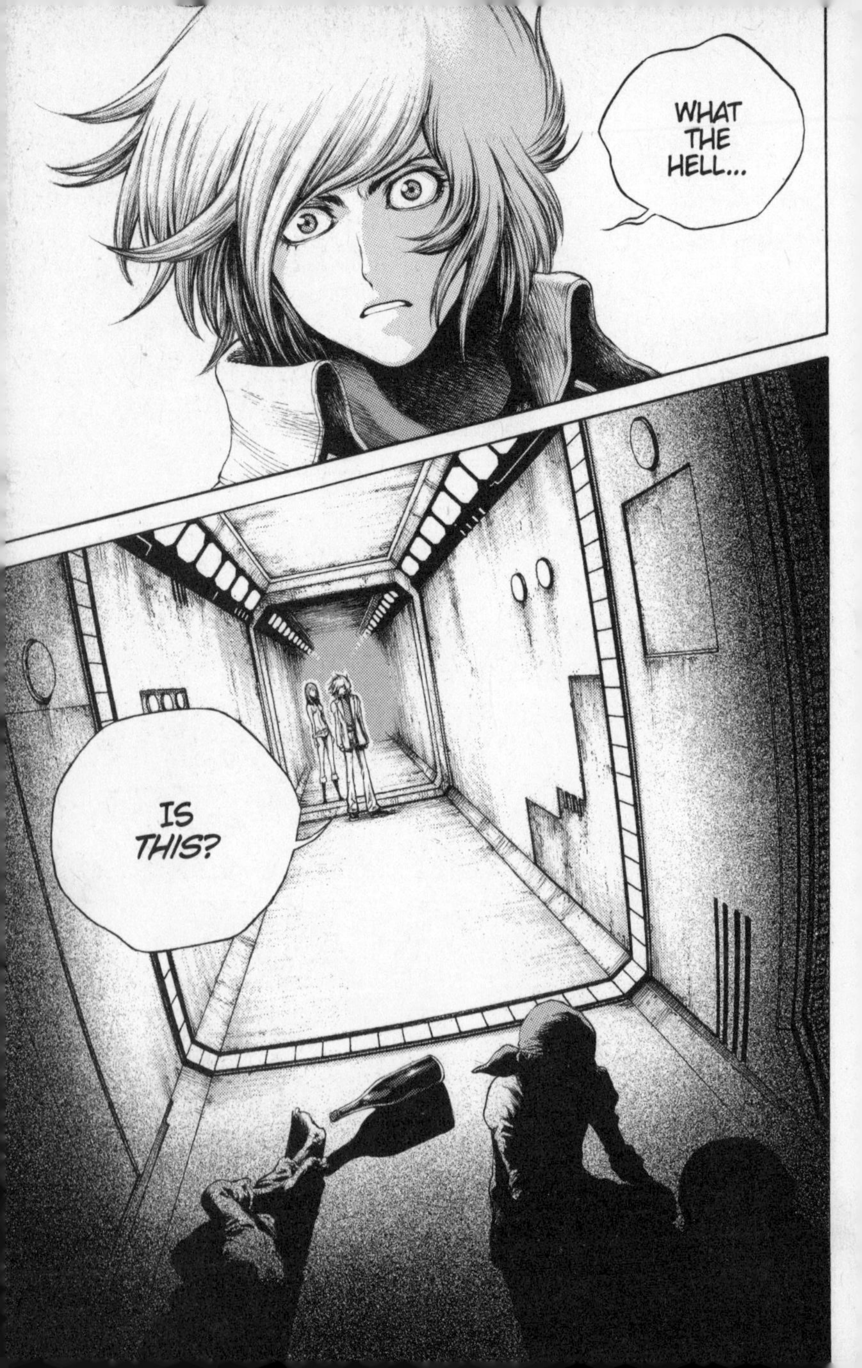
WHAT THE HELL...
IS THIS?

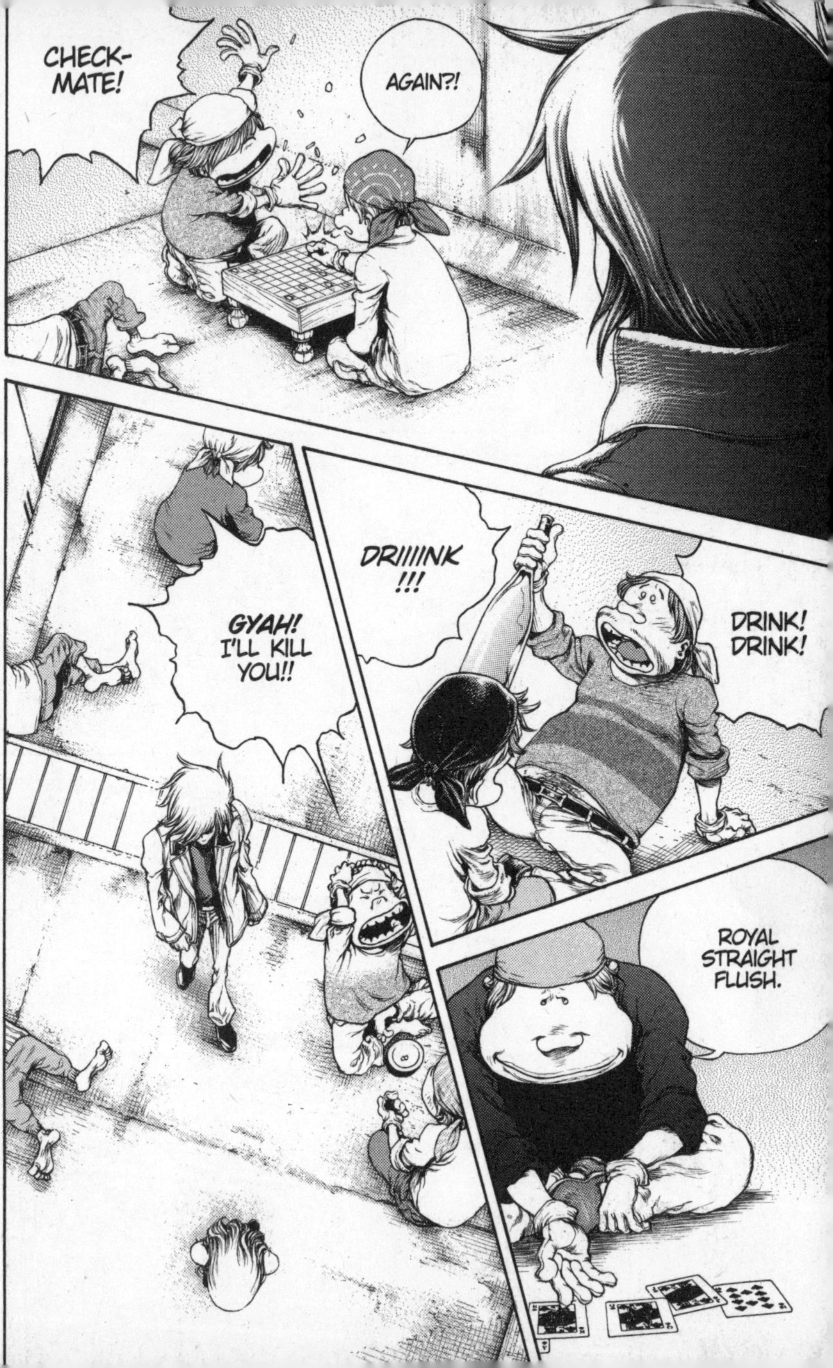
AGAIN?!
CHECK-MATE!
DRINK! DRINK!
DRIIIINK!!!
ROYAL STRAIGHT FLUSH.
GYAH! I'LL KILL YOU!!

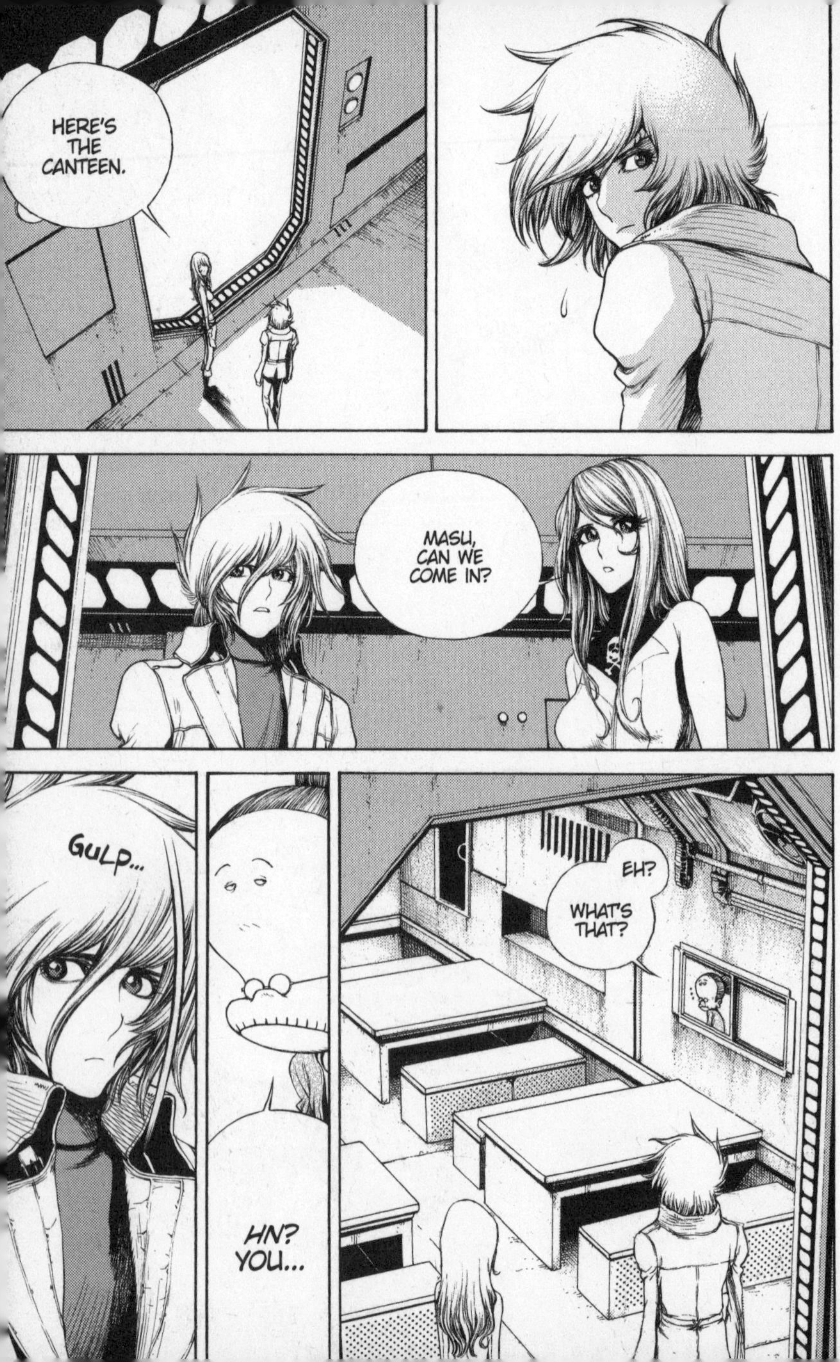
HERE'S THE CANTEEN.
MASU, CAN WE COME IN?
EH?
WHAT'S THAT?
HN? YOU...
GULP...

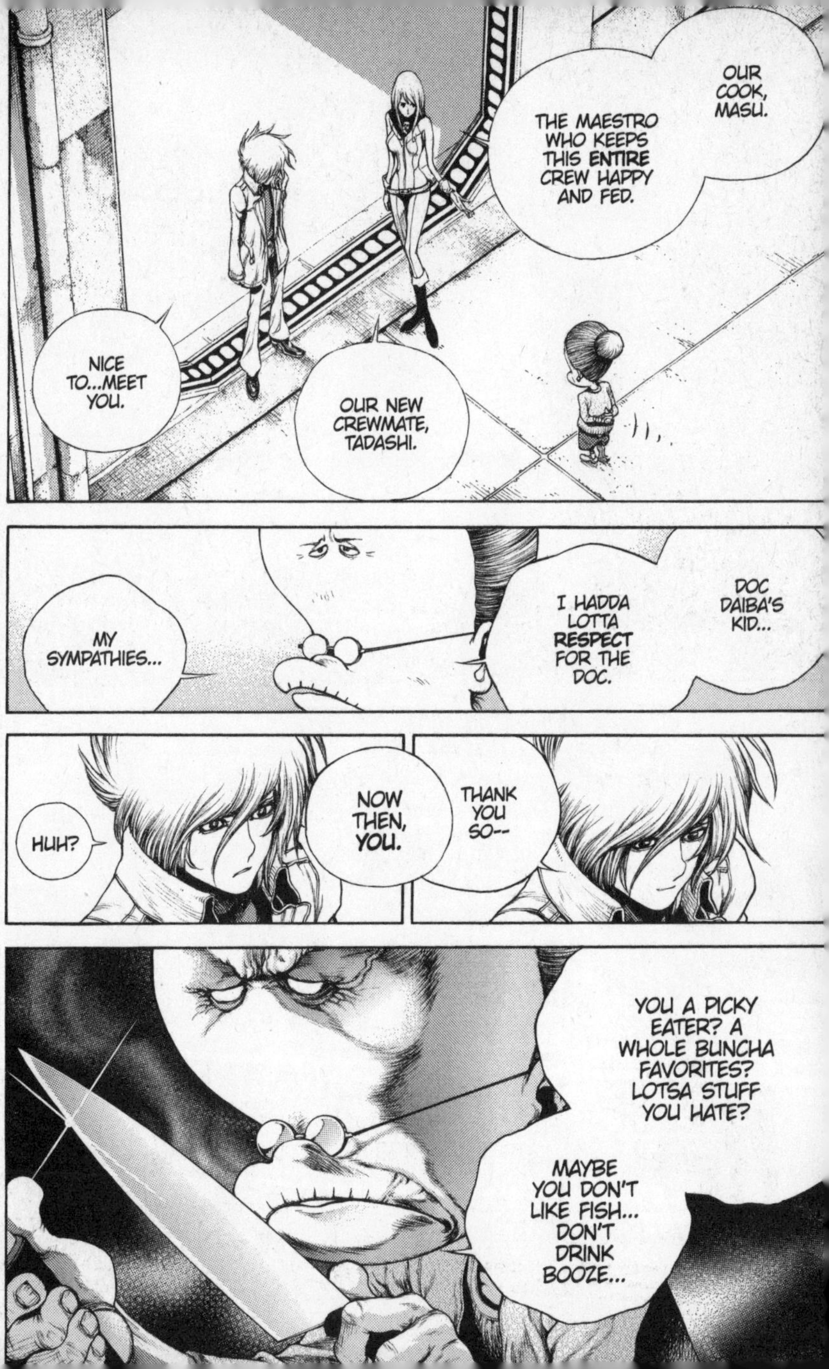
OUR COOK, MASU.
THE MAESTRO WHO KEEPS THIS ENTIRE CREW HAPPY AND FED.
OUR NEW CREWMATE, TADASHI.
NICE TO...MEET YOU.
DOC DAIBA'S KID...
I HADDA LOTTA RESPECT FOR THE DOC.
MY SYMPATHIES...
THANK YOU SO--
NOW THEN, YOU.
HUH?
YOU A PICKY EATER? A WHOLE BUNCHA FAVORITES? LOTSA STUFF YOU HATE?
MAYBE YOU DON'T LIKE FISH... DON'T DRINK BOOZE...

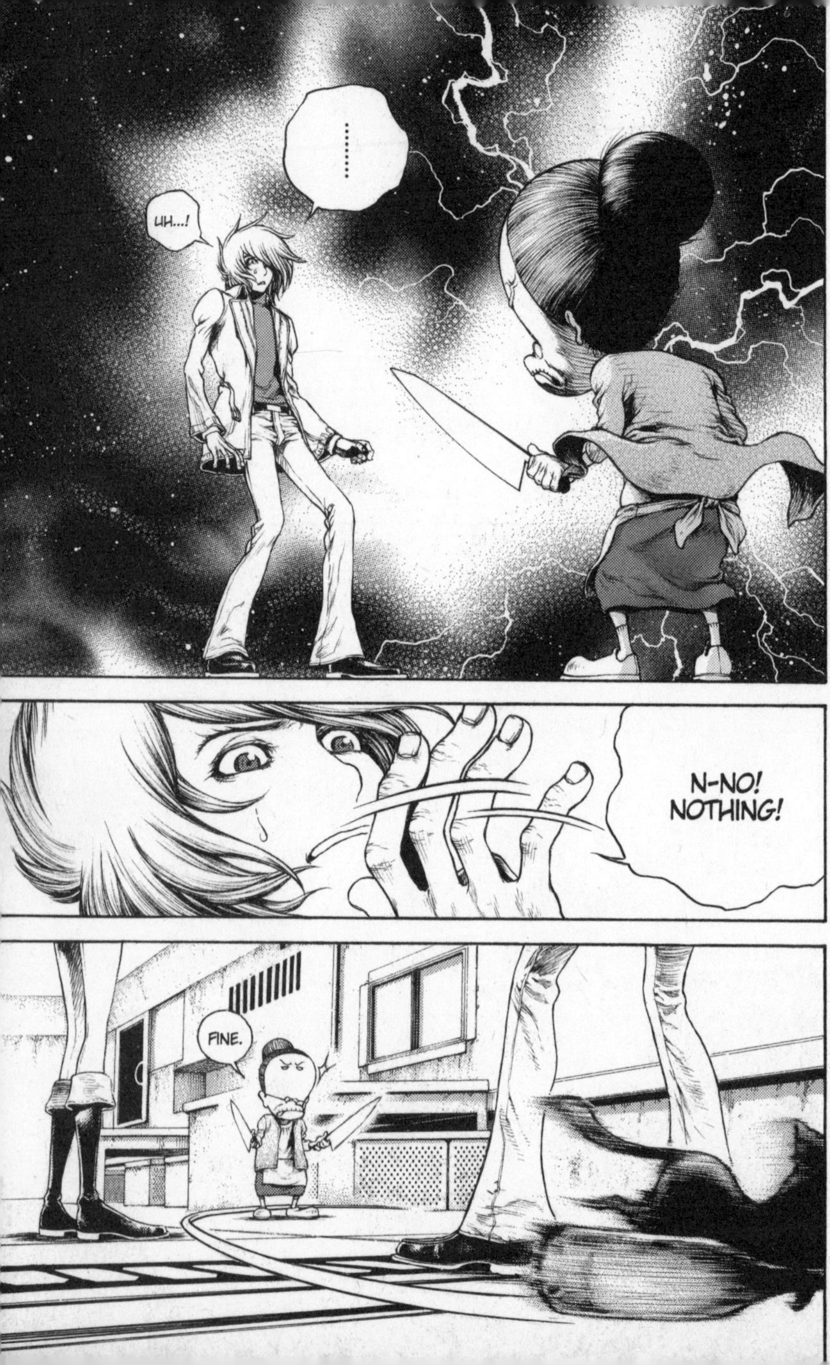
......
UH...!
N-NO! NOTHING!
FINE.

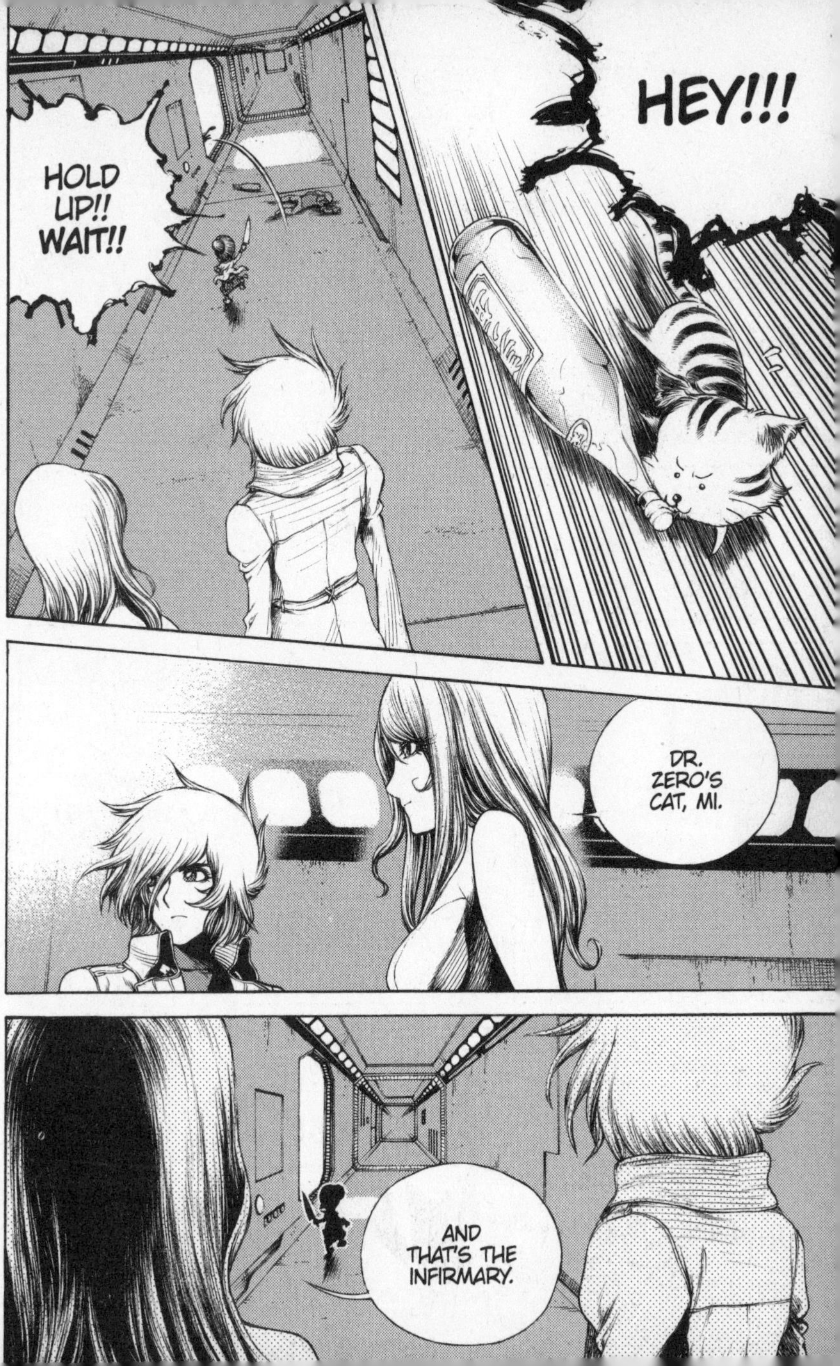
HEY!!!
HOLD UP!! WAIT!!
DR. ZERO'S CAT, MI.
AND THAT'S THE INFIRMARY.

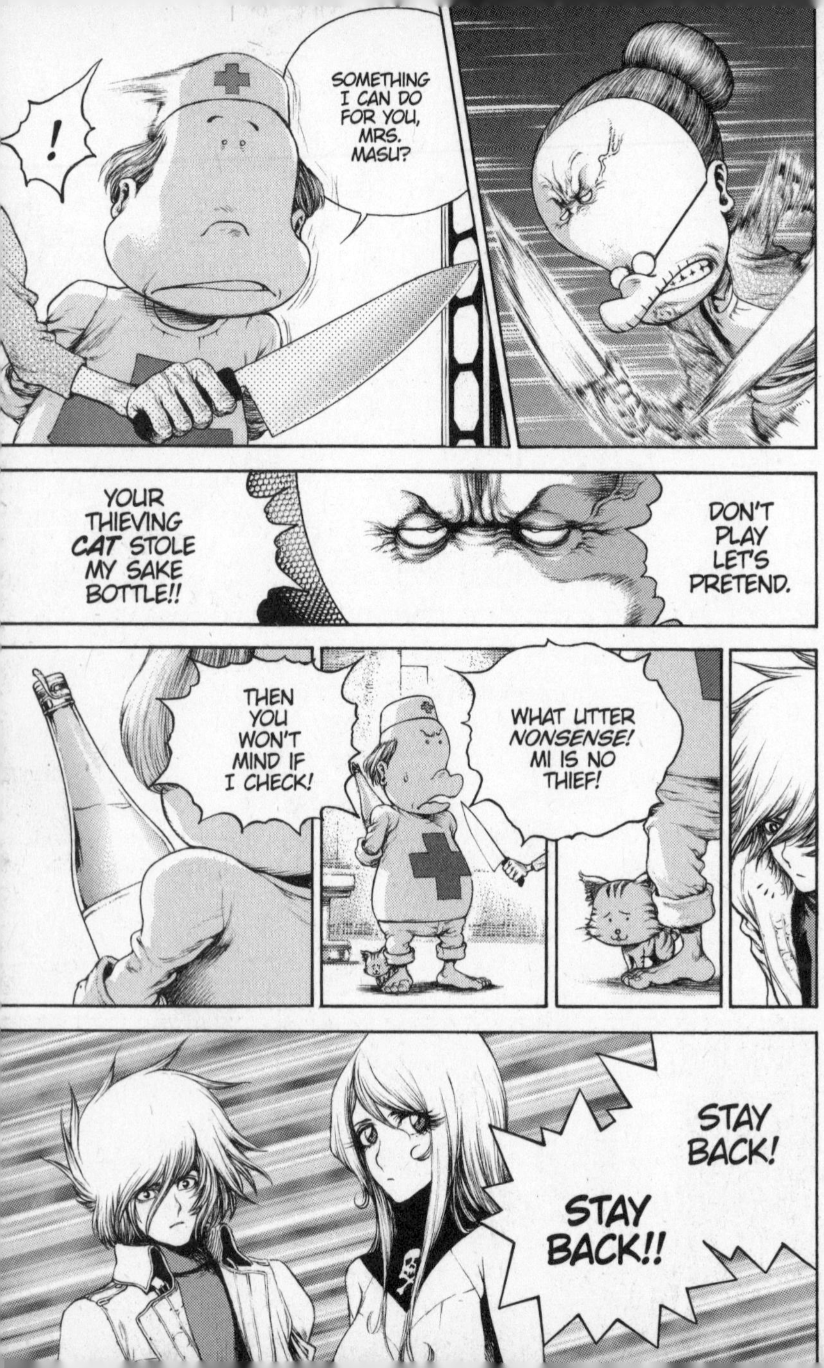
SOMETHING I CAN DO FOR YOU, MRS. MASU?
!
DON'T PLAY LET'S PRETEND.
YOUR THIEVING CAT STOLE MY SAKE BOTTLE!!
WHAT UTTER NONSENSE! MI IS NO THIEF!
THEN YOU WON'T MIND IF I CHECK!
STAY BACK!
STAY BACK!!

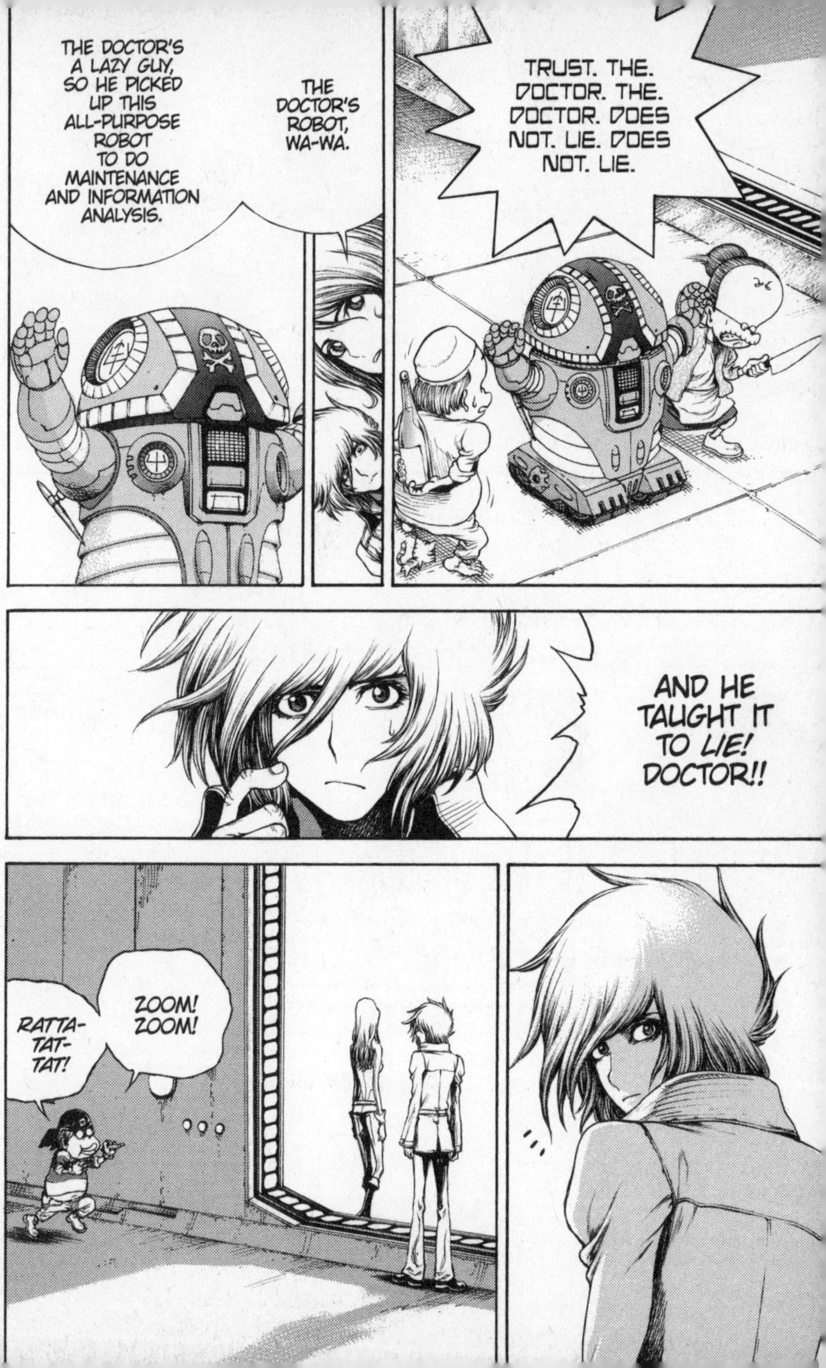
TRUST. THE. DOCTOR. THE. DOCTOR. DOES NOT. LIE. DOES NOT. LIE.
THE DOCTOR'S ROBOT, WA-WA.
THE DOCTOR'S A LAZY GUY, SO HE PICKED UP THIS ALL-PURPOSE ROBOT TO DO MAINTENANCE AND INFORMATION ANALYSIS.
AND HE TAUGHT IT TO *LIE!* DOCTOR!!
...
ZOOM! ZOOM!
RATTA-TAT-TAT!

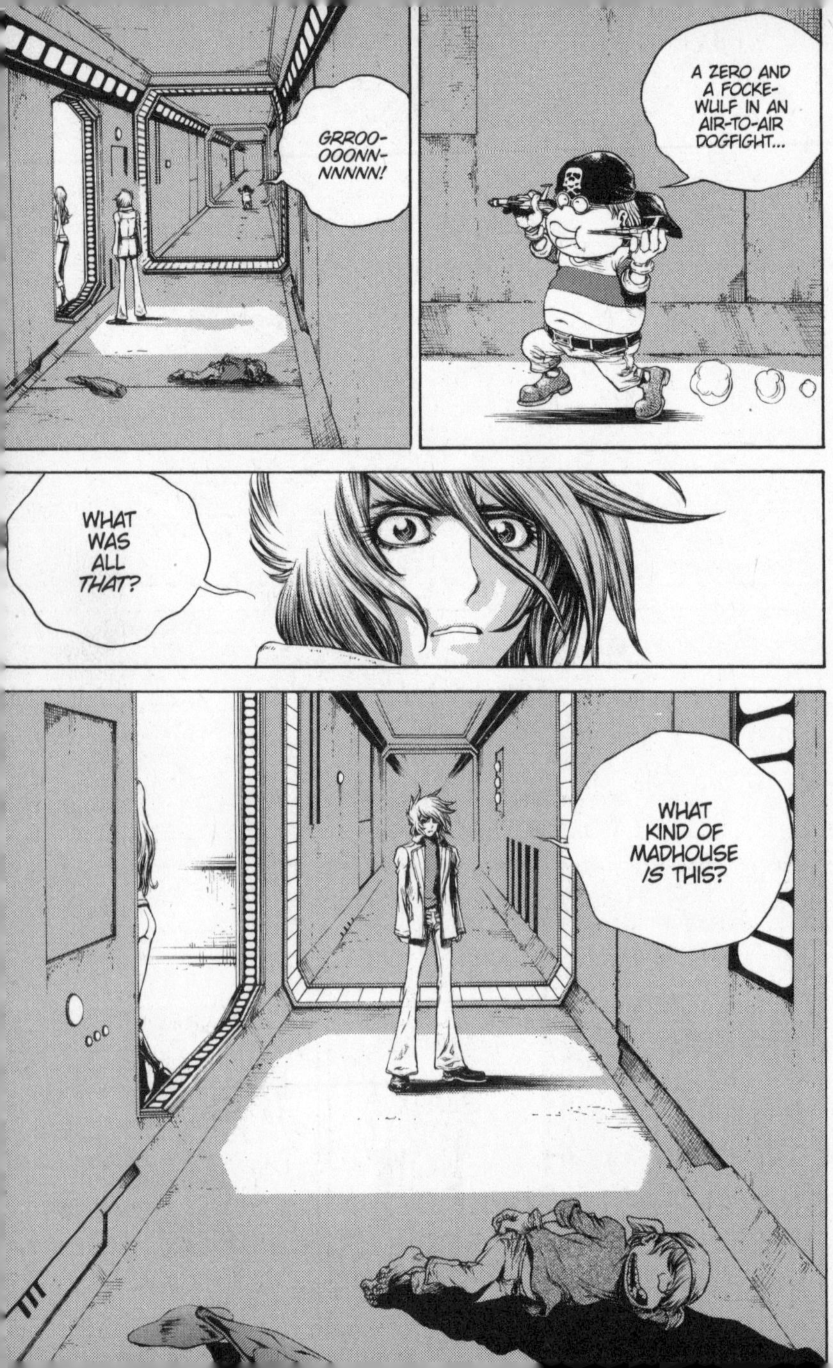
A ZERO AND A FOCKE-WULF IN AN AIR-TO-AIR DOGFIGHT...
GRROO-OOONN-NNNNN!
WHAT WAS ALL THAT?
WHAT KIND OF MADHOUSE IS THIS?

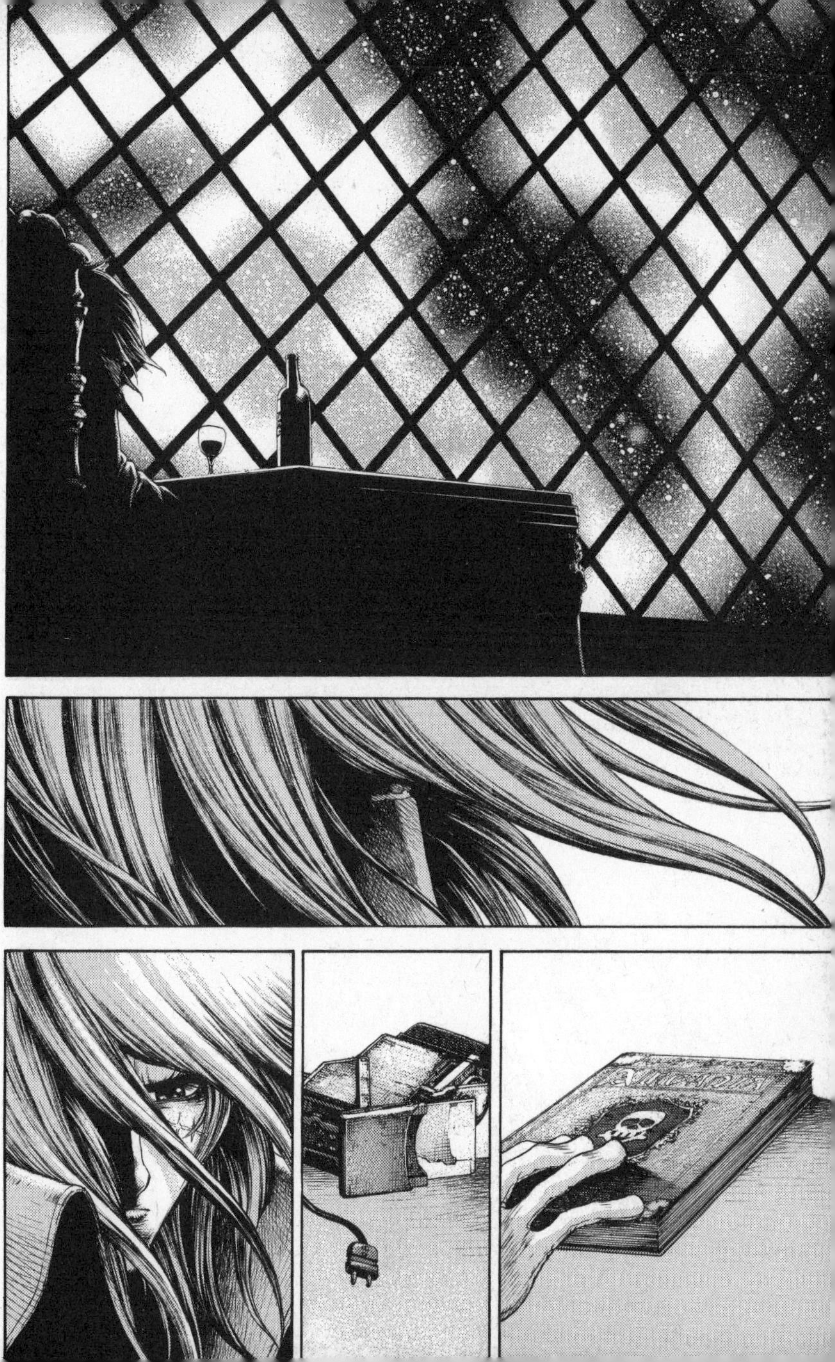

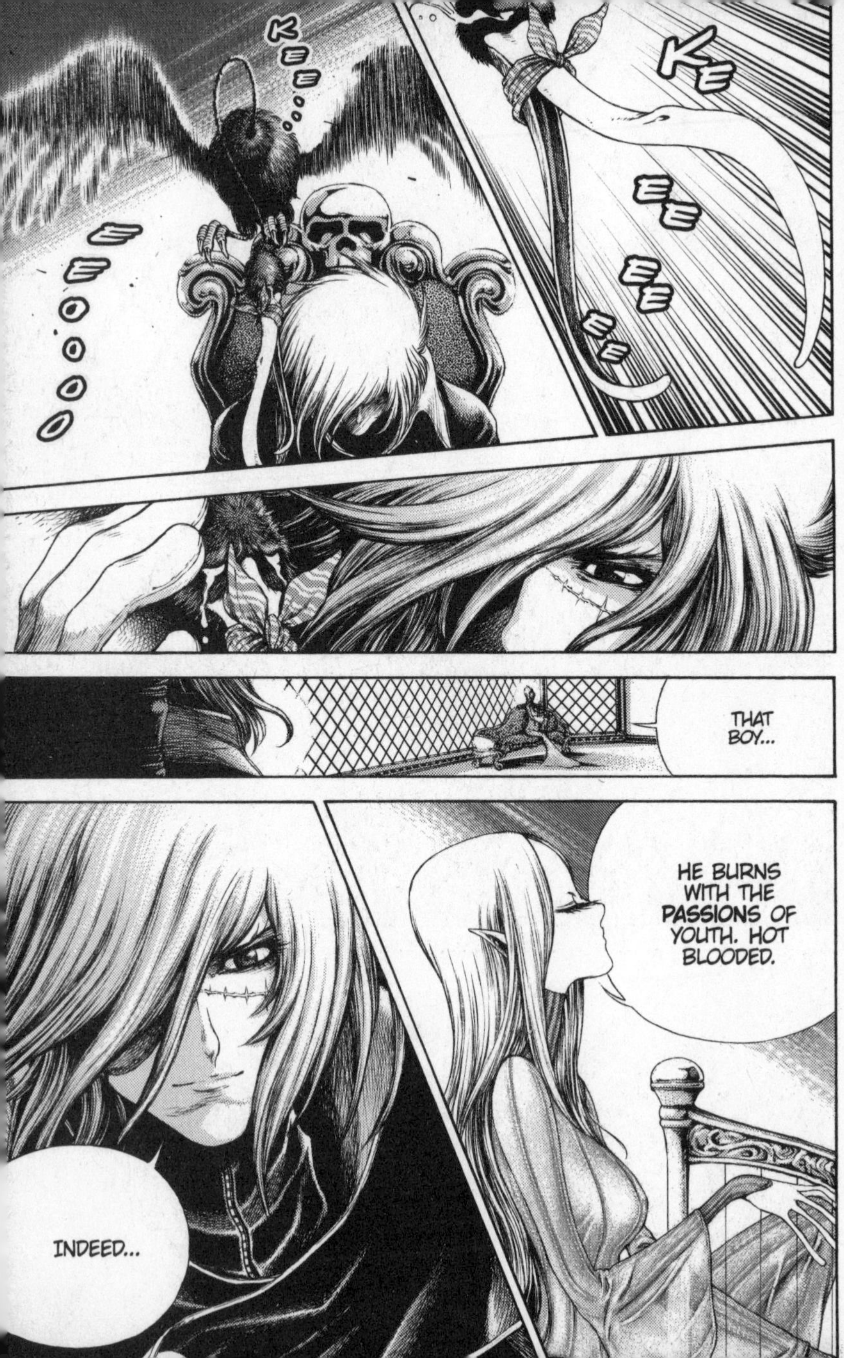
KE
EE
EE
EE
KEEOOO
EEOOOOOO
THAT BOY...
HE BURNS WITH THE PASSIONS OF YOUTH. HOT BLOODED.
INDEED...

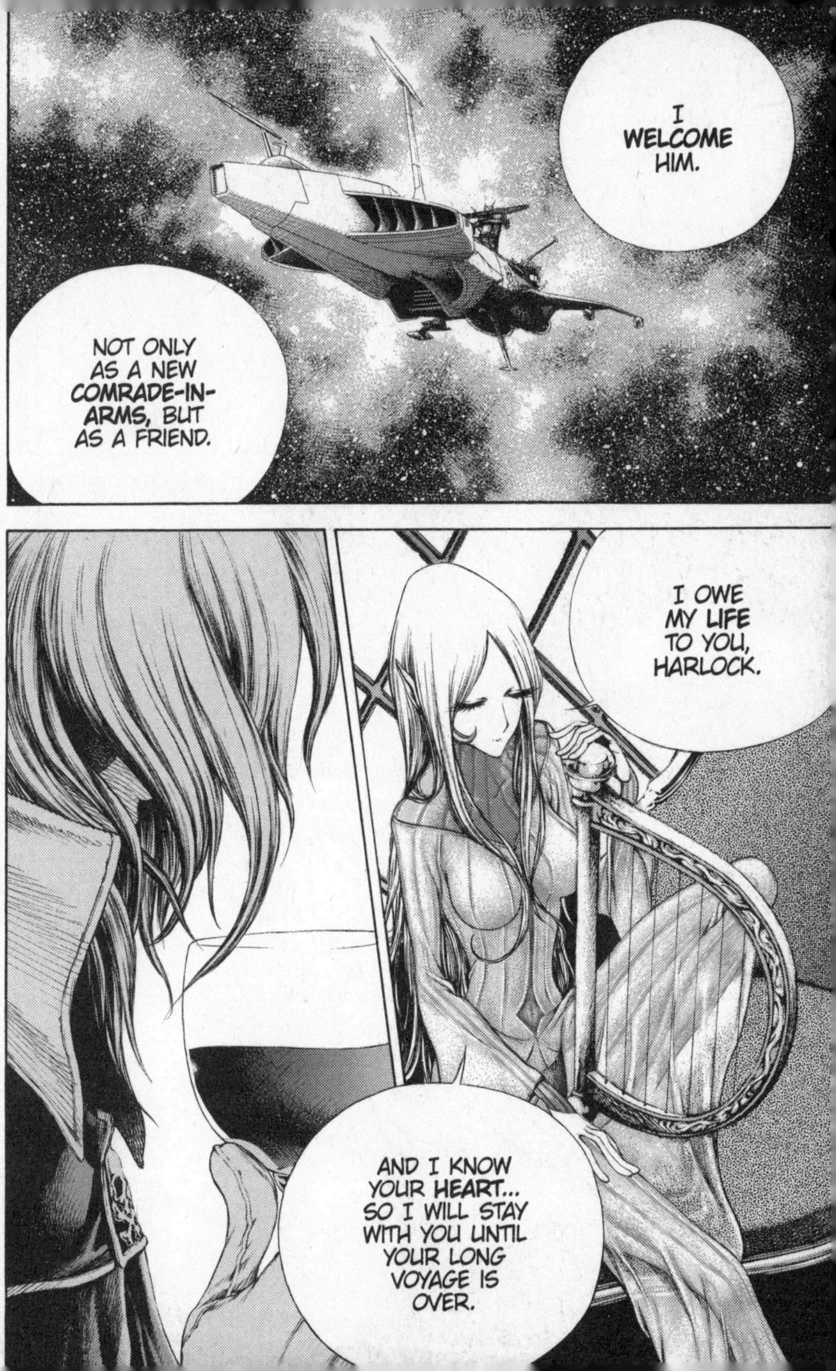
I WELCOME HIM.
NOT ONLY AS A NEW COMRADE-IN-ARMS, BUT AS A FRIEND.
I OWE MY LIFE TO YOU, HARLOCK.
AND I KNOW YOUR HEART... SO I WILL STAY WITH YOU UNTIL YOUR LONG VOYAGE IS OVER.

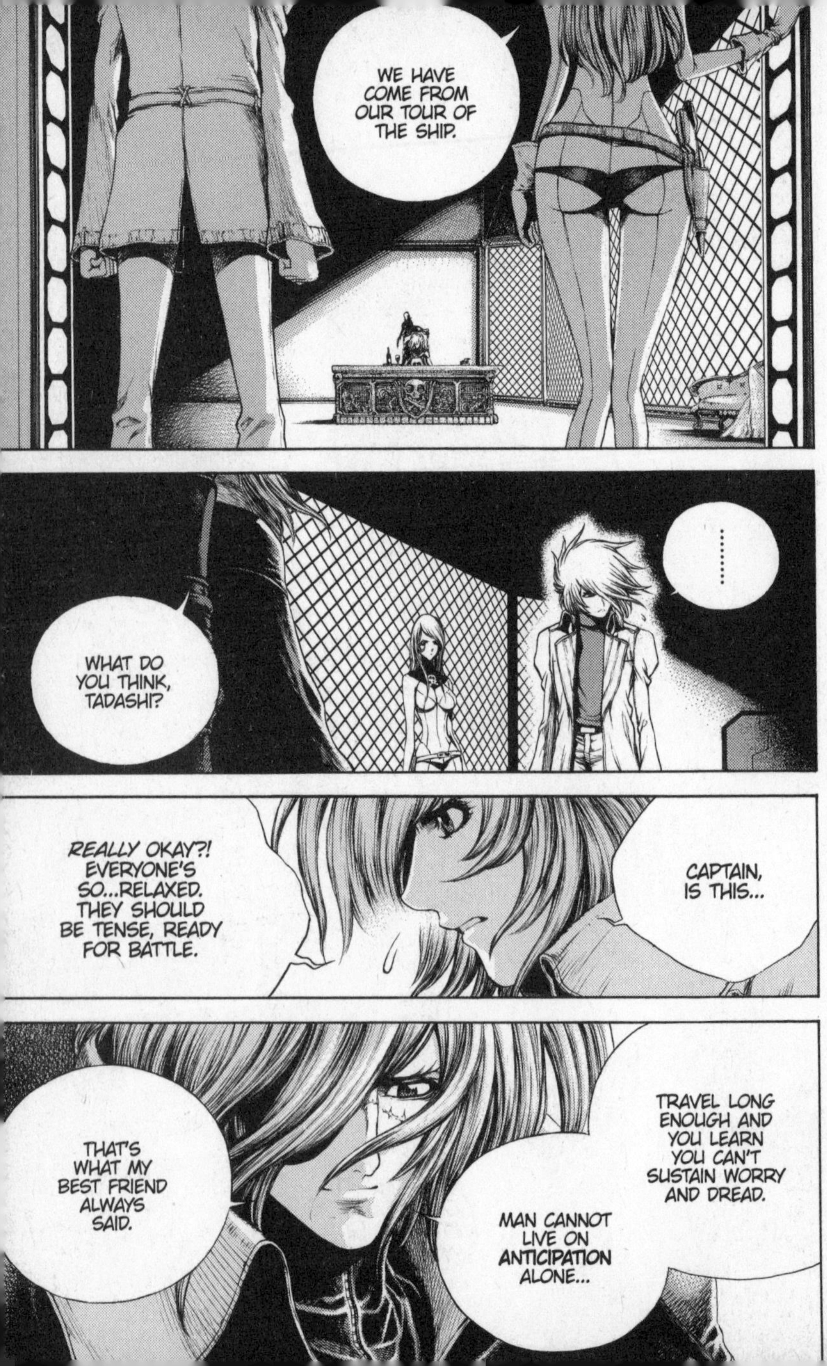
WE HAVE COME FROM OUR TOUR OF THE SHIP.
......
WHAT DO YOU THINK, TADASHI?
CAPTAIN, IS THIS...
REALLY OKAY?! EVERYONE'S SO...RELAXED. THEY SHOULD BE TENSE, READY FOR BATTLE.
TRAVEL LONG ENOUGH AND YOU LEARN YOU CAN'T SUSTAIN WORRY AND DREAD.
MAN CANNOT LIVE ON ANTICIPATION ALONE...
THAT'S WHAT MY BEST FRIEND ALWAYS SAID.

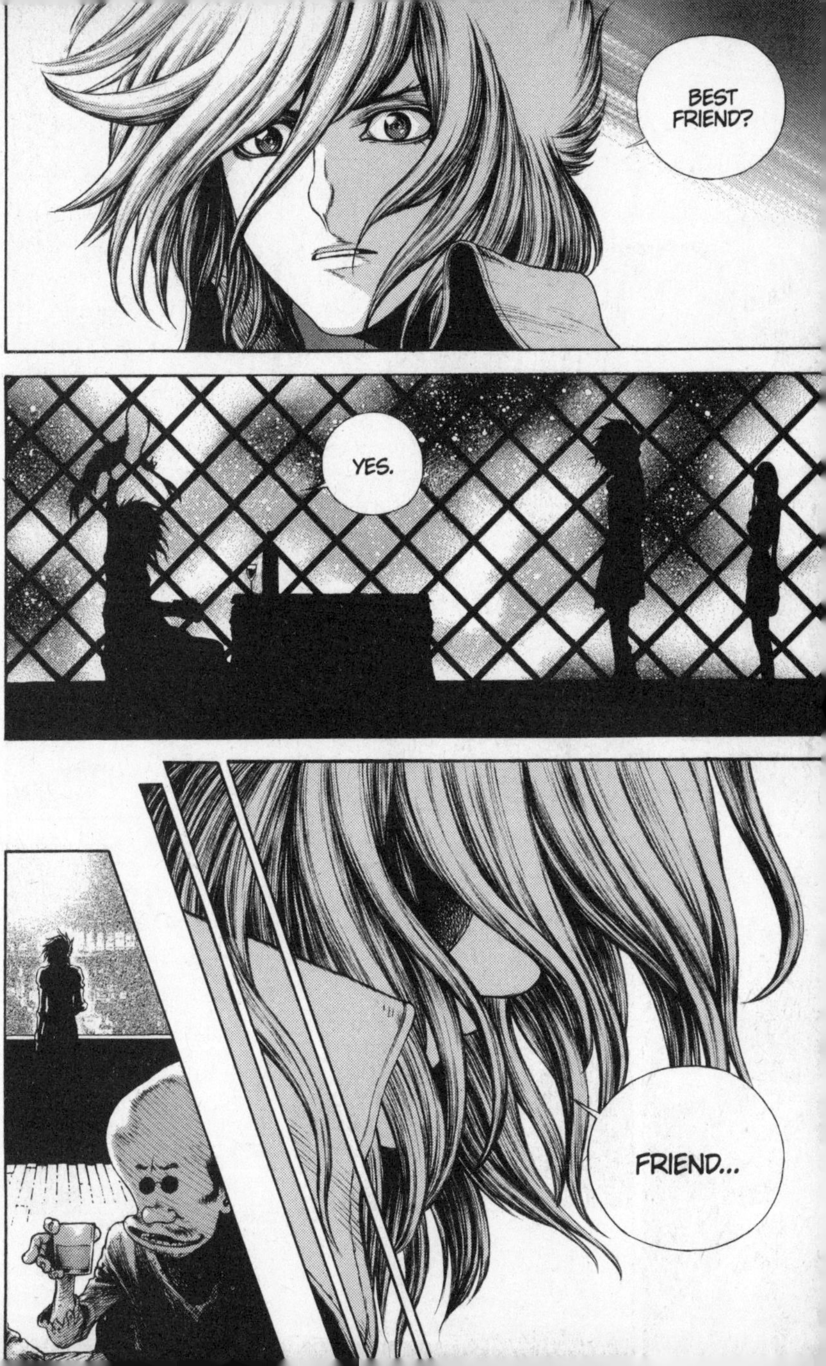
BEST FRIEND?
YES.
FRIEND...

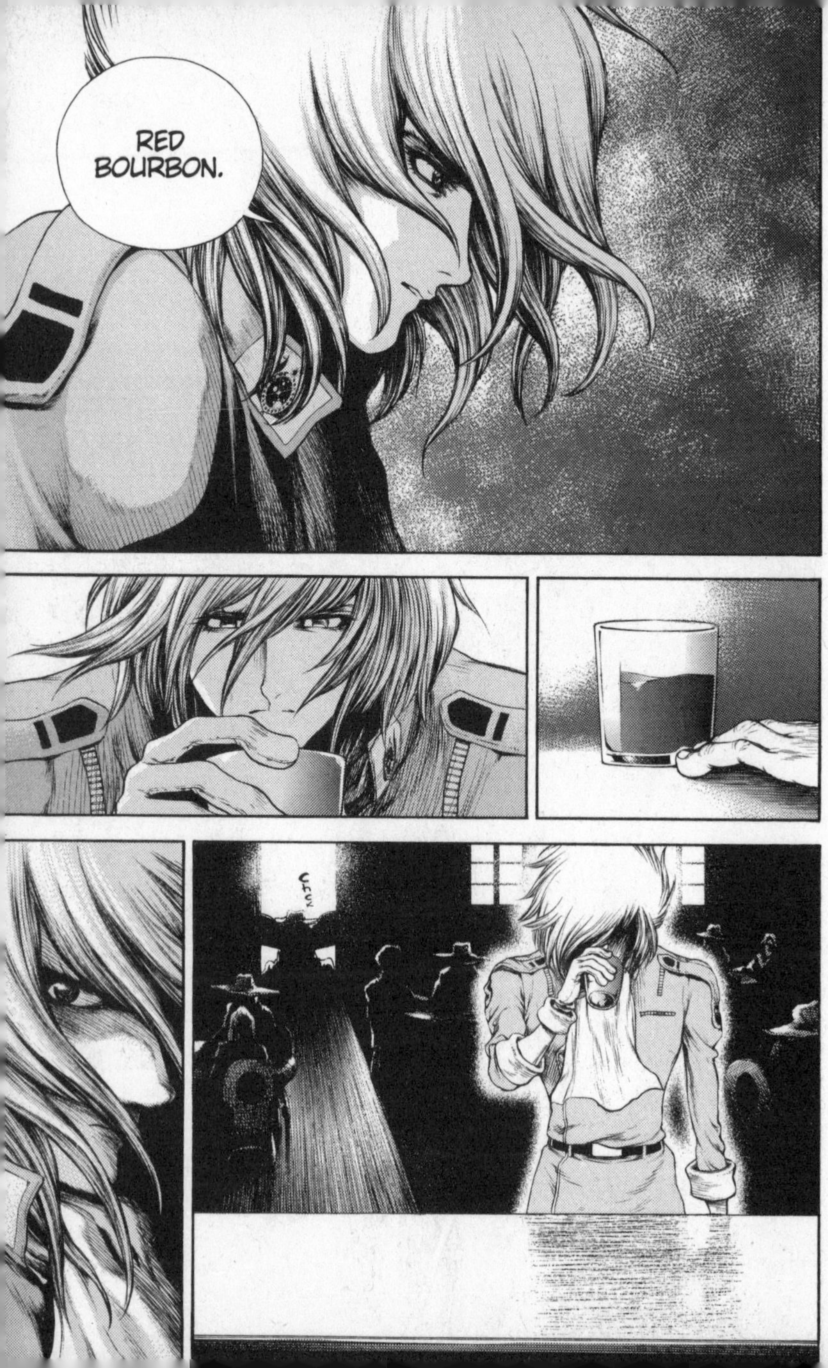
RED BOURBON.
CHCK

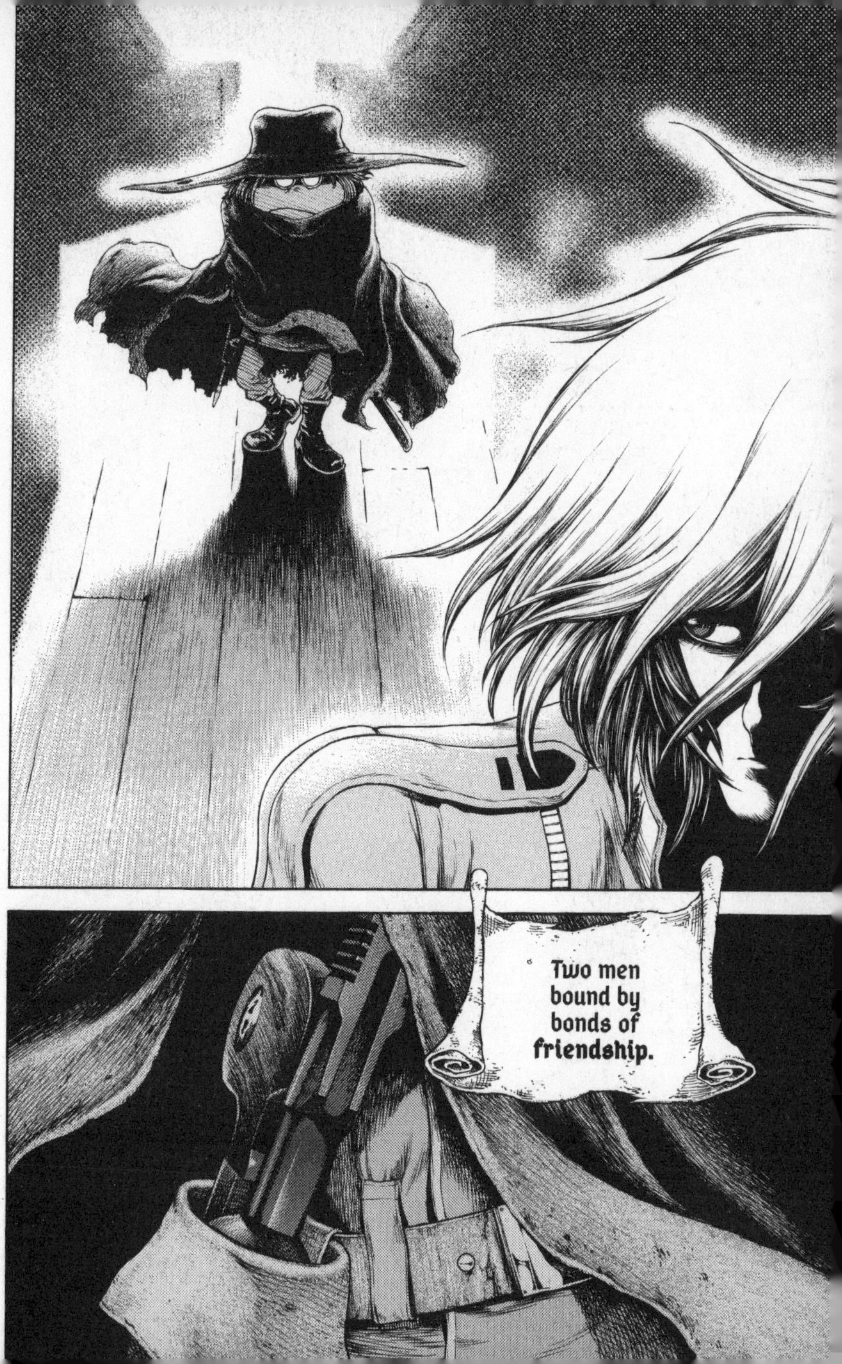
Two men
bound by
bonds of
friendship.

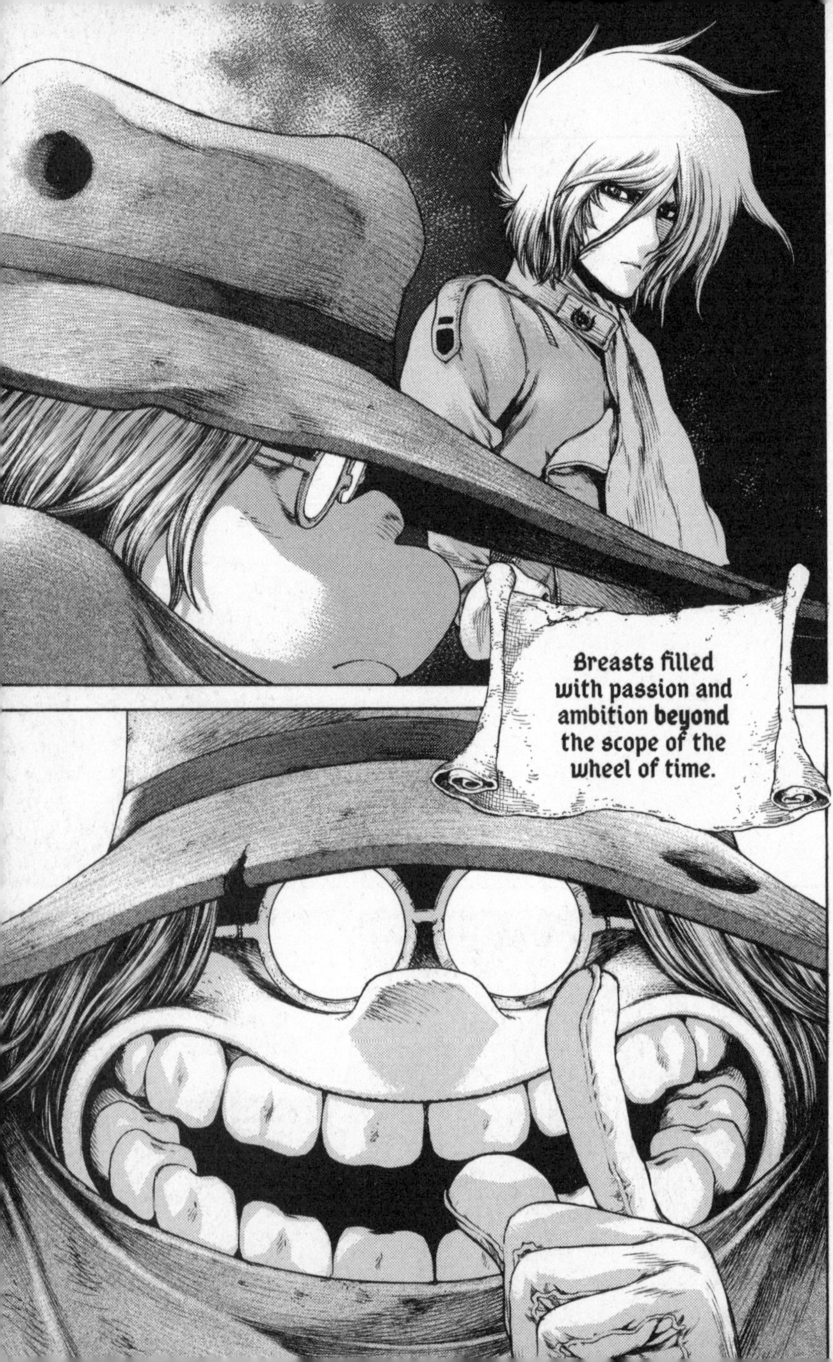
Breasts filled with passion and ambition beyond the scope of the wheel of time.

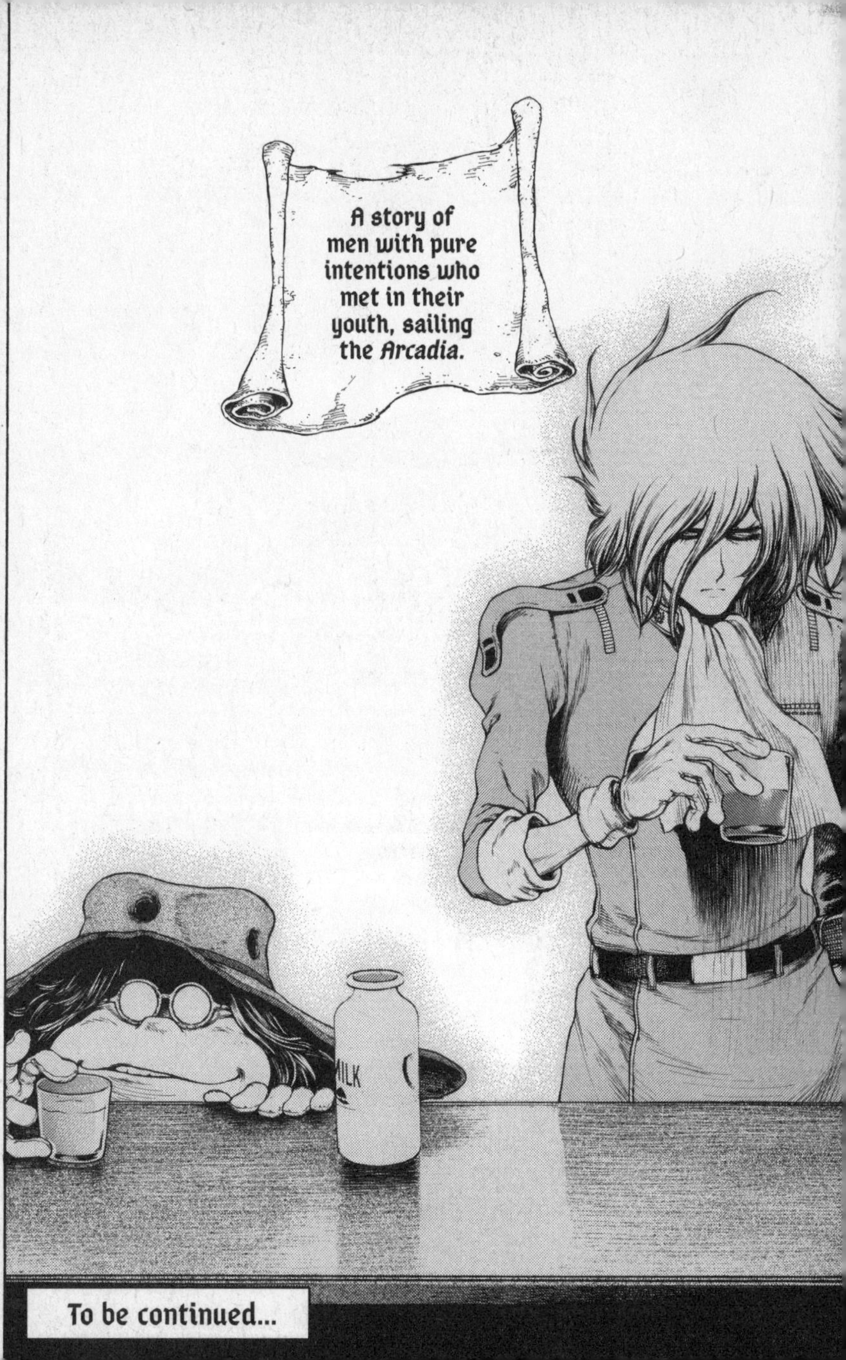
A story of men with pure intentions who met in their youth, sailing the *Arcadia*.
MILK
To be continued...